SHATTERED PIECES EVERYWHERE

a memoir

How I Found True Joy in My Most Broken Moments

CHRISTINA MARIA MARTINEZ

with
Aquila Mendez - Valdez

Cover Photography by
Elizabeth Homan

Division Street Books

Contents

From the Author

Shattered Pieces Everywhere is a work of nonfiction.

There are pieces missing from my story as it is a tell *some*, not a tell *all*. Others have read the manuscript and have confirmed the story being shared. However, some details, names and identifying characteristics have been changed to protect privacy.

To the young person who looks in the mirror and only sees shattered pieces.

To anyone who has experienced tragedy and keeps their scars inside.

To the warrior who fights the good fight.

To the friend who stands in the fray.

To you, the Reader.

Prologue

I t felt like they had been driving for days, or maybe it was time moving slower, according to her will. As if she had that kind of power. As if God would give a woman like her, who had made the mistakes she had, the ability to control anything. Shaking the demons of self-doubt from her mind, she pulls out a sheet of paper from her purse on the floorboard in front of her.

Taking off her sunglasses and squinting at the bright sunlight, she looks over the driving instructions one last time. She reads the address on the paper and compares it with the address on the sign in front of them. "This is it," she quietly announces to the two young girls in the backseat. He is there too, in the driver's seat, but she doesn't acknowledge him. She is deeply indebted to him, and she loathes that he is here at the same time—loathes the fact that she needs him at all.

"Vivian," he says softly. "You're doing the right thing."

How the hell would he know? Vivian shrinks at the harsh words that come to mind first. It's not his fault she's in this predicament and besides, how else would she have made this trip if not for his car? The man drives the creaky sedan up a winding road until they reach a red brick building perched high on the hillside. As the monstrosity groans into *park*, she takes a deep breath and sighs. There's no turning back now.

She looks over at the young girl seated behind the driver's seat first. A beautiful, little blonde-haired wild child with hazel eyes. She's barely six years old. Vivian gives the little girl a warm smile and, though it is unrequited, she softly touches the bottom of the girl's chin and gives her a wink as well. Vivian then turns her gaze to the back seat where the younger child is. This little girl is four years old, her thick brown hair held back with two tiny red barrettes. She has chubby cheeks and a sweet smile radiating from her eyes, which only gets bigger with Vivian's attention. *They know what's coming,* thinks Vivian. *We talked about this. It's not a surprise.*

The dusty drive had been long, crossing state borders and landing them in a city none of them have been to before. With the car idling in the gravel driveway and a curious mind itching to explore, the oldest little girl opens the door, steps out, and takes in the new surroundings. Her eyes follow the tall pine trees until they meet with the clouds in the sky. Gazing back at the car, she opens the back door wider. Her little hand reaches out to the smaller shy brunette, urging her to scoot across so she can help her out of the backseat.

Leaving the door to the car open, the two girls straighten and turn to look at the entrance of the building, the doorframe of which is now filled with two women walking towards them. The eldest girl immediately steps away from the vehicle and ducks under the shade of a pine tree, arms crossed in a pout, and refusing to utter a word. Her sweet face is now replaced by anger, but with a deep, unmistakable sadness in her eyes. Vivian walks over to her and winces in pain as she kneels—now eye-level with the blonde girl. She whispers something to her, out of earshot from the rest of the group. Attempting to mask her own emotions, Vivian offers the little girl another smile, but is met with only a scowl and a half-turned back.

Despite the stabbing pain of rejection, Vivian pulls her in for one last hug. She knows this could be the last time she ever sees

Santina. Struggling to hide the very real physical pain as she stands, she then walks over to the younger child. Kneeling once again, this hug is met with the open arms and warm embrace of a child who has not yet learned to mistrust. *Hold on to that innocence. Hold on.*

As Vivian brings the younger girl in closer for a final hug, she can feel the child's heartbeat racing against her own chest. Not wanting to let go, but also not wanting to draw out the pain of goodbye any longer, she pulls the little girl away to gaze upon her one last time. She wipes away the tiny tears that stream down those chubby cheeks. Before standing up for a final time, Vivian clears her throat, holding back her own tears.

"It's time to say goodbye," Vivian chokes out. "Your sister will take care of you, and remember, you'll always have each other." Pausing as she stands, she softly strokes the cheek of the younger little girl. "Christina, I will always love you."

Get it together, Vivian thinks. *He drove you all this way. There's no way out of it, even if you wanted one.* Sensing herself only moments away from a total meltdown, Vivian turns back toward the car, attempting to distract herself from the torture within her heart. She ducks into the back seat of the car and grabs a small brown grocery bag with a few pieces of clothing inside.

Christina's whimpers become louder and louder. As the two women from the building reach Vivian, she hands the bag over to one of them. Vivian looks stone-faced at them both and makes one last plea: "Please take care of my babies."

Turning on worn heels, Vivian walks away to get into the car as she hears Christina scream, pleading with her, "Don't leave, Mama! Don't leave! I want to stay with you! Please!"

From the reflection of the car window, Vivian can see one of the women pick up Christina and take both girls up the steps towards the intimidating building with its two-story facade and gray windows. She can't turn back. She'll change her mind. She can't bear to see the pain in both daughters' eyes.

Vivian closes the door of the car, but nothing can shut out the heartbreaking cries and howling screams from Christina and Santina

3

as they reach the building's heavy doors. A mother would hear that pain from across an ocean. "Are you ready to go?" he asks.

Has she been ready for anything in her life? Was she ready for motherhood? Was she ready to make this decision? There was no use fighting against all the tiny moments that had led her to this big one. Rather than answer, she places her sunglasses on her face to hide her tears and adjusts her seatbelt. Wordlessly, he puts the car in *Drive*, trying to avoid looking in her direction as she takes a punishing peek in the side mirror. Christina, the "quiet one," is visibly heartbroken and inconsolable as she stretches her arms towards the retreating shadow of their car.

As they approach the end of the driveway, Vivian tries unsuccessfully to catch her breath while wiping the tears from her face. She repeats the only thing that comes to mind. *This is what's best for your daughters.* Even in that moment, though, she doesn't truly believe it. But it doesn't matter. What's done is done.

Her emotions crash through the flimsy strongholds of her mind as she looks up and reads the sign in the rearview mirror: "Hillcrest Children's Home."

* * *

This is how one of my life's most pivotal moments felt as perceived by my mom, Vivian. Ultimately, though, *Shattered Pieces Everywhere* is my story.

Chapter One

Breathe.

 A woman is like a tea bag; you never know how strong it is until it's in hot water.

— **Eleanor Roosevelt**

Vivian grew up in California and was the oldest of seven children. On Christmas Day 1970, at the tender age of fifteen, my mom became a mother for the first time. With the arrival of my brother, Eddie, she abandoned her studies and dropped out of school before completing the tenth grade. In those days, the world was anything but a welcoming place for single mothers, much less ones who were barely old enough to have a driver's license. Even more challenging, was trying to find a job without a high school diploma. She often exaggerated her age while working as a server at a popular twenty-four-hour restaurant, coincidentally next door to the bar where her own mother had worked for years.

My mother struggled to make ends meet and provide for my brother and herself. I imagine those teen years must have felt overwhelming, each day so difficult, yet knowing the whole expanse of life was ahead of her—being tied to the ground but itching to fly.

Despite the challenges of her youth, she was a strong woman. Maybe it was in her DNA, or maybe it was just because she had to be.

My mother has always been beautiful. Her smile sparkled with a zest for life, and people always gravitated to her whenever she entered a room. Even as a teenager, with shimmering red hair, legs for days, and deep, knowing eyes at her disposal, she was a force to see and be seen. Her name means "full of life," and she was confident in all her curves. "Vivacious Vivian," as she was commonly known, was always undeniably comfortable in her own skin.

Dreaming of a life beyond California, my mom walked into a Navy bar with a fake ID at eighteen and, like a scene out of *Top Gun*, she smacked right into my father, Vincent Diecedue III. What an intensely Italian last name! Even the English pronunciation, DEES-ah-DOO, sounds like flirting. Fiercely Sicilian but born and raised in New Orleans, he joined the Navy when he was seventeen. My father was quite the debonair young man with his broad shoulders and chiseled face. With European blood coursing thick in his veins, he was strikingly handsome and, like my mom, had a smile that caught the attention of anyone nearby. Although he was reserved, he was also bold.

At twenty-three, my father looked every bit the part of a polished, handsome sailor, brimming with life, possibility, and unrealized dreams—just like my mother. At their first meeting, he assumed my mom was twenty-one or twenty-two. He would never have guessed that her fake ID was hiding many red flags, from my brother to her lack of education and her underage status, not that any of it would have mattered to him. He was smitten, and so was she.

After an intense but brief season of dating, he received his next deployment orders and was bound for Italy. He would go back to the land of his ancestors but, potentially, leave behind the girl of his dreams. One typical evening out at a local bar, not long after his deployment orders had come, my mother and my father stood outside casually watching a fight that had broken out, as one does when you're used to being up to no good.

"Come with me," he said to my mother, but they both understood the times and the world's opinion, should she choose to follow a man without a wedding ring on her finger. Though my father knew about my brother, my parents had kept their relationship casual for fear of how people would gossip about them if they moved too fast. This was not the long-awaited marriage proposal my mother had envisioned and so she told him in her matter-of-fact Vivian tone to try again. "You have to ask me," she said, and he did. My father proposed then and there without fanfare or pageantry. They jumped in a car and headed to Reno for a hasty ceremony in a church... next to a casino, no doubt. No sooner had the ink dried on their marriage license when they were shipped off to Italy, stationed near Mount Etna, an active volcano on the east coast of Sicily. Their proximity to nature's fury would be telling of their relationship.

In Europe, my mom was half a world away from everything she had ever known. Though my parents were equally obsessed with each other, it would take them all of five seconds to find the first thing to fight about. If you asked my mom, she would admit she was hard to handle. She deliberately provoked my father, which caused shouting matches that then turned into physical violence. There were plenty of reasons a fight would start well before she provoked one, and it usually involved my dad getting drunk.

Looking back, I think my parents had an undeniably toxic relationship—one where each partner needs the other and yet is dragged down into the worst version of themselves at the same time. My parents were dubbed "The Fighting Diecedues" because there was rarely a moment when they weren't squabbling about something, be it big or small. If they weren't at each other's throats, they were inseparable, feeding off each other's energy. To their Navy friends, they were the "fun couple." Sure, they were a blast to hang out and party with but, after the party was over, it was another story. So, while the countryside of Italy was a new and thrilling experience for my mother, life at home with my father was hardly a walk in the park. Even after the birth of my sister, Santina, in Naples, a new baby did not create marital bliss. And so began my mom's itch to leave my father.

It would have been hard enough to leave my father if my mother had been in the States with family to support her but, with a whole Atlantic Ocean separating her from them, it felt almost impossible. And my father knew it. During their most intense fights, he would throw the car keys at my mother and, with a smirk, say to her, "Drive home then," all the while knowing it was impossible. Little did they know their situation would change soon enough.

* * *

Though he was a passionate husband and loyal friend, I believe my father's one true love was the Navy. Besides drinking, he was perhaps more faithful to the Navy than anything or anyone else. For example, while in Italy, the Mafia approached him and politely *requested* that he sell his gas and cigarette rations to them—something provided free by the military to all the servicemen. Always ready to make a little extra cash, he eagerly complied, thinking this enterprise was a harmless hustle. A short time later, however, he ended his deal and stopped selling his rations. He feared being caught, and how it would negatively affect his career in the Navy. While he wasn't afraid of bending the rules in some aspects of life, he drew a hard line when it came to his beloved Navy, naively thinking the Mafia would accept his decision and fade away. He was wrong.

The following evening, his car was blown up while parked right outside their bedroom window. The explosion was so intense it melted the bowling ball in the back of his car. A message from someone? Maybe. But my father and the Navy weren't taking any chances waiting around to find out. My parents were immediately transferred to New Jersey, where my father was asked to instruct an officer's training program. Later, though, he was passed over for a promotion, and spiraled further into the grip of alcoholism.

New Jersey is where *my* story begins. Life in The Garden State held more turmoil and heartache for my mother and, although my parents would have their good days, family outings and time spent enjoying the company of friends, the bad days eventually outweighed the good ones. Despite my parents' issues and father's abuse, my mom truly loved my dad. It would take another three years before she finally gathered the courage to leave him.

On the cusp of having saved enough money to leave, my mother began feeling ill and hurried to the doctor. One blood test later, and her entire plan came crashing down around her. She was pregnant... with me.

Though motherhood until this point had been anything but a fairy tale for her, she loved my brother and sister fiercely. This pregnancy was entirely unexpected and unplanned, and she believed it would make it nearly impossible for her to leave my father. How could she support three children on her own? For my mother, she could see her window of escape closing, and felt as if a rope was tightening around her neck. *Where was Vivacious Vivian?*

Knowing my mother's desperation, a friend suggested she have an abortion and offered to help pay for it. My mother visited an abortion clinic in New York and scheduled the procedure. But when the day arrived to terminate the pregnancy, just stepping inside the doors of the clinic was enough to confirm the feeling in her gut; though the path would be difficult, she felt an overwhelming desire to keep this baby. So she did.

For much of my life, I didn't know that my mother was so close to ending her pregnancy. When she eventually told me the story, I felt awful. Part of my shock was that this was the first time I had heard anything resembling my darkest fear of being unwanted, said out loud. There I was, living proof that my mother cared for me, but I still couldn't shed the feeling. Knowing how tough life was growing up, maybe there was a grain of truth to my feelings that I had made my mother's life more difficult. She had done her best, and I knew she loved me. I just couldn't help but imagine how I must have added to some of the burden in her life during that uncertain time.

My mother's pregnancy with me was not smooth, no doubt exacerbated by the stress of our family's struggles and, despite being pregnant, the physical abuse continued. After a night out drinking with his friends, my mom "provoked" a fight when my father returned home without the milk he had promised to bring. Whirling to face her, he slammed her burgeoning body to the floor. In that moment, she knew what they had between them was over. It was clear to my mother that if he was willing to continue the abuse in her very pregnant state, it would never stop; the abuse could only worsen. A part of her thought bringing new life into the family would bring new hope. But that wasn't the case. No matter how much she loved my father, he wasn't the same man when he was drunk.

Sometimes, I try to imagine how my mother must have felt—waiting and watching her belly grow though she knew she wasn't meant to stay with my father. It must have felt like she was on the precipice of a new beginning, but with dangerous landmines littering her path. It would be easy to wonder why my mother didn't leave while pregnant or feel empowered to go at the first sign of trouble. From what she has shared with me, the love for one another still existed, along with the hope of long-term change. We all know survivors of domestic violence who have stayed and endured far worse circumstances. Outside of the fear, I wonder if the economic and societal challenges made leaving so difficult for her.

For my mother, it would take stashing some money aside, the help of others, and an invitation to stay with her family in California to make leaving my father possible. All these dominoes had to be in place by the time she felt the first sign of labor pains. Then my arrival would be the domino to set everything in motion.

On January 9, 1979, during one of the worst winters in New Jersey history, a snowstorm began bearing down on the city of Lakewood. Lying on the operating room table for her Cesarean section procedure, wide awake, and with a curtain dividing her chest from her stomach, my mother nervously stared at a ceiling of fluorescent lights and awaited my arrival. But instead of hearing the joy of my first cry when she knew I was out, she heard a deafening silence. I wasn't breathing. The staff was doing everything they could to save me. When the doctor came out to tell my father, he wrapped his thick Sicilian hands around the doctor's throat and insisted he "*Fix this!*"

It was quickly determined that I had meconium aspiration, which can be caused when a baby is stressed and gasps inside of the womb. With my airways blocked, I couldn't take those vital first breaths. The nurses and doctors whisked me away to begin resuscitations before my mother even saw me for the first time. After being placed on a ventilator, it didn't take long for the hospital staff to realize their facilities were not equipped to handle the severity of my case. Sixty seconds was all my mother was given for her first look at me. However brief, she would never forget the shock of seeing my tiny body, intubated, with my head shaved and wires springing from every which way as the medical team wheeled me away. I was flown by helicopter to a nearby hospital and placed in a specialized neonatal intensive care unit (NICU).

Separated from me and lying in the recovery wing, guilt and sorrow washed over my mother. She was convinced I was going to die. In the bed beside her, another mom had delivered a healthy, bouncing baby boy earlier that morning. She was being punished. Listening to another's joy, amidst her own despair, my mom wept.

Her downward spiral of thoughts was enough to convince herself that, had she not considered ending the pregnancy, her new daughter would have been born healthy. There was no persuading her otherwise; it's what she believed. At that moment, my mom prayed to God, begging Him to spare my life and, in exchange, she would change hers, committing to live a Christian life.

When my mother shared this story with me, I remember feeling heartsick for the young woman crying alone in her hospital room. Life had dealt her a series of increasingly challenging cards, but she shouldn't have felt the weight of that on her shoulders alone. In no way, shape or form did my health in my first few moments of life have anything to do with her past decisions. We make the best ones we can at every moment. We all need a little grace from time to time. I know that, and I think she does now, too.

They eventually released my mother from the hospital to recover at home. I wouldn't follow until several weeks later since I was still recovering in the NICU. Severe jaundice had set in not long after my delivery and, after being taken off the ventilator, I needed a little more time to regulate my breathing before the doctor felt comfortable releasing me. My mother later told me I battled a case of pneumonia, resulting in a hospital stay each year for the first four years of my life.

Upon arriving home, I was finally introduced to my big brother and sister. My brother, Eddie, had been enjoying life as an only child before my sister, Santina's, arrival two and a half years earlier and had reacted with an abrupt, "I don't want that baby. Give it to someone else." Luckily for me, he was accustomed to the joy of a sibling and was much happier when I was brought home. Santina, now a toddler, was beyond excited to be a big sister. As soon as I was laid in my swinging bassinet and everyone left the room, she quietly crawled in, too, snuggling her chubby arms around me. My mother walked back into the room and froze, panicking when she found her very hefty toddler lying with her very sick new baby.

In true Diecedue fashion, I was born with a full head of thick, dark hair, half of which was growing back after being shaved for my IVs. When my sister laid down next to me, she began trying to soothe me, stroking my head. Pointing at the shaved part of my head, she told my mother, "Owie."

While my mother recovered from my delivery, my father helped care for the kids. Even when I stayed in the hospital all those weeks, he never missed a daily visit. He knew his marriage had problems, but he truly loved having a family and never wanted us to be apart. Although it was far from the environment he was raised in, I guess, in his mind, this was how most families operated. The parents fought. Everyone was miserable. But you stuck it out for the sake of the kids and to avoid any social embarrassment. That was never the life my mom wanted, though.

I believe my father wanted to change; at times, he even sustained short bursts of recovery. But without professional help, it was impossible for my father to maintain his sobriety, and he eventually fell back into drinking. Often, those who suffer from severe addiction of any kind do not realize they may not be able to change for the long term by themselves. In fact, very few can achieve genuine change without professional help. The hold my father's addiction had on him was proving to be too strong. And he had no idea that he was on the verge of losing everything.

I was about six months old when, after a huge fight, my mother decided she had tried all she could to stay in her rapidly deteriorating relationship with my father. No more waiting to see if things would get better. They wouldn't. After my father left for work the next morning, she packed a bag and called a friend to come pick us up. This first step would prove to be the hardest.

Toting an eight-year-old, a three-year-old, and a six-month-old baby, my mom checked into a nearby hotel. Her friend promised to return after gathering enough funds to purchase plane tickets for us. Once again, all the pieces of our escape needed to fall into place. The only thing left for my mother to do was wait. With no money to spare, we spent three anxiety-ridden days hiding out in that hotel, with only some formula for me and peanut butter with crackers for my sister, brother, and mother. It was the best my mom could do until the flight would depart from New Jersey and take us to her family in California.

I imagine when the plane lifted off the ground, my mother could finally take a deep breath. She would have been fighting an absurd mix of feelings. Leaving my father meant there would be no father present for us and no financial support either. Yet living with him guaranteed abuse. Despite all of that, my father was the love of her life, making a hard decision almost impossible. But it had to be done. My mom knew the choice to leave was necessary for us. It was time to start over.

When we arrived in San Francisco, my mother was terribly relieved and thought the grass would surely be greener on the Pacific coast. Unfortunately, almost as soon as my mom settled into her own mother's cramped, one-bedroom apartment, a sense of "buyer's remorse" settled in. It was obvious that our new living conditions would not be the best fit for her or for us.

My mom hadn't lived in California for several years, much less seen her family, and she had let time soften the hard edges of reality there. My grandmother, Phyllis, had different values from my mother, which often strained their relationship. Phyllis had never liked my father and still resented that he and my mom had taken my brother away from her. So, where my mother expected to find a soft spot to land, she instead found tension.

My mother's fear of quickly wearing out our welcome became reality when all three of us children came down with chickenpox not long after we'd arrived. We were miserable and, therefore, made everyone else miserable with our tears, complaints, and incessant scratching. Though my mother's instinct to pack us up and leave gnawed once more, she had to wait until we were healthy before even considering her next move.

While we all itched in anguish, my brother began developing a knack for trouble. He was eight years old and, since my mother was the oldest of seven, her youngest sibling was only four years older than my brother. One evening, these two found themselves beyond the watchful eyes of adults, which wasn't hard to do, and my brother was introduced to smoking marijuana. He was in the second grade. If he wasn't headed down a perilous path before then, that first puff definitely set him on a negative trajectory for his young life. There wasn't anyone to blame except the turbulent circumstances that had led my family there.

Eventually, my brother explored other drugs, further fueling his troubles. But when his new past-time was discovered, my mom sped up planning for our next move. Whether or not she liked it, she realized she would have to consider reaching out to my father's parents, Evelyn and Vincent Jr., in New Orleans for help. *Would they take us in?* My mother always said having three children was the most challenging thing when trying to find someone to take you in. She would joke when considering her circumstances, repeating what someone once told her, "When you have one kid, sure! Two kids? Maybe. Three kids? Stay the heck where you are!"

She had miraculously escaped an abusive relationship, and now her only hope for leaving her current nightmare was halfway back across the country. And she didn't have a penny to her name to get there. My grandparents were fully aware that my parents were having marital problems, but they cared for my mother and us kids all the same. They couldn't bear the thought of us suffering alone, and I imagine my mother thought New Orleans offered a better environment for our family. She also knew she would have the support of my grandmother, Evelyn, who was traditionally minded and family focused. For the first time, we would experience a true extended family: great aunts and uncles who would gather for holidays; cousins to play with; and the support and stability that strength in numbers provides. After my mom confessed her struggles to my grandparents, they sent for us to be with them in New Orleans without hesitation.

Chapter Two

Gone.

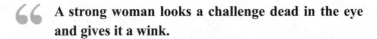 **A strong woman looks a challenge dead in the eye and gives it a wink.**

— **Gina Carey**

W hen I reach for the earliest memories from my childhood, I always end up in New Orleans. It's home in my mind. Even though there were many road trips which took our family to all ends of the United States, the magnetic pull of New Orleans always brought us back.

My grandfather had been drafted into World War II at nineteen years old and served in the Navy, as did his sons. He retired early after having a major heart attack. He spent much of his later years mending shrimp nets to not only earn a modest income, but to keep his mind and hands busy. Grandpa sported a thick Italian mane of hair like my dad, and his deep-set eyes seemed to contain a mixture of gruff masculinity and a soft spot for us, his grandchildren.

While my grandfather wasn't the greatest babysitter, he was always willing to watch us, and my mother almost always needed the help. In my faded memories of him, I see him sitting at the kitchen table just off the living room in his favorite chair. His faithful dog, Pasqua (meaning "Easter" in Italian), was well fed and showed signs of being given too many treats, which probably explains why he rarely left my grandfather's side.

Food was the top priority when Grandpa was in charge. He would wake each morning primarily concerned with breakfast, and after dinner he always had a snack of Little Debbie Star Crunch® cookies. Wearing his suspenders and house shoes, he'd shuffle from the kitchen to his bedroom and return with his special treat. Hiding them in his room created the suspense of wondering when he might bring one out to us. He knew the way to our little hearts!

Grandpa Vincent kept a tidy space, always making sure everything was in its rightful spot. His newspaper, special folded towel on the kitchen table, eyeglasses, and brown coffee mug filled with whiskey always lay next to the latest copy of *TV Guide*.

He had his routine, and I was content sitting on the couch quietly playing or enjoying whatever he was entertained by. My mother didn't like us watching television but, when we were in his care, he would flip between his regularly scheduled shows like *Perry Mason* or *The Price is Right* to Nickelodeon's *Pinwheel* just for us. He would, that is, unless the Chicago Cubs were playing. The Cubs trumped everything. Looking back, I think this is how I became a Cubs fan long before I ever stepped foot in the Windy City.

My grandmother, Evelyn, was extremely well-educated, earning her degree in finance. She worked as a bookkeeper for Nikelson's, a locally owned grocery store, and her routine was like clockwork. She was up at four in the morning, working long shifts at the store before stopping at her mother's home to care for her. Finally, she would return home to cook dinner and eventually fall asleep at the table, over a crossword puzzle.

Grandma Evelyn's office at the grocery store was near the bakery, so she always smelled like freshly baked bread when she arrived home. I have fond memories of climbing up on her lap the moment she sat down and before she had time to settle in. She was incredibly warm and loving, precisely the way you might imagine an Italian grandmother would be.

She was, to quote my mother, "an 'actual angel of God.'" I never saw her wear makeup or dress in anything that wasn't conservative. My mom dedicated Sunday evenings to my grandma, washing and putting rollers in her hair while they talked about everything under the sun—something both my mother and grandmother looked forward to each week.

The Evelyn my mother knew was giving, non-judgmental, and full of integrity. She was not a high maintenance person by any stretch of the imagination, spending all her extra money on her grandchildren. Her presence alone meant everything to my mom. Quite simply, our grandmother was our family's anchor. She provided a steadiness and stability in our life which hadn't always been present amidst the drama in our family.

After sixteen years of service in the Navy, my father didn't reenlist. Instead, he returned to New Orleans… and his parent's couch. Although we were all in the same house, we were rarely all together. It wouldn't be an exaggeration to say that he was either working (if he held on to a job), out drinking, or passed out on the couch. This didn't prevent my mom from trying to get him to be present in our lives, though. She would dress us up and braid our hair, only for my father to not show up. If he did, it was only after he had been drinking too much. Consequently, the positive memories I have of my father have more to do with his family than with him.

I'm not sure if it was because of the times they were living in or their own personal preference, but my grandparents slept in different bedrooms. This left only one bedroom for my mom, my brother, my sister, and me to share. As we all grew, in their tiny house, we had to become more strategic with our sleeping arrangements. This led to my sister and me fighting over who would sleep with our grandmother. Truthfully, most nights I would regret sleeping in her room because, being a full-figured woman, grandma snored... and *loud*. But if I could go back in time, I would gladly enjoy the opportunity to snuggle next to her and appreciate the rhythmic sounds of her sleeping, if only for one last time.

Long before we arrived in New Orleans, my grandparents had purchased the home where they would raise their family and live until their final days. It was not too far from the eastern bank of the Mississippi River, next to the Lower Ninth Ward of New Orleans and the Jackson Barracks, all of which is chock-full of incredible history.

My grandparents' home in St. Bernard Parish, or "da parish" as the locals would say, was simple and quaint. Outside, grew a beautiful magnolia tree which, to this day, makes me think of my grandmother every time I see one. It's fitting because a magnolia is considered a symbol of purity and nobility, and that describes her perfectly.

Located on Prosperity Street, their one story home was probably no larger than nine hundred square feet. The next two streets, similarly named, were Easy Street and Success Street. I'm not sure my mom would agree any of these street names were a fitting description for her life back in that time and in that neighborhood. I can only imagine the cruel irony she felt walking for miles, pulling her kids behind her in a loaned red wagon, the only transportation we could afford, down Success Street.

Prosperity Street, however, was a very neighborly block where everyone knew each other and everyone's business, including my mother's. The rear gate on the fence of my grandparents' home provided us front row seats to watch the annual Mardi Gras parade passing along Judge Perez Drive. This was the same major thoroughfare where my father fell asleep at the wheel after drinking too much, leaving my sister, only seven years old, seated next to him, holding the wheel and me praying we would make it safely back to Prosperity Street.

Each Mardi Gras season brought a celebration of its own kind, regardless of our circumstances. My grandmother, always thinking of us, would inevitably arrive home with a King Cake from Randazzo's. Snuggled somewhere inside was a little baby Jesus, and we fought over who would get the lucky slice containing the tiny plastic figurine tucked underneath.

My mother would walk onto the porch to help grandma with her packages and sigh, "Oh, mama, you shouldn't have. The girls will fight over the baby."

My Grandma, however, was always one to think of the details *and* the silver lining, responding, "No Vee, I already thought of that; I asked for an extra baby for the girls."

One of my favorite photos from Mardi Gras includes my sister and me bundled in big jackets. I'm about three years old, smiling as happy as can be while clutching a beer bottle. We were comfortably snuggled up in the back of a pickup truck watching the elaborate costumes and carnival masks pass by.

"Throw me somethin', mista!" I'd yell with all my heart. By the end of the night, we would be *rich* with beads, doubloons, cups, trinkets, and toys that had been tossed our way. It was times like Mardis Gras when it was easy to forget our problems and circumstances.

While New Orleans is perhaps most well-known for its traditions and history, it is painful that many of the places I remember as a child are no longer standing. In 2005, during Louisiana's battle with Hurricane Katrina, the surging water reached from fifteen to twenty feet high, breaching the levee in St. Bernard Parish and decimating the area. The force of the water left hardly anything recognizable on my grandparents' street. I'm grateful they didn't live to experience Hurricane Katrina's fury and the aftermath. With so many homeless and displaced, it would have devastated them.

Our first few years in New Orleans consisted of bouncing from place to place. Yes, my mother always had my grandparents' home to turn to for shelter, but this meant she had to deal with all my father's drinking and arguments. Regardless of him being there, she always preferred the independence of living on her own. Even if that meant struggling in poverty, unlike the rest of our family. So, my mom would save up enough money for us to move out of my grandparents' home for a while. Inevitably, though, jobs would dry up; unfortunate circumstances would arise; and we would move back in as fast as we had left.

Though she fought it, my mother continued to love my father far longer than she would probably care to admit. The attraction the two had for one another was as strong as the pull New Orleans had on our family. It was so powerful that, by my second birthday, they had married, divorced, remarried, and divorced *again*. I think my mother was always in search of something better, not only for us, but for herself. Sometimes, she would place her bets on my father and, other times, she would bet on herself. As much as each of us wanted to be one big, happy family, it would never happen.

When my mother was approached about receiving food stamps on welfare, she said she believed they should be saved for others who needed them more. That's debatable but, for her, government assistance meant answering lots of questions about my father, and that didn't sit well with her. Although many didn't agree with her decision, my mother had made a private vow to Evelyn that she would keep the family's affairs confidential and not do anything that might land my father in jail. In return, Evelyn promised my mother she would always make sure we were taken care of despite never formally receiving child support from my father.

My sister and I found a way to make our own "contributions" for support. When my father passed out on his parent's sofa, loose change and dollars always spilled from his pockets as he tossed and turned. Our chubby fingers would quietly scoop them up one by one, making a game of it to see how much we could gather before Dad woke up. Some might call this stealing but, the way we saw it, we were helping expedite the delivery of what our mother was owed.

As kids, we were also accustomed to picking up an odd job here or there for a few dollars. On the rare occasion my father was present, Santina and I would do our best to hustle him. One partic-ular season, I worked for my father in the cold months, up to my elbows in mud, to tend to his creole tomatoes. I'd like to say this was a classic daddy-daughter bonding time. That wasn't the case. After he gave his instructions, I did as I was told. Even as young as I was, I thought by always obeying and doing a good job, I could "earn" his love. When I would get a few dollars from him, I'd pass them on to my grandfather, knowing he would put it in a safe place and save it for me. Eventually, I had saved up a whopping twenty dollars! The next weekend, my mom took my sister and me and with some of the money, we splurged on Rally's French fries. We couldn't have been happier.

Over the years, there was no job my mother wouldn't do to bring in money. She worked as a school bus driver, bartender, carpenter, housekeeper, plumber—anything she could do to earn a living. One summer, she took a job as a painter's assistant. During a lunch break, my mom felt vulnerable enough to confide in a coworker, Walter, about some challenges she was facing. She told him how she was raising us three children alone. Not to mention, she was dealing with the drama that came with an alcoholic ex-husband and the never-ending roller coaster of moving in and out of my grandparent's house. She just wanted to create a home of her own. It was too much, and she was tired.

In that same conversation, my mom casually mentioned to Walter that, a few weeks prior, she had been walking to work along the busy Judge Perez Drive when, just for a second, she imagined stepping off the curb into oncoming traffic. Though she never seri-ously considered harming herself, the thought alone scared her. *If she was gone, who would take care of her kids?*

My mom felt like no matter how many steps she took forward, there were too many steps back. She couldn't get ahead. She couldn't get out from underneath the weight of poverty and toxic relationships. It was a rare and vulnerable moment she shared with Walter. Immediately, he stopped my mother in her tracks and encouraged her to speak to his wife, Sandra, about her thoughts.

The following day, she called Sandra and was invited to visit their home if she ever wanted to talk.

That same night, to Sandra's utter shock, my mom grabbed my brother's bike, all she had to travel with, and rode it a few miles to Sandra and Walter's home. As my mother caught her breath, Sandra began sharing the Bible with her. From that day forward, my mother started attending church and working to change her life as she had promised all those years before in the hospital where I was born. She was at another low point in her life, but this time, she was surrounded by people who wanted to help.

My mother's spiritual outlook on life changed radically. She regularly attended church with Sandra and embraced the opportunity to belong to a community who would rally behind her. Feeling confident and inspired, my mother began changing the way she spoke and the way she acted. Sandra and Walter, with two young children of their own, took my mom fully under their wing.

I remember playing at Sandra and Walter's house with all their kids' toys and marveling at the fully stocked refrigerator. I remember sleeping over many nights, having dinners together, and going to functions with their family. After church on Sunday, you could find us at McDonald's, playing on the playground without a care in the world. Sandra would strategically purchase and divide hamburgers and fries for all the kids, and we were always part of the fold.

Sandra and Walter even included us in their family summer vacations. They were so generous and had to have known we could never repay them. It was part of their fiber to help where they could.

As my mother became more and more entrenched in her faith, she began viewing Sandra and the women in her church as examples of lives she wanted to emulate. Rather than wallow in the despair of her circumstances, she found joy. She still wasn't perfect, but she made every effort to build a better life for our family. It wasn't long, however, until her newfound values would be put to the test.

By this time, my father was a free man, hanging out at the bar again while enjoying the company of various women. My mom still couldn't count on him for support and, on the rare occasion she would ask for help, inevitably he would let her down. Having a spiritual sister to walk alongside her, Sandra and Vivian were a force to be reckoned with when they put their minds together.

One afternoon, my mom exploded after my father broke yet another empty promise to spend time with us. To his credit, he did show up, but only to water his creole tomato plants, then left quickly. My mom called Sandra, fuming, sharing how upset she was. She exclaimed, "He cares more about those stupid tomato plants than he does for his own children!" Trying to break the tension, Sandra jokingly suggested, "I'd pull them up."

Brightening, my mom responded. "That's a great idea!" As she hung up the phone, she could hear Sandra's protests not to do anything she would regret, but it was too late. My mother hurried out to the backyard on a mission. Over six feet tall, she ripped each and every one of those precious tomato plants from their earthy homes and tossed them over the fence towards Judge Perez Drive.

After the dramatic event, grandma would tell her, "Vee, why did you do that? You know I love those creoles." Of course, upsetting my grandmother made my mom feel terrible. Not only because of how much she loved her, but because she had been trying to "change her ways." Later, she would apologize to my father. She would not continue to allow his behavior to dictate hers. But as much as she would try to take the high road, invariably he would find ways of bringing her back down, especially when it came to us kids.

And that's exactly what happened the day my mom came home to find the three of us alone, with no adult supervision. She was furious. Immediately she called Sandra, who picked all of us up to go with my mother to find my father, so my mother could let him know exactly how she felt. Pulling up to a nearby cul-de-sac, we found my father sitting outside drinking with a group of friends, including one ex-girlfriend, Jenny, who had been bad news from the start. Jenny had already been taunting my mother for years with vulgar comments about the fact that she was spending extra time with my father.

Again, trying to be a better version of herself, my mom decided she wouldn't let Jenny upset her and did her best to ignore her. On this day, however, it was going to be difficult, with emotions already running high. Meanwhile, we kids were squeezed in the back seat along with Sandra's kids, all with front row seats to what was unfolding before us.

My mother marched up to my father and said, "I need to speak with you," in a calm yet threatening tone.

My father didn't move from his spot, simply tossing her a casual, "Later."

"Vincent, tell this b**** to leave," Jenny interrupted, though my father ignored her entirely.

My mother quickly retorted, "This is none of your business," and tried her best to focus on my father. Turning to face him once more, she said, "I need to speak with you now about leaving the kids by themselves."

Jenny interjected for the last time, snarling, "Vincent, tell this b**** it's my birthday and she needs to leave."

That was all it took. With no patience left for any of it, my mom yanked Jenny out of her seat by her hair and whispered intensely, "I've got your b**** right here." Blow after blow fell on the birthday girl, leaving Jenny on the ground and the surrounding group in bewilderment and chaos. Before turning to walk away, my mom spat out one last decree, "Now every time you see me, you'll say 'Ms. Vivian.'"

"This wasn't for you," my mother growled at my father, making it clear this wasn't about jealousy; it was about us kids. Jenny had taken the brunt of all that frustration. Getting back in the car, still in shock, my mother looked over to see Sandra staring wide-eyed and with my sister, Sandra's girls and me, stunned and crying in the back seat.

"I didn't know you were going to beat her!" exclaimed Sandra.

"It happened so fast," my mother justified. "The devil got a hold of me." But almost instantly, my mother regretted the incident and how she had let Jenny's taunts get the best of her. This wasn't the first, or last, fight I saw in my childhood, but this one stayed with me. She had worked so hard to let go of her old self and be what she believed was a good example of a Christian. Fighting in cul-de-sacs was not who she wanted to be anymore.

Years later, Jenny was injured in a horrible car accident that nearly took her life. While still struggling with very little money for our own family, my mom brought Jenny groceries and cooked a meal for her. When my mother announced herself on Jenny's doorstep, Jenny was nervous to let her in, no doubt remembering their last encounter. Reluctantly, she allowed my mother to enter and, as she was about to leave, my mom asked, "Do you mind if I pray with you?"

Jenny agreed and, as my mother turned to leave, Jenny whispered, "I don't know why you are doing this for me."

"God loves you, Jenny, and everyone needs someone," my mom stated. With years of distance between their fight in the cul-de-sac, Jenny didn't need another enemy; she needed a friend. Jenny wasn't a bad person. She just lacked the precious community and faith that my mother had been fortunate enough to stumble upon—a support system that wasn't tied to my father's double-edged sword.

Despite her struggle, my mother finally felt free enough to look forward to what the future could hold. She had a job which provided her a vehicle and a steady income which allowed us to be in a place of our own. Though life seemed to move in the right direction, without warning, she experienced a year-long period of constant bleeding. It wasn't painful, but it caused her extreme weakness and fatigue, making her miss too many days of work. After visiting her doctor, he recommended she undergo a hysterectomy. When the recovery took longer than expected, though, she was forced to stop working altogether. Without the job, she was without a vehicle once again, and things began to quickly fall apart. She kept telling family and friends her situation "isn't good" but they would tell her to keep her faith.

By this time, my father had remarried and now that he had a wife, my mom felt moving back in with our grandparents would not be appropriate. Besides, my brother continued to find himself in trouble, so she felt it wasn't fair to put that burden on my grandparents. She felt she was out of options and the slippery slope of poverty called my mother's name once more. In the months following the surgery, my mom struggled to feed us, much less herself... and the first day of school was right around the corner.

For my mom, there were two times of the year when the constant pressure of living paycheck to paycheck became suffocating: the first day of school and Christmas. Instead of sharing our excitement about new teachers or school supplies, no doubt my mom only saw the money she didn't have. We three kids would need new clothes and shoes, as well. We hadn't stopped growing! If it had felt overwhelming in the past, the feeling was nearly unbearable the July after her hysterectomy. When she confessed her despair to her pastor, he introduced her to the idea of placing my brother, Eddie, in a boys' home and my sister and me in Hillcrest Children's Home.

Her pastor proposed this as a solution to her problems. She could heal and get her life back together. The organization responsible for running the Hillcrest facility was associated with the church my mother had been attending, and he was confident this was the path she was meant to take to get her life back on track. When her friends in the church heard of her agreement to this plan, they begged her to find an alternative solution. But the financial recession in the early 1980s left many people struggling to take care of themselves, much less offer financial help to others, and my mom felt the guilt of needing to be rescued. Again.

Although many of her friends were upset with her, begging her to reconsider, my mother believed she had no other choice. It wasn't a decision she took lightly, but it would be an opportunity for her to return to school and get an education. She just needed a car to get us there. Hillcrest Children's Home was seven hours away in Arkansas.

Fortunately, she had befriended a co-worker, Warren, who might be able to help. Although he was interested in her romantically, my mother didn't reciprocate his feelings. Warren graciously offered my mom the transportation she needed to get to Arkansas. He was a kind enough man and, having no children himself, saw no problem with dropping us off at a children's home in the care of strangers.

Though I was only four years old, I do hazily remember when the children's home came into view—a lush green yard with several buildings grouped together to form a small community over many acres of land. The main house opened inside to a large assembly room of sorts with cottage-like buildings branching off into all directions in the woods. When we arrived, there were many other children staying at Hillcrest, all with differing backgrounds, but there was one thing we all had in common: our parents had left us there. They were gone. *She* was gone. My mom was gone. Although I was surrounded by smiling people, doing their best to help navigate this unimaginable path my life had taken, I couldn't imagine anyone filling the void left inside. *Mama.*

I missed the feeling of her. The feel of her warm embrace when she snuggled me on the couch, wrapping her curvy thighs around me to squeeze me tight. Her smile when she put on her lipstick; she never left home without it. I missed the way her hand felt in mine, as we walked to the park down Judge Perez Drive. Though she never liked the veins on the back of her hands, to me, they were perfect. Because they were hers. And I missed those, too.

Imagine finding yourself in school all day. You patiently wait for the time you'll go home. Except... you don't. You never go home because *this* is home.

There was a great room where many of us would gather, especially on days when prospective adoptive parents came for a visit. The staff would dress us up in our "Sunday Best," asking us to behave in hopes of attracting a family to adopt us. I didn't want another family. I wanted *my* family. But I was unwanted. At least I felt I was.

I remember, one day, sitting isolated in a large, open room eating lasagna. As I sat there, I thought about being at my grandmother's table on Thanksgiving, surrounded by our family and all the food she would make. One thing I don't remember at Hillcrest is being with my sister, Santina, very often. Besides being separated from my mother, not having my sister at my side was jarring. I was used to being with her twenty-four hours a day, hand in hand, and doing absolutely everything together—from the moment I woke in the morning until the moment I fell asleep. Santina was my constant. A part of me felt missing at Hillcrest almost immediately.

For most of the day, and into the evening, we were separated by age groups. Outside of scheduled activities and playtime, we were assigned chores and tasks, but this was common for my sister and me. The days were very structured, and we were expected to obey. If you chose not to cooperate, there was a simple solution: the paddle. Back in that day, spanking was common. While I recall being on the receiving end of the paddle a couple of times, I seem to have blocked out what I did to deserve it. Most likely because I wanted to stay with my sister. Nights were especially hard.

Walking in the room filled with other children sleeping, I would look around, searching for my sister's blonde hair. Tip-toeing over and standing beside her bed, I'd quietly whisper, "Santina, I want to stay with you."

In the darkness as I crawled into her bed, Santina panicked, knowing it was against the rules for me to leave my designated area. "Shh, Christina. What are you doing? You're going to get in trouble." My sister whispered back intensely.

"I'm scared. I want to stay with you." Feeling alone, as I'm sure she did, tears welled up in my eyes.

"I know, but you need to be strong." Santina lifted the covers and got out of bed. Reaching out her hand, she took mine and quietly walked me back to my room. Instead of leaving, she helped me into bed and snuggled next to me.

"I'll stay here with you until you fall asleep, but you have to stay." Knowing she was inviting whatever consequence there would be for leaving her room, she preferred it over me getting in trouble.

My sister and I will always share a bond from being the only two people on earth who truly understand what we went through our entire lives… both the shared joyous memories and, of course, the challenging ones.

When I look back, I think my time at Hillcrest showed me a type of independence rarely formed at such an early age. In that environment, everything had a routine and order. Even as young as I was, and still today, I appreciated when my belongings and surroundings were organized and tidy. It was something I could control, something predictable and a way to maybe even perfect the imperfect. It helped me cope when everything else felt so out of control.

I remember asking the houseparents a few times, "Where's my mom?" and only receiving vague answers. I wanted to be with her, and the sense of abandonment I was feeling was a complex feeling for my little heart. I can still feel the joy when I received a package from a "sponsor family" while everyone was gathered in the great room. When I opened the box, I found a beautiful light pink night-gown and a stuffed teddy bear. I remember feeling special and thinking, *Wow! Someone knows I'm here. Someone is thinking about me.* I loved that teddy bear.

Since my mother had full custody of us, she could decide to give us away without my father's consent. We had not lived with my grandparents in several months, so they were unaware of my mother's plans. Without my grandparents knowing, there was no family to urge her to reconsider. With the advice of those she deeply trusted, she believed that, as difficult as it was, this was best for everyone involved, including herself. For my mother's part, she says the moment she signed the papers that day and said goodbye; she realized what a terrible mistake she had made. The advice of leaving us at Hillcrest did not align with her heart.

On the returning drive back to New Orleans with Warren, she was silent as she tried to figure out how to reverse what she had just done. What she didn't know was that crossing state lines further complicated things.

Once my mom discovered that regaining custody would be full of hurdles and red tape, she was devastated. Ultimately, she would have to prove to a judge that she could care for us by securing a home and a job because she had fully surrendered her parental rights to the children's home. If that proved too difficult, however, she simply needed a husband.

Never mind that she had been raising us as a single mother for years already by this point; in those days, a woman wasn't regarded as truly stable or legitimate until she was connected to a man. Though she had decided to fight to get us back as soon as she left, the sad reality was nothing about her situation had changed. She still needed recovery time because of her hysterectomy, so she had no job, no vehicle, and no apartment. My mom was also out of money, so she was left with only one option—to find herself a husband.

If she wanted us out of Hillcrest Children's Home, and she desperately did, there would need to be a wedding ring on her finger. With this realization, she and Warren said, "I do." Her new marriage, combined with an impassioned letter to the judge, conveyed her pain and earnest desire to be reunited with us kids. This worked, and a few weeks before Christmas, as the Arkansas fall was rapidly turning into winter, my mom burst through the doors of Hillcrest to finally take us home.

I remember returning home with a separation anxiety which lasted for many years after. My mom says not only had I changed, but the bond between us needed to be rebuilt. Even still, if my mom left a room or was gone too long for work, I would feel my heart quicken in my chest. It didn't matter who was watching me. I would become overwhelmed with emotion, sure that she was gone forever this time. As a child, it was hard to shake that feeling of abandonment, and into adulthood I found it permeated many of the relation-

31

ships in my life. I was young and already accumulating scars. It made it hard to trust people and accept love, not sure how long a relationship would last. *Who else would leave?*

With the Hillcrest custody problem behind us, my mother and Warren agreed to dissolve their marriage. Although this is a time in her life she doesn't like to discuss, I know my mom has always been grateful for what he did to help her get us back. It was an act of kindness she can never repay.

Chapter Three

Pancakes.

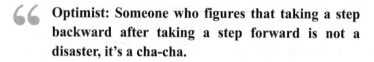

Optimist: Someone who figures that taking a step backward after taking a step forward is not a disaster, it's a cha-cha.

— **Robert Brault**

It seemed we had barely set our things down upon our return to New Orleans when my mother abruptly decided we were taking a road trip to see her family. Everywhere she turned, it was a reminder of what we all had gone through with Hillcrest. With one borrowed car and no radio, all we had were the songs in my mother's head from "The Big Easy" to the California coastline.

Music went hand in hand with my mother. Perhaps that's why I've always loved to sing. She was the first to admit that she couldn't carry a tune to save her life, telling me "If I had a voice like yours, I'd be dangerous!" If we were cleaning the house or doing a project, you better believe Aretha Franklin was right there with us in spirit. My mom always listened to soul music, and she loved to dance. I felt her passion for life through those dance parties in the living room.

When she would start the first few notes of a lullaby, I would put my finger to her lips and say, "Shh, no mama, don't sing. I'll sing to you." On all our road trip escapades you could bet there was one song we were eventually going to sing: "California, Here I Come." Our version of the lyrics went something like this:

"California, here *(we)* come right back where *(we)* started from…"

Then we would proudly name all the states we had visited or lived in, attempting to name them all in order. I wasn't very old before it became a pretty long list. That's the summary of my childhood in general. My mother was spread too thin trying to raise us children, and my father was off somewhere focused on his own happiness. Just when I had some sense of routine, just when I had made a few precious friends, life's circumstances would throw us a curveball and we'd be back to square one. How could I feel secure in my identity when my family seemed to be constantly changing ours? Shattered pieces everywhere, across state lines, and different homes. I was caught between a father who couldn't be bothered with his children and a mother who was struggling to provide for them.

Not only did she have myself and my sister to worry about, but my brother's problems were growing worse. As he got older, when he was not helping to care for us, he got into more and more trouble —stealing, using, and selling drugs. My mother was not able to send him to the boy's home when we entered Hillcrest. His behavior made him ineligible for the home and his problems were only increasing with his age. Eventually, he stole a gun out of a police detective's vehicle. With that, my mother felt she couldn't handle the downward spiral he was on. When she would confront him, inevitably it would turn physical, which should never have to happen between a mother and son.

While Eddie was a gentle big brother to Santina and me, we were also witnessing their physical fights unfold in front of us. My mom decided to take him to California to live with her family for some time. As soon as he arrived, he ended up getting in trouble and, eventually, arrested. My brother would, unfortunately, be sentenced to an intense youth correctional institution at the age of sixteen years old. While there, he was diagnosed with paranoid schizophrenia.

After he left us, whenever the song "Stand by Me" by Ben E. King came on the radio, I couldn't help but think of when he danced with Santina and me. He would remind us it was "our song" and to always think of him when it played. Even today, when I hear that song, I can't help but think of our time together. During those years, Eddie would write to us, and he always referred to Santina and me as his "Heart and Soul." Despite my brother's troubles, I remember how incredibly sad we all were without him. A piece missing from our little family.

We extended our stay in San Francisco so long that I began kindergarten, but I didn't finish there. This California visit started out mundane enough, but Santina quickly became a handful for the family. This included getting into fights at school, often after sticking up for me. Soon after, at the insistence of our California family, my mom sent my sister back to New Orleans early.

In my sister's absence, I soaked up all the attention I could get. My great grandmother, Dorothy, or Omie, as we called her, was such a tiny woman that, at six years old, I fit into all her clothes and shoes. When my mom was at work, she loved to dress me up and take me all around San Francisco. While she may have been a little grumpy with everyone else, she showered me with attention, and I looked forward to everything she planned for me. We would ride the trolley, visit the zoo animals and, of course, stop in Chinatown. It was the only time I've ever experienced the Golden Dragon or "Gum Lung," the star of San Francisco's Chinese New Year festival. I felt a connection with Omie as each day I spent with her felt exciting, but the attention she gave me made me feel as special as the dragon.

This California trip was unique in that, for a short period, time seemed to slow down. I remember a couple nights when my mom would cuddle up with me and read my favorite book, *Mr. Bell's Fix It Shop* from the *Little Golden Book* series Omie had gifted me. I was happy enjoying the short-lived opportunity to be the only child, receiving a lot of one-on-one attention, particularly from my mom. I got to experience a mother with just one child to care for, and no ex-husband or the drama that followed him. Sadly, all good things must end, and I was soon off to New Orleans. As was always the case with my life, the winds of change were never far away.

* * *

Living off and on with my grandparents and managing life with us as young children, my mother had little opportunity to date. Her life was filled with work or with us. That was it. Over the years, my mother was introduced to various suitors, including an heir to a family fortune. Although she was enamored with the promise of a financially secure future for a time, she wasn't ready to take the risks associated with a relationship. No one had been able to capture her attention quite like my father all those years ago until that moment.

What moment? The moment she met Isaac. He was charming and kind, and genuinely showed tender care for my mother in a way that most men never took the time to do. Isaac was a pilot and Captain in the Navy. He always looked very sophisticated, dressed in his uniform. He also wasn't intimidated by my father, like most of the other men were.

Though her life was full, with us getting older and a new interest in Isaac, my mother did all she could to let us see my father often. Unfortunately, his sober moments were so few now, it seemed impossible to catch him at a good time. My mom confided in my grandmother about meeting Isaac and how much he cared for her and us. After hearing this, she agreed my mom should move on. My grandmother, although a traditional woman, understood her son's faults, including his drinking habits. I imagine even she could see from his actions that it was difficult and unrealistic for my mother to expect much from him as a father.

When I was about six years old and not long after Isaac came into our lives, Grandma Evelyn fell ill and had to be admitted to the intensive care unit (ICU) of the nearby hospital. My mom would visit her every day. It was summertime, so Santina and I were out of school. She would leave my sister and me in the waiting area while she would spend every opportunity she could at my grandmother's bedside. At this age, I would use my imagination to make up games. In the hospital waiting room was where I drank coffee for the first time, stealing a sip from the waiting room carafe, finding entertainment while stirring around cream and sugar.

There weren't many other children who visited the waiting area. However, I remember a little girl who walked in one day with a new baby doll. The doll resembled a real newborn baby, and I had seen other little girls my age toting them around when we were out. It even came with a hospital bracelet and birth certificate.

Usually keeping to myself, I depended on my mom to help soften introductions by making them for me. Without my mother with me, I only stared at the baby this little girl was holding, wishing I could have one myself. Watching this little girl cuddle and coo with her baby painfully reminded me I had never had a baby doll of my own. My heart ached. I wanted to hold it so badly. Usually, the only time we got to play with new toys was if we went over to a friend's house. It was out of the question to ask my mother for a new toy because, even as young as I was, I knew we never had enough money.

While my grandmother was in the ICU, my mom would talk to her with the only acknowledgement from my grandmother being a squeeze of her hand. My mom got a tape recorder and recorded us talking to Grandma Evelyn, since we weren't allowed to be in her room. I vividly remember sitting in the back seat with my sister. My mother held the tape recorder while I belted into this little device my best Whitney Houston impersonation for my grandmother to hear.

My mom played my song along with everything we wanted to say to her. She knew my grandmother could recognize the voice coming over the speakers by the tears that streamed down her face. We all believed our words would heal her and she would come home. No matter how much we wanted her with us, she never came home, and her passing devastated my mother. Even today, I still remember the moment my mom heard she had died. She was standing at a payphone, calling to check on my grandma, and couldn't stop crying after she hung up. My mother always tried to be strong around us children, like most parents do. She was transparent with us about what was happening when times were tough, but she always tried to model a good attitude and keep things light at the same time.

In times like that, when the tough facade would crack and we'd get a glimpse into the actual human behind my mother's imposing strength, it made us stop in our tracks. Grandma Evelyn had made such an impact on her life that, for years after, just thinking of her would make my mom cry. When my grandmother comes up in conversation even now, tears still well in her eyes.

Unfortunately for us, those early years after my grandmother's passing in New Orleans felt like a giant game of pinball, with us bouncing from one home to the next. Sometimes we could afford a place on our own, but it was usually short-lived. Oftentimes, we were staying with friends. Being as young as I was, I didn't think about how we were homeless. All I knew was that we moved a lot. With so much change, we weren't anchored to anything or any place. We were just holding on to navigate the next storm.

* * *

My mom had secured an apartment so that we could all be together, finally in a place of our own. We were so excited. I remember it vividly. We had no furniture except for an old television, found alongside a dumpster, now proudly resting on a blue, plastic milk crate that we turned upside down and a mattress on the floor in the single bedroom we three shared. No electricity, just the sunlight provided by nature and some creativity until a couple of weeks when my mom could afford to get it turned on. "We're on a camping trip in the wilderness" my mother would tell us, in an attempt to distract us from the reality of our circumstance. We listened to music, danced until we couldn't anymore, and swam for hours at the apartment pool. We were beyond happy just all being together, and my mother did everything she could to keep it that way.

On the eve of my sister's eleventh birthday, my mom had a surprise proposal for her. "Do you want a birthday party, or do you want to go to Florida?"

Well, that was an easy answer. In fact, I think I helped Santina reply by speaking up on her behalf, unrequested, of course. "Florida, Florida!" We both cheered and jumped up and down with so much excitement! Little did we know there was an ulterior motive behind her offer. There usually was. My father, who in no way, shape or form could care for us, had decided at the urging of his relatives to file for full custody. That idea terrified my mother.

As the court date grew closer, my mom's panic grew, too, so she decided she would hide us by taking us to Florida. She knew that if she kept us in New Orleans and the judge ruled in my father's favor, she would lose us almost immediately. My mom wasn't willing to take the risk, so she devised a plan to get us out of the state, and my sister and I were totally oblivious to the drama going on behind the scenes.

We drove the entire night, nearly ten hours, in the car with Ms. Anna, one of my mother's trusted friends. Like her friendship with Sandra, they were glued at the hip. Besides giving the best hugs that you could sink into, Ms. Anna treated us like we were her own. She took us into her home, when needed, and she was always there for my mom.

We finally arrived at the St. Petersburg home of Anna's daughter, Linda. A beautiful woman, Linda traveled the country as a professional ballroom dancer, entertaining audiences from all over the world. She shined like the sequins on her dress, so being around her made you feel like you were in the company of a celebrity. I wanted to be just as elegant as her, but I felt far from it.

We didn't really have traditional vacations in my childhood, but like all things, my mom made this one sound exciting. Our hopes, however, would be deflated. After a day of sand, playing games and spending time together, my mom announced she needed to leave us for a few days. She promised she only needed to return to New Orleans briefly and would be back to get us before we could get the sand out of our clothes.

Would she return? With our Hillcrest history always fresh in our minds, we were terrified this could mean another long separation. Although Ms. Anna did all she could to keep us happy, and my mother trusted her with our lives, my mom's departure for however long removed any fun from the rest of the trip for my sister and me.

We tried to fill the days, but they were still long. Not to mention the humid weather was suffocating us on top of our worries. Linda's home was more than a quick walk to the beach, so we often weren't up for the long hike. While my sister and I found the beach to be exciting at first, after my mom left, it was a reminder that she wasn't with us. Besides, there's only so much you can do with sand, since water was not an option.

"It's 'red tide' and I can't afford for you girls to get sick, so no swimming." Our mom had told us. Knowing I had suffered with breathing problems in the past, she wasn't willing to take the risk that comes with red tide, a type of harmful algal bloom known to cause skin and respiratory irritation. Especially in her absence. So, she gave clear instructions before leaving back to New Orleans: "I'm sorry, you two are going to have to find something to do. Entertain each other. Get creative." *Creative?*

As our luck would have it, television wasn't an option either. Every network was covering Oliver North's congressional committee hearing. *Great.*

So, as an alternative, we found exploring Linda's home, filled with mementos from her world travels, to be an interesting source of entertainment.

Ms. Anna would always say "yes" when it involved turning Linda's porcelain into a royal tea party. It was my favorite thing to do—pretend I was very regal, polite and distinguished over water and crackers. Linda's souvenirs included a two-foot-high jar filled with matchbooks from every special place and restaurant she had ever visited. I remember organizing them, categorizing them by type and color; imagining the day when I traveled to all these places, living a glamorous life of my own. Although I could pass the time for hours doing that alone, it wasn't enough. The long idle days only made us miss our mother more. I recall staring at a crumpled Yahtzee scoresheet with my mother's handwriting on it and keeping it safely in my pocket. It was the only thing I could physically hold which would connect me to her as I waited and hoped, praying for her safe and quick return.

Two long weeks passed before my mother made her way back to St. Petersburg. Ecstatic to be reunited, my mother seemed to float on air the moment she walked through Linda's front door. We, including Ms. Anna, were all eager to pack our bags and head back home to New Orleans. The judge had ruled in her favor, and that meant no more running, no more hiding. But we were never promised we would stay in one place.

Life moved on, as it always does. My mother and Isaac were becoming a sure thing. They had a steadier relationship than I had ever seen my mom have with my biological father. Isaac would intentionally spend time with us, take us out for ice cream, and bring us presents regularly.

With Isaac's stable income and dependability, soon he helped my mom secure a duplex. This would be the start of our life improving dramatically. Our new place had two bedrooms so my sister and I were able to share a room of our own. "Furniture shopping" entailed my mom spending a late night with Ms. Anna sifting through nearby dumpsters for hidden "treasures." On one such adventure, my mom found a pullout loveseat sofa and placed it in our bedroom instead of a bed. In her sleep, my sister would kick feverishly and stretch out, leaving no room for me. So, each night, I would place the two sofa cushions on the floor with a sheet over them to fashion a bed. I didn't complain, though. Everything around us was more than we ever had before.

This included food in the refrigerator on a regular basis. After Isaac would visit, we would always find new things popping up around the house like Easter eggs. Each time he left, my sister and I went on a scavenger hunt of sorts. We would "ooh" and "ahh" as we opened the cabinets and closets, finding an array of things commonly found in any other household, including our grandparents. They were simple things: a small toolbox placed in one of the many empty kitchen cabinets; a matching set of dishes and utensils. We had lived with these items before, but they had never been *ours*. We even found a great big jar of whole pickles. Pickles!

If Isaac did nothing else, he won us over with this gesture! We were easy to please because we were accustomed to an almost empty pantry. Before Isaac, my mother would offer choices like: "Do you want pancakes with sugar or pancakes with peanut butter?" There was a time when this was our entire menu of options for breakfast, lunch, and dinner. That's it. When things were good and my mother had a little money while trying to make it on her own, it was a bit fancier, and we would splurge on tuna sandwiches. Even better was the rare occasion we would wake up to the smell of eggs, with pancakes of course, being prepared by our very own Chef Vivian.

Believe it or not, before Isaac entered our lives, the lack of options often made eating fun when we received a box of donated food. It was almost like a game. Although we were used to receiving a lot of grown-up food like minestrone soup, now and then, we would hit the jackpot with a can of Chef Boyardee ravioli. Now that was a special day.

As you might imagine, my sister and I were very intense about sharing this treasure trove of goodness, carefully counting each ravioli. If there was ever an uneven number, the little ravioli was cut perfectly into precise portions. Even the sauce was carefully ladled out in equal spoonfuls—*one for you, one for me*—until the entire can was scraped clean. Were we trying to share? No. On the contrary, this was a very strategic plan to ensure neither one of us received even one more spoonful than the other.

Maybe Isaac knew the impact he was making during that period or maybe not, but he made a home for the three of us. He helped provide stability, which we greatly needed. We experienced other changes, as well. Isaac was calm, patient, understanding, and never raised his voice. My mother believed the popular saying: "Spare the rod, spoil the child," but this didn't sit well with him, so she agreed to hold back on spanking us. But she was still known to give us the occasional swat, or secret pinch, all the way through our high school years.

The closer my mother and Isaac got, the more my sister and I considered him as part of the family and, truthfully, the more we imagined him as our stepdad one day. When his time in New Orleans came to an end, he invited all of us to join him just outside of Chicago. I imagine the decision to move for my sister may have been hard, since it meant moving away from our father. While my sister was more than thrilled to have even a few moments in our father's occasional presence, I was often put off by broken promises, the smell of alcohol on his breath, and had grown increasingly uninterested in being around him.

For me, although I would miss the Diecedue family, following Isaac to Chicago seemed like an easy choice. For my mother, she understood it might be her only opportunity to escape the stormy waters of New Orleans and start over. Isaac's promise to my mom:

In six months, if you don't like it, I'll send you back. With my mother in agreement and Isaac's steady hand to guide us, we were on our way to Illinois.

Chapter Four

Hiding.

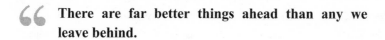 **There are far better things ahead than any we leave behind.**

— **C. S. Lewis**

Surrounded by packed boxes of what few belongings we had accumulated, my sister and I laid on a mattress in the back cargo area of a moving truck as we made the long journey from New Orleans to Chicago. A new school and a new set of friends were waiting for us, and we couldn't wait.

Truthfully, moving had already become our norm. Regardless of the challenges each move held, there were times when we all eagerly anticipated a move. I suspect those were the times when we had stayed in one place for so long that problems accumulated, and we craved the adventure of starting over in a new place. It's like driving a new car. After a while, the new smell fades; the dirt and dust accumulate, and over time, you get the urge for a different model. The urge was especially strong in my mother because of all her practice moving when she was desperate to get away from my

45

father. So, I couldn't tell you the number of times we moved homes and I've found that my expectations in a move haven't always met reality.

While being the "new kid" seemed like such a fun idea, really, it wasn't always the case. The realness of the first day would quickly set in, as I awkwardly walked into a new environment filled with complete strangers. This was especially true when we moved from Louisiana to the suburbs of Chicago. Children can be brutal, making fun of you for just about anything: what you wear; what you look like; or how you act. Many of our new school mates were put off by our New Orleans accents, making us feel like we didn't belong or fit in. We were teased quite a bit until our Midwestern Chicago accent took hold.

By the time I began my new elementary school, I was nervous about several things, but there was one thing I knew for sure: I love music and I love to sing—just not out loud. When it came to singing in public, my insecurities would get the best of me, and my throat would close tight. At home, though, you could hear me singing my heart out within the safety of my room to a Whitney Houston album from start to finish.

Home was my singing sanctuary. No one in my house, or our neighbors, ever complained about the music or me singing. They let me pour my soul into the moment. My mom loved to show me off to family and friends by asking me to sing. By "asking," of course, I really mean telling.

Don't misunderstand. Like any young girl, I imagined myself on a stage singing in front of a large audience but doing so wasn't authentically me; it just never felt natural. I was never the person who wanted "all eyes on me." Instead of me taking center stage, my sister would take my place. She would lip sync and dance in front of me as if she was on Broadway. Meanwhile, I would stand in the shadows, belting out any song my mother requested. This was our gig, and it worked.

Unfortunately, my uneasiness for singing spilled over into being dissatisfied with my appearance. When I looked at myself in the mirror, I didn't like what I saw. I felt as though every flaw was screaming back at me. Baggy second-hand clothes, crooked teeth, bushy eyebrows, a bump on the nose. As a little girl, my father would call me names based on my appearance—names I would never call another person, much less my own child. These insults, even said jokingly, only made me feel more self-conscious. Not beautiful. Not wanted.

With my dark hair, dark eyes, and olive skin, I looked a lot like my father. Our similarities went as far as having matching moles on our respective left thighs. When I was a kid, I remember that same mole seemed to be the size of a half dollar. I would rest my hand over it, trying to cover it in the summer whenever I was wearing a bathing suit. The truth is, it's the size of a chili pepper flake, but I passionately hated it, along with every mole on my face.

You're not pretty enough. You're not good enough. These were the things the mirror would say to me when I stood in front of it, and sadly, I believed it. It's easy to believe the voice in your head when it's the only one you can hear, or really the only one you're listening to.

Consequently, my self-esteem was always crushingly low.

My mind continued whispering negative thoughts as I navigated the treacherous waters of middle school. On the outside, I fit in. On the inside, I felt I didn't. After Christmas, when everyone in my school was bragging about what presents they received, I was hiding that my gifts were donated from a sponsor family. Although I was grateful, it was just another thing to hide about my life.

I was hiding my time at Hillcrest, hiding how money was always a struggle, hiding how I never felt I was ever enough. I confused having less with being less. It seemed impossible to feel special and, heaven forbid, if anyone knew our family secrets. Sadly, I often wished so much to be anyone but me.

I carried shame for our circumstances and with that, many details of my childhood I would spend a lifetime trying to forget.

But there was one thing I would never allow myself to forget. The promise I made to never grow up and live life the same way. I didn't know how or when I was going to make good on that promise—but I had enough faith to believe I would figure it out someday.

Switching schools didn't switch our circumstances, nor did it make my lack of confidence magically disappear. In the words of the ancient Chinese philosopher, Confucius, "No matter where you go, there you are." My sister was also there. As the teenage years hit for her, our differences became more and more noticeable. Despite the same blood running through us, my sister and I couldn't have had more opposite personalities or appearances.

Sure, I was a Diecedue, but I wasn't always very proud to be one. Even my last name was ridiculed in school. If someone wasn't saying something about how I looked or what clothes I was wearing, they would certainly create interesting variations of my last name to make fun of me. It's interesting how, as children, we are more than willing to abandon our heritage at the first signs of bullying. I could only dream of the day when I would get married and take on another name, praying it would be a more easily pronounced one like "Smith" or "Williams."

Maybe my sister battled with her own insecurities, but from my point of view, my sister wasn't given any cruel nicknames, just the usual compliments. "Oh, you're so beautiful! Look at all that blonde hair and those pretty hazel eyes." My sister's face resembled that of our late grandmother, Evelyn. She would catch the attention of everyone; it was impossible for her not to with the amount of confidence she exuded.

I know I can't be the only one in the world whose family inadvertently made insensitive remarks on occasion, or whose sibling would joke that the differences in our appearances were because I was adopted. It didn't help that I was already struggling with self-doubt and insecure about how I looked. My sister added gasoline to the fire when she questioned whether or not I "belonged" to my family. I can't blame her. I just could never understand how very different we were. Same mom. Same dad. So different.

* * *

In the fifth grade, I befriended a girl my age who shared with me her Latin family traditions. The first time I ate guacamole and experienced mariachi music up close was an evening out with Mariana and her family. From that night on, I was hooked.

This was one of my first exposures to Latin culture, despite Isaac's Mexican heritage. His first language was Spanish, but he didn't speak it with us. He would always shock people when he would begin speaking in his native tongue, as his looks would never hint that he was Hispanic.

Spending an afternoon with Mariana, over freshly made empanadas, I caught the bug to learn Spanish. I loved the way the language sounded. "How do you say 'red'?" I would inquire, looking around the room for other random things she could translate for me. She was eager to teach me so she would play along by answering back in Spanish. Trying hard to come up with a more complex word, I blurted out: "How do you say 'piano'?" She laughed and replied, "Piano."

Feeling a little stupid, she would eventually help me realize how many words were similar in Spanish and English. Instead of making me feel embarrassed, she pointed out that this meant I was closer to fluency than I thought. I had a long way to go, but it was still an entertaining and easy way for us to build a friendship.

Isaac in our lives meant there was much less drama compared to the past, but that didn't mean more wouldn't eventually find us. Mariana's family lived in the apartment directly above ours, so it was easy to hear most everything happening in her home, including when her stepfather returned from out of town. The late-night yelling and physical abuse we could hear hit too close to home for my mother, and she couldn't help but intervene.

The next time Mariana's stepfather left town for a work trip, my mother moved Mariana, her mother, little sister, and aunt into our tiny two-bedroom apartment. Though the family had moved just a few feet away, they eagerly welcomed this sanctuary of safety and security. Despite having seven people all crammed into our tiny space, I remember that period fondly. Our time together felt like one long sleepover to Mariana and me. I doubt Santina felt the same.

My mom helped Mariana's mother and aunt enroll in English classes and eventually taught Mariana's mom how to drive. This would offer her mom an independence she had not experienced before. Ultimately, they returned home with a promise of change. But, like my mother had experienced with my father, a couple of years later, they would return to our home once more for a safe place to heal and regroup. On their last return home, Mariana's step-father forbade her to be friends with me. I was more than devastated. Mariana saw the details of my life that no one else did. I didn't have to hide with her; I could be me. The loss made me feel isolated. The rejection was heartbreaking for me and would change the way I approached friendships forever. We shared more than a childhood friendship; we had spent every waking moment together. Living so close to each other and now forbidden to be friends, it felt like I was losing a sister.

My mother knew all too well the realities of life and tried to protect us from ever being harmed. The darkness she experienced in her life growing up are details I could never imagine. This meant she was overprotective; *always*. She was normally willing to loosen her restrictions within the confines of the church. I cannot recall a time when church was not a part of my life since my mom's conversion to Christianity had occurred very early on. So, I never thought twice about going and the church often provided transportation when we didn't have our own. There were always activities to participate in, and we didn't have to worry about money there. Church was a familiar environment that we welcomed, and it welcomed us.

During my preteen and teen years, my mom encouraged me to take part in youth group outings, retreats, and eventually, even mission trips. It was in these settings, where I always felt the most independent outside the protective boundaries of my mother. I was a high school freshman when my first two-week mission trip took me about twelve hundred miles north from the Midwest to Canada. The following year, I traveled approximately fifteen hundred miles from Illinois, south through Texas, to across the U.S. border where we worked in a small town outside Juarez, Mexico. Eventually, I would return to Mexico for a thirty-day mission trip. Although each time I missed my family, the offer of independence more than made up for the absence.

Our group traveled for miles down dirt roads to unfamiliar parts of town, spending most of our time working with families and children, setting them up with the necessities in life and sharing the Bible with them. In Mexico, I was introduced to construction as we helped the community build a church. It was labor intensive as we spent days digging trenches, quickly learning how to construct a church building using mortar and cement cinder blocks.

The youth mission trip was the first time I felt comfortable singing in public because music was an easy way to connect with anyone, no matter the language barriers. During the evenings, when all of us would gather around and goof off, was when the singing would start.

A year prior, I discovered a dual language song, *Via Dolorosa*, performed by Sandi Patty, a native English speaker. Because Sandi's first language was English, the idea of learning *her* song in Spanish didn't seem too daunting, so the practicing began. Coincidentally, by the time I was in Juarez, I knew the song backwards and forwards.

"Does anyone know any Spanish songs?" Julian, one of the team leaders, asked. We all looked around at one another, waiting for someone to speak up first. No one did. Not fully understanding what I was doing, I raised my hand and said, "Oh, I might know one, but there's some English in it."

"Perfect. You can sing it tonight at our community gathering!"

Wait, what? I'd unknowingly volunteered to put myself right in the center of the spotlight. I hadn't even allowed my closest friends to hear me sing. My only saving grace was that no one in the group went to the same school as I did. So, I prayed that any embarrassment would stay behind in Juarez.

From that day forward, I would perform *Via Dolorosa* nightly. With each passing performance, I gained some confidence in my public singing, mostly from the encouragement of others. It translated into confidence in other areas, too, as I heard myself speak up more in conversations and volunteer for more activities within the group.

* * *

Back in Chicago, Isaac and my mother married just as I was completing the sixth grade. Having Isaac move in and become a permanent part of our lives helped slow down the pace considerably. My mother and step dad worked extremely hard, but when they were around, they were intentional about being present with us. If Isaac was fixing something, he'd ask me to join him, teaching me how to use various tools. I was always eager to learn from him, as he would patiently explain things to me. It felt good to have a "dad" in my life, even if he wasn't my biological father. He was as close to having a father in my life than I had ever experienced before.

There were some ups and downs during our initial transition to the Midwest. Our life was better in Chicago in a lot of ways. However, my mom and Isaac had to work long hours to manage the cost of living there, which was much higher than in New Orleans. The two of them were always adding a few side hustles to make ends meet. It wasn't uncommon to have children work with their parents to earn extra money, and our family was no different. Besides taking traditional side jobs like babysitting, we went door to door and sold pot-pourri sachets, stuffed envelopes, counted lug nuts and, if we were at the office, we helped file, staple, and sort. If they took a cleaning job, we were cleaning right along with them. If they were at a warehouse making kitchen countertop coverings for kosher cooking, my sister and I would sweep the floors and clean up late into the night.

You could even find us squeezing fresh lemonade at Chicago's Buckingham fountain or serving up bratwurst at Oktoberfest or the Taste of Chicago in Grant Park. Working the events and festivals was hard work because doing so usually included setting up, serving, and breaking down the vendors' products and facilities. Working these events was still a favorite; while working, we could experience the excitement of the city and its events for free. Maybe we whined a little but, knowing my mother's response, I doubt we complained much. Teaching us to have an unbreakable work ethic was vital to my mom.

My sister and I knew working would help our family, as we needed the extra money. When working on some of the jobs, we were hidden from public view, like cleaning offices late at night. Others required us to be in plain sight, which was harder. It felt like a scene in a movie to watch kids from our school walking around, enjoying the fair while we scooped ice cream into their root beer floats and counted out their change at the cash register. Ironically, I was living more comfortably than I had ever before, but still felt "less than" in this environment with the kids surrounding us not having to work and being substantially more well-off. In New Orleans, I was poor, but maybe there weren't as many opportunities to notice. Even when we made it a few rungs up the ladder in Chicago, there were others who were still so far ahead.

There was never a dull moment in our household, though most of our time was filled with side jobs; there were evenings and weekends spent like any other family. Always prone to reaching out, my mom befriended all our neighbors. She needed to make sure they were safe enough for my sister and me to be around, but she also truly loved people and loved to help others when she could.

One Sunday, when I was around eleven years old, we were out along the apartment community pond having a barbecue with some neighbors when a little boy walked right up to me and tapped me on my side to get my attention. I took one look at him and instantly fell in love. He was so adorably cute! I picked up a royal blue rubber racquetball we had with us and bent down to play with him. After a few minutes, I looked up to see a woman walking toward us. She was beautiful. With flowing blonde hair and a beaming smile, she looked like she had walked off the *Charlie's Angels'* set. She sweetly approached us, introducing herself as Kathy, the apartment manager and mother to Tommy, the precious two-year-old we had met earlier.

She stayed a while to visit, mentioning that she also lived on the property. Later in the conversation, Kathy confided in my mother that she was looking for a babysitter and didn't trust just anyone with her son. Kathy's apartment was located right next to her office, and she was looking for someone who wouldn't mind watching Tommy at her place over the summer.

I wasn't confident enough at this age to negotiate for myself, so my mom did all the talking and, quickly, I had my first babysitting job. Did I know what to do with a toddler? Absolutely not. I only had experience helping my mom when she babysat for some extra cash. So, while I arrived at Kathy's apartment early that first morning on my own, soon after, my mother was right behind me, teaching me how to care for this cute little boy.

From the beginning, I thought Kathy was amazing. She was single when we met, but soon was engaged to her true love, Steve. Her refrigerator and freezer were stocked with every snack a kid would love. Including me. When she arrived home each day after work, she would ask me questions about my life, and we would chat like girlfriends. Her genuine interest in me made me feel like a beloved niece, and I loved being around her. She was also a successful businesswoman. Who wouldn't look up to her?

When Kathy married Steve, they blended their two families into one big happy family, the Wolskis. Over the next couple of years, the Wolskis truly became family to us when what began as a small babysitting gig turned into so much more.

Eventually, Kathy helped me get my first real job as a lifeguard, and I continued babysitting for her on occasion. Otherwise, I spent time with my friends or volunteered at church. Life was looking pretty good to me... right until my mom and Isaac made a family announcement around the spring of my sophomore year in high school. They had decided the time had come to pick up and move yet again. This time, however, it would not be across town like we were accustomed to since moving to Chicago. We were moving 1,241 miles away to San Antonio, Texas.

After the shock wore off, I tried to wrap my mind around moving to a new city for what seemed like the umpteenth time in my life.

Isaac benefited from this cross-country leap, as the move would bring him closer to his mother and family. My mom agreed that moving away from the brutal cold winters in the Midwest was also a good idea. This wouldn't be our first time in San Antonio. Isaac's mom would pitch in for plane tickets and open her home for us to spend our most recent summers and Christmas breaks with her. Thanks to these trips, we were somewhat familiar with the city.

I'll admit San Antonio was lovely to visit—so full of food and culture. Like most tourists, I was charmed by the famous Riverwalk with its boats passing on the water, and the sounds of live performances playing in the background. This might sound silly, but at the time I had never been to Europe, and this is what I imagined it to be like. Except, this version of Venice had engines on the back of the gondolas.

The Riverwalk was especially romantic in December. All the trees were draped in lights, and the water sparkled with the reflection of them. I remember several times walking along the Riverwalk with my family and imagining what it would be like to stroll along with a special someone by my side.

While I loved the romance of San Antonio, the only challenge to our visits was knowing how much it would affect my mom. She was the type of person who would give you the shirt off her back if you needed it but fight you if you tried to steal it instead. She was both the person you wanted to care for you when you were sick and the person you didn't cross.

My stepdad's family, however, didn't want to take the time to learn, understand, or appreciate my mother. They only saw the overly confident and, at times, too forthcoming Vivian. In that state, my mother was often very polarizing. Some of Isaac's family deeply loved her, while others couldn't stand her. During one get together, of which there was one almost every weekend, my mother and I walked into a backyard barbecue to find several of Isaac's family members. Without tossing so much as a glance our way, some of them switched into Spanish.

"Mom, they're doing that, so we won't understand them," I whispered, protective of my mother to a fault.

"Shh, do you think I don't know that?" she whispered back under her breath as she pulled a water bottle from the cooler. "Let it go." And with her final word, she smiled flawlessly before ushering me to take a seat.

Even if I didn't always agree with my mother, I would protect her to the ends of the earth from anyone who would want to hurt her. This made being at those first San Antonio family functions especially challenging. Behind the smiles, I knew who didn't care for my mother or us. Nevertheless, my mother raised us to be kind and loving no matter how we were treated. And it seemed she was trying, for Isaac's sake, to put her fighting days behind her.

My first impressions of Isaac's relatives weren't all bad. Some of them treated us with love and kindness. I hadn't really grown up with a lot of family around us after leaving New Orleans, so although they were far from perfect, it was nice to visit and have a large extended family. The culture in San Antonio was also quite different from New Orleans or Chicago, and I embraced every part of it, from the mariachi music to breakfast tacos. Homemade potato and egg stuffed inside a flour tortilla—it was hard to say no to one.

Because of this dynamic with my mother, when my stepdad mentioned starting a new chapter in San Antonio for him and my mom, I was intrigued to join them, but torn. I finally felt like I was coming into my own in Chicago. I had great friends and had gained some new freedoms. I had earned a shiny new driver's license earlier that year and was feeling more independent as a result. On the other hand, I knew San Antonio was a fun and romantic city from our visits. The itch to wipe the slate clean and begin again seemed genetic, and it was hard to resist.

It was no secret my mom operated in crisis mode nearly my entire life while raising me. Good decisions or bad decisions, including Hillcrest. She always tried to do what she thought was best. At this point I was old enough to navigate life on my own and she trusted I wouldn't get myself into any trouble. I had never given her a reason to worry.

With that, my mother offered to let me make the final decision. If I wanted to, she would allow me to finish my last two years of high school in Chicago and live with who I now called my "Aunt Kathy." My mom saw Kathy and Steve as an extension of her "village" to help raise me. I felt conflicted being so young and trying to make such a complicated choice. Should I stay in the life I knew and with a stable family or take a leap of faith and move to San Antonio with the family that, while volatile, had been my people my entire life?

Aunt Kathy and Uncle Steve, for me, had the most ideal family life. Spending time visiting with Aunt Kathy's extended family in southern Illinois was like watching a scene in a Hallmark movie.

As much as Aunt Kathy and Uncle Steve showed love for and spent time with their children, they always set aside time for each other and their own relationship. Uncle Steve would wait patiently for Aunt Kathy in the family room while she put the final touches on her makeup. Sitting in the chair, he would place his arm around her waist as she passed by, making her pause, laugh, and spin around to sit perfectly on his lap. With a gentle kiss and a sly grin, he would ask her if she was finally ready to go out, to which she would giggle and nod in agreement. It was beautiful to watch them together, and I was taking mental notes for my future relationships.

Truth be told, there was always love in the air when Aunt Kathy and Uncle Steve were around. They had a Disney magic type of relationship, and it didn't seem to be something they had to work hard to maintain. Watching the two of them set me on my own path to find the same in my future husband. I wasn't sure if this type of relationship would be a reality for me, but I knew I wanted it. Thus far, I had seen my father and mother, who while they loved each other, fought like bitter rivals, and then I'd watched my stepdad and my mother caring for one another, but with a far more business-like relationship than what I saw in the Wolskis.

It was easy to want the life they had created together. It seemed to be a more steady, consistent one with the type of predictability I knew I would enjoy. Maybe a whole and healthy relationship was one of the keys to healing a broken piece of me? The movies had told me it was as easy as that. If it could happen for them, I could cling to the possibility that it could happen for me. My only remaining question was whether *I* would be enough to have "a whole and healthy relationship" of my own.

Before they left for their night out together, Aunt Kathy would always stop and give each kid a goodbye kiss, saving the last one for me. Aside from her thoughtfulness towards me and consistently making time for me, I was always in awe of her. She was kind, beautiful, and her love seemed endless. Never short of gratitude, she would often smile at me and say, "Thank you, Christina, for being here. We always love having you with us." I remember thinking even back then that the pleasure was always mine.

Again, from the outside looking in, it might have seemed like a simple choice to ditch my biological family and pick a more idyllic life with the Wolskis. Ultimately, though I truly loved them, I wanted to live with my family. Not to mention, the possibilities of starting in a new city were so tempting. The allure of a new place, a new identity, was calling me. I mean, it had been at least a few years since I changed schools, so why not?

And while I was given the choice to stay in Chicago by my mother, I knew what was expected of me, and I couldn't disappoint. So, I took the path of least resistance, allowing the winds of change to blow me in the direction that would please everyone. In June, when my family transitioned to Texas, I spent the rest of the summer in Chicago and planned to join my family in San Antonio just before school started. The Wolskis were thrilled to have me spend the summer with them, and how could I resist soaking up a bit more of this wholesome goodness before starting over again?

Thanks to Aunt Kathy helping me get the lifeguard job, I was not only getting the best possible tan, but earning some extra cash, which allowed me to soak up my last few moments of having fun with friends. More than that, I was officially a Wolski for the summer and Aunt Kathy made my last memories in the "Windy City" happy ones. We spent quality time together at the movies, going to the kids' sporting events, and often heading to the ice cream shop for a treat afterwards. Before long that summer, Aunt Kathy and Uncle Steve realized we had maxed out the amount of fun we could have in Chicago, so they planned a surprise—we were heading to Disney World.

Growing up, I had always dreamed of going to Disney World. If I'm being honest, I'd always fantasized of being a singing Disney princess. What little girl doesn't?

But eight years after my traumatic first visit to the state, this trip to Florida would be different. We weren't running from the threat of custody battles. Instead, I was with the kind of family that read bedtime stories every night, without fail. I wasn't wondering when my mom would return; I was old enough to take care of myself.

As summer drew to a close, my new school half a country away was starting in a few weeks. Placing the last of my belongings in my backpack, reality set in. I looked around the room I had called home with the Wolski family and felt a sense of dread coming over me. It was going to be terribly hard to say goodbye. I couldn't deny I had been happy in Chicago between the stability I'd found with the Wolskis and the friends that had become family.

I heard a honk outside letting me know the time had come to hit the road. Peering out the window, I noticed a sedan parked in the cul-de-sac. There was one person already sitting inside the vehicle that I was especially excited to see. She was perhaps the best thing to come out of my mom's relationship with Isaac—my stepsister, Nicole. Only three years apart, Nicole and I shared the same birth-day, which made me always feel an instant connection with her.

Though she was now a full-fledged sister to me, I could remember the moment I met her at a birthday party for her father, my stepdad Isaac, like it was yesterday. We shared similar features with our dark hair and eyes, but she exuded confidence and calm in a way I never could. Nicole has always reminded me of Snow White, cheerful and sweet. She sees the best in people and is incredibly thoughtful. She immediately took on a big sister role with me, finding opportunities to make me feel special. "Oh, you'll look so amazing in this Christina!" Smiling brightly, Nicole would grab a dress off the department store clothes rack and put it up next to me. Sure enough, not only would it be something I would like, but a perfect fit. As if she had memorized everything about me. I found we shared so many things in common, not just our birth date. It didn't take long to think back then that maybe, just maybe, I had found my soul sister.

I was elated that Nicole had agreed to make the drive to San Antonio. As I opened the door to Aunt Kathy's home, she gave me a big smile and waved as she eagerly stepped out of the car to greet me. I finished my tearful goodbyes with the Wolskis and hurried towards the car. In typical Nicole fashion, she asked, "Christina, do you want to sit in the front seat? We can always switch at the rest stop." I beamed at her thoughtfulness and switched my attention from my summer as a Wolski to the road trip ahead of us.

Despite my joy at the prospect of uninterrupted time with Nicole, thinking about the eighteen-hour drive to San Antonio made me sigh. I had learned that things always change with road trips, so I hated long car rides and was not looking forward to this one, even if I was excited about the adventure and the company.

I could feel the gloomy emotion setting in with each turn we made as we came closer to the interstate. From the front seat, I looked in the side mirror at the Chicago suburbs disappearing behind me and, for a moment, seriously reconsidered my mom's offer to let me stay. I didn't want to say goodbye. I had said goodbye so many times in my short sixteen years. Why did this have to be another one?

Some decisions in life we make, and some are made for us. I had experienced plenty of twists and turns in my childhood that were not of my own doing, but this was my chosen fate, and I would need to accept it to have any chance of happiness. The states blurred past from the window of the car as I hurtled towards my new hometown, like it or not.

Chapter Five

Sing.

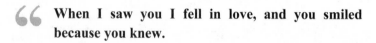

> **When I saw you I fell in love, and you smiled because you knew.**
>
> — **Arrigo Boito**

When we arrived in San Antonio, my fears that those feelings of animosity I had sensed from some of Isaac's relatives during our visits had not been imagined. They were very real, in fact, and they weren't going anywhere. My family was the result of Isaac's second marriage, his second wife, and some of his family would never approve, at least not wholeheartedly. It wasn't our fault, yet it felt like we were stepping into a party that had begun without us, and we were not naturally a welcome addition.

On the contrary, Nicole was excitedly welcomed since she was directly related to everyone we visited. Although we were greeted with hugs, there was a noticeable difference between the warm hugs Nicole received and the apathetic glances my mother, sister, and I walked into at family functions. Despite our protests, we spent most of the last weeks of summer bouncing from birthday parties to casual get-togethers with Isaac's extended family members. There were many of them who genuinely were kind and loving, while others were not. With each visit, I became increasingly tired of those pretending to like us. And we certainly didn't want to keep acting like we didn't notice their disapproval of our mom.

I just didn't think we fit in, but I wasn't sure where we did fit in either. Between my mom's family and my father's, it was as if we weren't tethered to any family group. With all our moves, we lacked deep roots. We missed all the years of memories which bring families together. The "I've known you and watched you grow since you were born" kind of connection, the inside jokes only a family shares, the happy memories, and the sad ones. Since leaving New Orleans, we had been without deep family connections like the ones we could see between Isaac's family. While some opened their hearts to us, others didn't feel the same way. I just assumed they preferred the original family, which included Nicole. So, I did what I could to pretend it didn't bother me and tried to be on "my best behavior."

One Saturday morning, my mom announced, "We're going to a family event tonight." Not knowing who would be in attendance, my sister and I immediately dreaded going to another family function.

"We have nothing to wear, so we're going to head to the mall," my sister calmly explained to our mom.

"Well, be back by two or we're going to be late for the ceremony."

Walking out of the door, my sister shouted, "Okay, will do, Mom." She looked at me with an eye roll.

"I'm tired of this," I told my sister, frustrated as we buckled our seat belts in the sweltering car.

"I know. I'm tired of the family functions, too," she agreed.

"Why do we have to keep going? Why can't she go without us?"

Making our way to the mall, we parked and walked inside. A

couple of hours passed before my sister glanced at her watch. "It's getting close. We need to head home," she said.

Once again, I sighed and shook my head. "Why can't we 'get lost' like we always do? If we're late, she'll have to leave without us." We both looked at each other and agreed it was a brilliant plan.

We continued shopping, never thinking twice about the clock after assuming we were off the hook with our ingenious plan. After a few hours, we headed home. Pulling into the driveway, we noticed my mom's car was still parked at the house. Frantically, we looked at each other and then looked at the time. "It's five. Why is she still here?"

My sister shrugged and said, "Maybe she feels the same as we do and changed her mind about going."

Hesitating, we both slipped through the back door. Like a gust of wind, my mom angrily bolted into the kitchen yelling, "Where have you been?! I told you to be back by two!" My sister and I immediately began talking over one another. We explained how we had gotten lost, giving her all the details we could make up to calm her down and, finally, apologizing for having missed the event.

My mom looked at us and said, "Get dressed. We need to leave now!"

My sister protested, "Mom, it's probably over. I'm sorry we missed it."

Ever the most stubborn of us all, my mom retorted, "We did not miss the entire thing. The ceremony was at two, but the reception is at five. Get dressed. You have ten minutes to get in the car; I don't care what you look like."

As my mom stormed off, I thought to myself that we must be heading to a wedding. With dread, I realized not only did our plan fail, but we were going to look awful. *Great. Nothing like really living up to the whole ugly step daughter image.* I ran upstairs to change, and I quickly found some black pants and a white dress shirt. Stepping into the bathroom, I pulled half of my hair back in a barrette, leaving the remaining half down. I slipped on some black patent leather dress shoes, grabbed my makeup bag, and started heading for the door.

If there's one thing I knew, it was that I could not stand to see my mother angry with me. She's not someone you want to upset and, by that point in the afternoon, we had clearly upset her. We'd expected our mother to have already left for the evening, and we would deal with the consequences of our "getting lost" plan later. I would have never knowingly walked into that storm. We ran to the car where she was waiting and drove off to what we assumed would be the wedding reception of some distant relative.

As I awkwardly entered the reception and looked around the room for any familiar faces, the bride was presented with the wedding party. Then another girl walked in dressed in what appeared to be *another* wedding gown with *another* groom. *Another* wedding? Two weddings at the same time? The brides looked to be about my age, I couldn't believe it. *Wow, they marry the girls young down here in San Antonio;* I thought to myself. I hoped they didn't think I'd be next.

We walked to the far right of the dance floor and found an empty table towards the back of the room. We sat our purses down and stayed there, hoping the night would be over soon.

By this time, I needed some clarification. "Did both girls get married?" I asked my sister. Not knowing the answer, either, she shrugged. A woman standing behind us overheard my question and broke in to solve the mystery.

Laughing, the woman explained, "Oh no, this isn't a wedding. It's a quinceañera." We looked at each other in bewilderment and then back at her, puzzled.

"What is that?" I asked.

"It's a celebration of a girl's fifteenth birthday and her transformation from childhood to adulthood. I can see how it can be confusing," she added laughing again, "since there is a ceremony, and what looks like a bride, groom and wedding party."

She continued to get a good chuckle at our confusion.

Thinking back to our earlier plan to get "lost," I made a mental note to make some adjustments for next time. We had failed and were rewarded with another forced family function.

Scanning the crowd for a familiar face, I spotted Uncle Richard, Isaac's brother, walking towards our table. With a sweet smile and an incredibly warm and inviting disposition, Uncle Richard was one of the few in Isaac's family who didn't make me feel unwanted. In fact, when we visited during Christmastime and prior to our move, Richard and his wife, Linda, went out of their way to purchase gifts for us, so we never felt left out. Tonight, it was no different. He walked up smiling and exclaimed, "I'm so glad you made it!"

Our quick conversation was interrupted by the sounds of my mother. "Christina! Santina!" waving us over and yelling our names.

We both got up and started walking towards my mom. "These are my daughters," she explained to some distant relatives of Isaac. We did what we always did—nod and smile, nod and smile. As we were being introduced, a mariachi took to the floor, which eventually broke apart the conversation. I was thankful for the interruption.

Everyone went their separate ways to their tables, but I stayed, and so did Uncle Richard. A woman dressed in a mariachi traje de charro (translated "suit of the horseman") walked up and belted out a song. I was so taken aback. This was amazing. I always thought mariachi music was fun, but I'd never seen a woman sing along, and she did so with such passion. As she sang one of the songs, I heard the voice of Mariana in my head and with all the linguistic strength I could muster, I tried to memorize the title of the song. "Tú, solo Tú."

You. Only you.

Although I couldn't speak Spanish fluently, I knew I wanted to learn how to sing like this. While I stood there awestruck next to Uncle Richard, I casually glanced to my left toward the entrance. As I turned my head back to the mariachi, I felt my gaze being pulled once more to the same spot at the front doors. About thirty feet away was a group of people around my age who had gathered at the entrance of the dance hall. But amidst the crowd, I couldn't take my eyes off *him.*

Trying to go unnoticed, I attempted to listen to the mariachi while sneaking subtle peeks at the entrance. Dressed in black jeans and a maroon polo shirt, his skin was deeply warm with light brown hair and green eyes. He was so handsome that I couldn't help but want to watch what he was doing. He was standing with a tall, slender girl at his side, smiling at her in a way that indicated this had to be his girlfriend. Truthfully, I'm not sure what it was, but something made him stand out from the crowd he was gathered with at the door. It was as if a celebrity had arrived and made their entrance.

Soon my mom popped up next to me and snapped my attention back to her. "I want you to sing that Spanish song you know. I'm sure Uncle Richard would love to hear it."

Groaning silently to myself, I shook my head "no" and spoke up, "You mean 'Via Dolorosa'?" No, Mama, I don't want to sing. Not in front of all these people. Not that song."

Glaring at me square in the eyes, she insisted. "Christina. I want you to sing that song for Uncle Richard. It makes my heart so happy to hear you sing." She began to beg. "Please, Christina. Please sing the Spanish song. Please!" Really, she was telling me; there wasn't much asking going on. The word "no" wasn't an option with my mom.

I don't want to sing the song! I screamed in my mind. While the song was a beautiful one, we were at a quinceañera and it wasn't appropriate for the function. She knew I was always so embarrassed to sing anything, much less sing in front of hundreds of people I didn't know and a song which was intended to convey the message of Jesus' crucifixion. I wanted to hide. But as fate would have it, before I even realized what was happening, my mom's wish for me to sing at this function would indeed be granted. It didn't matter that the song was inappropriate for the occasion, and it didn't matter that

I was terrified. Sometimes life has a way of stepping in and shoving you in a new direction.

The DJ suddenly got everyone's attention. "Good evening! Before we get started on the dance floor, let's have a singing contest! The contest starts in twenty minutes. If you're interested, come talk to me." I was not interested.

A singing contest? I thought to myself. Oh no! This evening just got worse. My mom walked right up to me. "Okay, are you ready?" She was smiling so broadly; I wouldn't be surprised if her cheeks were hurting. "Let's go see if he has the music for you to sing."

Right, because it's the most requested song for karaoke, I thought to myself sarcastically. I would never say such sass out loud, since I knew my mom was not above giving a good spanking well into our teens.

Before I could even fully process what was about to happen to me, my mom grabbed my hand and walked me towards the DJ's table. My heart stopped as we got closer, and my eyes connected with the green eyes of the guy I had noticed earlier, but this time, he was sitting alone on the stage. Embarrassed, I made my way up the three steps onto the stage where the DJ was set up. *Please don't fall. Please don't fall,* I silently begged of myself.

Walking towards the DJ, all I could do was think of the green-eyed dreamboat behind me. I could hardly say a word to the DJ or talk coherently, knowing every breath could be heard. *I can't believe this is happening to me. Why is this happening to me? Oh, I remember... because of my mother.*

Interrupting my thoughts, the DJ said, "I don't have that song. How do you spell it again?" Quietly, I told him the song and the artist's name again. Looking further, he glanced up again at me. "Right, I don't have it. I'm sorry."

Immensely relieved that I didn't have to sing, I looked at my mom and said, "It's all right, it's not meant to be. Another time, Mama."

I was halfway to the steps to exit the stage when my mom spoke up. "What if she sings with no music?"

Shocked, the DJ looked from my terrified expression to my mom's insistent stare, and said, "A capella? Uh, sure, if you want to, you can."

Rest in peace, Christina. This was it. This was how I was going to die—of embarrassment—at my first quinceañera. Smiling weakly at the DJ and with no fight left in me, I said, "Thank you." I started to walk away towards the steps, the same steps where the green-eyed man was a mere five feet away. I could practically smell him; he was so close. Repeating to myself, *please don't fall. Please don't fall.*

As if I was floating, I tried my best to chassé. Gliding gracefully, at least in my mind, I wove between the tables, feeling like he was watching every step I was making. I've never wished for eyes in the back of my head to see what someone was doing more than in this moment. I was confident if there was ever a time there was something stuck on my butt, it was now. It was like an out-of-body experience; every inch of me was screaming with nerves.

Participants in the contest sang, and I faded into the crowd, desperately hoping the DJ would forget my mother's request. Song after song floated through the air, cumbias and Selena's greatest hits rolling through the attendees one by one as I got the hang of the traditional dance moves and Spanish lyrics.

As the night went on, I lost sight of my handsome "friend" who was sitting on the stage. The crowd swelled inside the room, and he became harder to spot from my vantage point. My teenage disappointment in this scenario was instantly replaced by terror when the DJ came back to announce on the microphone, "We've now got an a cappella addition to our contest!" *Dead. Wheel me out, folks, I'm ready to go.*

The DJ turned off the ballroom lights and turned the spotlight on the dance floor. He took a few smooth strides to walk off the stage. I noticed the green-eyed heartthrob wasn't moving from his place, seated in the darkness on the edge of the stage.

For a self-conscious teenager, allergic to attention, this was absolutely my worst nightmare. How could I sing in front of this gorgeous man, much less the hundreds of people surrounding him? There was a rapid pulse pounding in my throat. My body trembled, and I started to sweat.

I knew I shouldn't have worn pants and a long-sleeve shirt in this ridiculous Texas heat. I couldn't breathe. I began to walk toward the stage and him, trying to not make eye contact, but I couldn't help it. Our eyes met once more for the briefest split second, and my stomach dropped to the floor.

As I got closer to the stage, we exchanged smiles, mine small and timid, his warm and encouraging. This quick encounter was instantly interrupted by the DJ as he handed me the microphone, saying, "Are you ready?" I smiled and nodded "yes."

"Well, you don't need any music from me, so just start singing when you're ready," he said.

Start when I'm ready, I repeated in my head. *I'm not ready.* I turned around and stared into the shadowy crowd of hundreds. At this point in the evening, plenty of drinks had been served, and the room was far from quiet. Glasses were clinking, guests were talking, and children were laughing. There was so much noise, but I gave in to the moment and began to sing, softly at first.

The noise quieted, and immediately the room became eerily silent. For a moment, I forgot who was standing behind me, quietly watching me with his smoldering gaze. But in the next instant, I remembered, and the nerves returned. I continued singing, thinking that I could sing faster without the music, speeding up the process and, hopefully, ending the pain of my embarrassment sooner rather than later. While I had been initially mortified at the idea of singing a capella, it might have been what saved me.

As the last notes rang out across the packed ballroom, I turned to my side, not acknowledging the eruption of the crowd. I handed the microphone back to the DJ, who looked at me in astonishment. I smiled awkwardly and walked away, embarrassed at what had taken place. Refusing to meet the eyes of the mystery man still seated on the stage, I made a beeline for the safety of my family. I was relieved that it was over and tried my best to enjoy the rest of the evening.

After the formalities of the traditional quinceañera were complete, it was time for the DJ to get the real party started. I was along for the ride and never would have imagined the fiesta was barely beginning. But this is where I didn't need any introduction or warmup. I loved to dance and started loosening up to have fun as I joined the others on the dance floor.

I had a few years of dance classes back in Chicago to thank for that. Though I had desperately wanted to take singing lessons around the fifth grade, my mom enrolled me in ballet, tap, and jazz classes like Nicole instead. I think my mother thought dance would add some confidence and self-esteem in me. Her plan initially backfired, though. I resented the lessons because I wasn't comfortable in my skin, and girls my age began training when they were four or five years old, like Nicole.

I must admit, the dance classes in those early years taught me how to fight through discomfort. They helped me develop stage presence and smile when there was absolutely nothing to smile about. More importantly, I learned how to move my hips and feel confident doing so. I guess my mom's plan had worked out after all. It only took a handful of years and one move to San Antonio to pay off.

I spent the rest of the evening on the dance floor with my cousin, James, Uncle Richard's youngest son. Swaying and clapping along to the music, I finally looked at James and summoned the courage to ask, "James, who's the guy sitting on the stage?" To my surprise, I wasn't embarrassed to let someone know I had an interest. It was weird. In the past, I always kept my feelings quiet for fear of ridicule, especially when it came to "love interests." Call it insecurity, being more reserved with my emotions, or just plain shy to rejection, I'm not sure. Maybe I was feeling more confident in my skin or just blinded by it all and hadn't processed exactly what I was doing.

James was a couple of years younger than me, but we clicked from the start. It felt natural to be his friend. He was sweet and warm-hearted, had a great sense of humor, and was spontaneous, making any time we were together fun. When I moved to San Antonio, he became my one true confidant, someone I could count on to fill me in on all the things I needed to know about adjusting to life in a new city. James was handsome and played football for the high school team and, unlike me, who didn't know anyone at my new school, was popular with a lot of friends.

In response to my question, he looked over and shrugged at me, saying, "I don't know, but I'll try to find out." I was fine with that, and I trusted him with my secret interest in this mystery man.

After a few more songs, I anxiously asked James once more, "Anything?" He shook his head "no," and we continued to dance. Much more familiar with the crowd than me, James meandered through the groups of dancers, with me in tow, to ask a few more people. "Do you know who that guy is?"

No one knew. Who is this guy? Not a single person could answer it. Throughout the night, I became more and more detective-like, trying to solve my own mystery. *Who was this green-eyed, beautiful person? Did anyone know him, or was he just a quinceañera crasher? Was that even a thing?*

I hadn't realized how much time had passed and that the evening was coming to an end until the ballroom lights were abruptly turned back on. I frantically searched for James so we could make a quick dash for the door. Finally, I looked around and spotted my cousin. *No way.* He was standing next to "the guy" and talking to him. At that moment, I heard my name being called from across the room: "Christina!" I looked around and locked eyes with James. I was in shock. I changed my mind. *Who was I kidding? I didn't have enough courage to talk to this guy, and there was no way he would be interested in me.* James called my name again. "Christina!" and waved me over to where he was standing. Suddenly, I couldn't cross the room fast enough.

Like a *terrified* moth to a flame, my feet carried me involuntarily, as I held my breath. I wanted to go so badly, yet I was dying inside. *What was this conversation going to be like? What was I going to say?* As I walked towards the two of them, I stared at this mystery man. I could not look away. Still seated on the stage, he was smiling at me and the closer I got to him, the more handsome he became. This man at a distance was nothing compared to the up-close and personal version.

I was certain this was going to be embarrassing, but had to see how this one played out. *Here goes nothing.*

I smiled shyly and waited for him to speak first. I couldn't be the one to break the ice; I knew I would screw it up. Finally, his warm baritone voice broke the awkward silence. "My name is Tomas. What's your name?" he said in the most beautifully comforting voice I had ever heard.

In my mind, I fainted and came back to life, just in time to answer him and mutter weakly, "I'm Christina." I was sure James was watching this entire interaction with glee, making mental notes so he could mock me mercilessly afterwards.

Focus, Christina.

"Nice to meet you, Christina. Are you in college?" Tomas asked. I giggled like a foolish schoolgirl, I'm sure, looking at everyone and feeling the weight of their eyes staring at us. I answered with an embarrassed, "No."

"Are you a senior?" he asked.

"I'm not," I answered back.

"Okay. How old are you?" He questioned, trying to solve his own mystery now.

"I'm sixteen," I answered. Tomas smiled graciously while he stood up. Adjusting his stance, he extended his hand, trying to shake mine, and as I shook his, he calmly said, "It was really nice to meet you, Christina." Suddenly turning, he walked out the door.

That's it? I thought to myself. I turned and looked at James, confused and in disbelief. Just like that, Tomas was gone.

Chapter Six

Mercy.

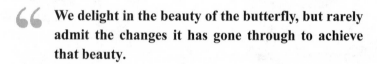

> We delight in the beauty of the butterfly, but rarely admit the changes it has gone through to achieve that beauty.

— **Maya Angelou**

With my heart still fluttering and my breath still taken, I could hardly focus on anything else but what had just happened. It was surreal. It was like being in a movie, meeting the person of your dreams, only to have them slip through your fingers like sand on the beach. Tomas and I had only spoken for what felt like five seconds, and then, like magic, he disappeared. He was gone.

Looking back, the craziest realization for me is how I really shouldn't have been there that night. If my mom hadn't met Isaac, Texas wouldn't have been on the radar. If I had stayed with the Wolskis and not joined my family in San Antonio or if I hadn't gotten home in time for my mom to take me to the quinceañera, I would have missed him entirely. But more than that, with my mother being the overprotective mama bear she was, had she been there for the end of the dancing, I wouldn't have been able to get within ten feet of any boy, much less one I had been stalking all night.

The whole encounter with Tomas was still burning in my mind. James and I casually strolled to the car like two teenagers with nowhere to be but, in my mind, I couldn't stop replaying the scene. His name was scrolling through my mind like a news ticker in Times Square. Tomas. TOMAS. Tomas.

Replaying the conversation for the millionth time, I realized with horror I had only gotten his first name, no other details. I didn't even know his last name. I was never going to learn it, much less take it in marriage like my teenage brain was already dreaming up. *Would that be the end of it?*

The conversation had shifted the moment I had confessed my actual age. I could only assume that meant he was not interested in a little girl like me. Although he never shared his own age, I could tell by the way he carried himself he was not a high school kid, he was more mature. I'm sure he saw me as a little schoolgirl, at best, potential jailbait, at worst.

We spent the entire night trying to figure out who he was, and no one knew him. Now I had spoken to him, and I couldn't forget him. *Sigh.* Tomas.

James was one of the few cousins from my stepdad's family I genuinely enjoyed spending time with, and it was one of the main motivating factors my mom used to convince me to attend the school she preferred. It was James' high school, too, so at least I would know and trust *someone*. When we arrived at his family home later that evening, we sank into their comfortable and cozy couch. James was eager to watch a scary movie and promised he would warn me to cover my eyes when a scene was about to get bad because I've always hated scary movies.

As I laid on the sofa curled up with my favorite blanket from James' personal stash, my mind drifted away from the horrors unfolding on the television in front of me and went straight back to thinking about Tomas. *How was I going to sleep tonight?* All I could think of was my fleeting encounter with a beautiful, green-eyed, handsome stranger named Tomas. The only detail James and I had to work with was that he could possibly know the DJ from the quinceañera. He *had* been on or near the stage quite a bit that night. Somebody at some point had said he lived in Austin, so, like a lovesick puppy dog or creepy stalker (depending on where you think this story is going), I found myself researching Austin DJs named Tomas as the movie credits rolled. Sadly, I found nothing and was left with no answers and no idea how I would ever find him. Perhaps it wasn't meant to be.

As the weeks went by, I became more and more immersed in Texas culture which, as any Texan knows, is almost a religion in and unto itself. The minute people discovered I was new to San Antonio, they would start listing the places I had to go or experience, more importantly, what food I had to eat, and so forth. I had people telling me repeatedly, you must try "Water Burger!" *Why on earth would I want to try a wet burger?* It made no sense to me. Eventually, I gave in when even James insisted I try one. I found myself stepping under a neon orange "W" and walking in to experience my first "Whataburger." *Oooh!* What. A. Burger. I was totally confused about the name. There was no "water" involved, and they were pretty delicious!

James' mom, Aunt Linda, was also an incredible cook and enjoyed introducing me to all kinds of food I had never experienced. Breakfast, lunch, and dinner, I couldn't pass up anything she would whip up in her welcoming kitchen. Although I missed the Midwest, San Antonio was starting to feel like home.

Two weeks had passed since the quinceañera, and I had been enduring a slow torture, as I still couldn't get the image of Tomas out of my head. I kept repeating our conversation word for word in my mind and berating myself, wondering what went wrong. I realized I had hardly said anything. Maybe that was the problem?

I couldn't explain why I felt such a powerful pull to Tomas. It was indescribable. I only knew I needed to know who he was. I had to find him.

Cheesy as it may sound, I remember lying on my bed, staring at the ceiling, thinking of *him*. I watched as the late afternoon sun stretched the last of its light across the room, when I heard James' familiar footsteps pounding up the stairs.

James smiled at me as he entered my room and, in his best attempt at singing, said, "I have new information." The look on his face said it all: he was relishing his chance to break the news to me in the smallest bites possible.

"Spill it!"

James continued, "I hear he's from Austin. He's with the DJ."

I groaned. *The DJ?* I'd already been down this path and it didn't add up. But maybe my detective skills weren't enough to crack the case? No, I'd already let the DJ story go in my mind. It couldn't be true. Really, nothing made sense. Letting my mind race, James finally interrupted. "Maybe Kat knows who he is."

Of course! Why hadn't we thought of this before? Kat was one of James' cousins and was the girl who was having the quinceañera that magical evening. She would've known everyone there that night. "Let's call her!" I half-yelled, unable to mask my excitement.

Grinning from ear to ear, James grabbed my phone and called Kat. I could only hear his side of the conversation, and I was dying a slow death inside.

"Okay. Uh-huh. Really? I'll let her know."

Over two weeks of waiting and I was only getting grunts and one-word sentences?! The only thing I could do was frantically mouth to James. "*What*?!" I felt helpless.

Smiling a wicked grin, he continued his conversation and shooed me away with a flick of his hand. "You ready? The number is (210)-"

Things had gotten real. That was my number! He had given her my number. *What does this mean?* Before I could get out another peep of protest, James hung up the phone and looked at me proudly.

"Well, Kat is going to make some calls." I couldn't help but wonder if I was setting myself up for rejection.

"What? Who is she going to call? Does she know Tomas??" I asked, practically hyperventilating at this point.

"Not directly, but her friend was the other birthday girl and, apparently, she's the one who has a connection with Tomas. Kat is going to see if she can get Tomas' information from her," he assured me.

For the next twenty minutes, James and I sat on the edge of my bed, staring at the house phone. No phone call. Thirty minutes passed. Nothing. I was on the edge of my seat, silently begging for the phone to ring and trying to stay distracted, when finally, the phone rang.

James reacted faster than I did, picking up the receiver before I could even begin to reach for it. I hit him softly on the shoulder and gave him the sharpest look I could muster. Despite the daggers I was shooting at him with my gaze, James smiled demurely and answered, "Hello?"

He listened for a brief second while I was on the edge of my seat, wondering who the person on the other line was. Finally, the tension broke as he said, "Sorry, she's not here right now. Can I take a message? Thank you. Goodbye."

"It was a telemarketer," he said, laughing, and walked back to where I was seated, tossing one of my pillows to the side. Just then, the phone rang again. James looked at me and shouted, "I'll get it," making two long strides back to the phone. I ran after him and as we both simultaneously reached for the phone, his long arms reached a little farther than mine, grabbing the phone from me. "Hello? Hey Kat."

My heart froze, and I stared at James with wide eyes, wondering what Kat was saying and trying to find hints in James' facial expressions. *Did she find him? Did he actually live in Austin? Was he even real?*

After James got off the phone, he smiled genuinely at me this time and said, without a hint of irony or jest in his tone, "He's looking for you."

"He's looking for *me*?" I asked, shocked. I could feel my heart beating in my toes. Was that normal?

A million butterflies sprang to life in my stomach. I was so excited. *He wants to talk to me. Me!* My mind raced. *What am I going to say? What is he going to say? I'm not good at this. He's going to think I'm an idiot.* Ugh. After so many weeks of anticipation, I realized I hadn't truly believed in my heart that we would find him until now.

Before I could doubt myself any longer, my friend Callie entered my room after getting off the other line talking with her family. She had arrived from Chicago a couple of days prior to visit over Labor Day weekend and was a friend I had kept in contact with after I moved. Callie had long, curly, model-like hair, blue eyes, and eyelashes for days. All the guys chased after her, and it was a blessing. However, as her friend, it felt more like a curse for a chance at love. I had told her all about this mysterious encounter, and we had mulled over all the possibilities of Tomas' whereabouts as I had shown her around the city.

"Tomas is calling Christina," James announced proudly.

"Really?! Tomas?! Green-eyed guy, Tomas? He's calling you? No way!" Callie screamed, jumping up and down. She wrapped her arms around me, giving me a big hug. "I'm so happy for you!" Just then, the phone rang. Callie reacted, releasing me from her hug and jumping on the bed. With two bounds, she was landing on the other side and beating even James to the phone.

"Hello?" she answered in a sweet, sultry voice. "No, this is Callie, her friend from Chicago. Who's this? Oh, hi Tomas, how are you?" I looked at James, and he rolled his eyes in annoyance. From the moment she arrived, James could see how much Callie loved the attention of others, particularly of the male variety, and he was not impressed.

Shrugging his shoulders, he walked closer to Callie, waving at her and pointing to me. He quietly said, "Christina can talk to him." Callie pointedly ignored James, sitting on the bed and falling back on a pillow to get more comfortable. She wasn't planning on giving up the phone any time soon. I couldn't believe it.

James looked at me again and said, "That's your friend. Good luck. I have to get going."

I gave him a hug as he left and, for what felt like forever, I listened to Callie laugh, talking about everything possible with the boy I had waited weeks to talk to. I tried to act like it wasn't bothering me. Somewhat numb, I distracted myself the best way I knew how—organizing anything. Choosing to start in my closet, I made sure not to go too far away, in case Callie ever felt inclined to pass me the phone. After about thirty minutes, I grew frustrated and doubted Tomas would even want to talk to me.

It was obvious he was enjoying Callie. By this point, he probably didn't even remember who he was trying to call in the first place. I walked over to where Callie was, mustered up some confidence, and whispered, "I want to talk to him."

Once I finally spoke up, she nodded and, after a few more minutes, she surprised me by interrupting their talk, saying, "Well, here's Christina. It was nice talking to you."

Here we go. The butterflies immediately returned so fast I almost felt nauseous. I picked up the receiver and muttered a faint, "Hello." When he finally spoke, it was as I remembered it from two weeks ago. "Hi Christina." His warm tonality was burned in my memory from that very first night. I was having an out-of-body experience. It felt unreal—like when you call a radio station, and the personality has a near-perfect voice. Soothing and interesting. His voice was not at all what I imagined my own sounded like in that moment. I was a nervous wreck, and there was no chance he wouldn't notice.

"How have you been? Callie mentioned you just moved here. How are you liking San Antonio so far?" he asked.

Breathe. Deep breaths, Christina. "Um… I like it. I miss Chicago, but San Antonio is okay."

"I get it. I just moved here too and I'm trying to get used to a new city myself. Have you found any restaurants that you like?"

Interesting how everything comes back to food. "There's a Puerto Rican restaurant right down the street from where we live. It's really good."

"Did you know that I'm Puerto Rican?"

"I didn't; that's really cool!"

"Yeah, my dad moved from Puerto Rico to New York when he was a kid, so I grew up eating a lot of Puerto Rican food. Maybe we should go check out that restaurant together."

A little hesitant, I answered, "That sounds good." I tried hard to deflect, knowing my mother would never agree to let me go out to eat by myself with a guy I just met. "So, you just moved here?"

"I moved to San Antonio with my dad after my last semester playing basketball at Wayland Baptist. He's helping me pay for college and I'm staying with him and my stepmom. My mom still lives in Buda, so I've only been here for about two months."

"That's cool and you play basketball? I'm hoping you like the Chicago Bulls and not just the San Antonio Spurs? Do you like any other sports, like hockey?" I laughed a little as I hinted at my midwestern ties.

He laughed "That's funny, I'm probably one of the biggest MJ fans you've ever met! I'm into other sports but I pretty much only play basketball so no, I don't play hockey, but we can always go to a game together."

Wow, he's persistent. Everything inside of me wanted to say "Yes!" But the reality was I needed to get past the guard, my mom. So, instead I offered a shy "Maybe."

"We need to talk about how well you sing. That night at the quinceañera, it was awesome. How did that get started for you?"

"Oh, uh… I grew up singing, but mostly at home. Recently I started singing more at church. That night was pretty embarrassing for me. But my mom loves to have me sing in front of as many people as possible. Even when it's totally not the right time."

"It was really good. I can't wait to hear you sing again."

I could feel the heat in my cheeks as I blushed and took in his encouraging compliments. Once we got the initial awkward exchange out of the way, we quickly moved into an easy flow of conversation.

Despite my nerves, I took in everything he said and added it to my memory bank so I could replay it over and over when the call ended. Tomas was so easy to speak with. He asked me what it was like, living in the Midwest, and what I liked to do. I learned about how he had moved from Buda, a small town between San Antonio and Austin (go figure) to San Antonio and was in college. As we spoke, it was clear he was more than just good to look at. I could talk to him for hours, but that dream was interrupted after a paltry ten minutes. Callie had gotten three times that amount of time with him. "I'm sorry, Christina, I have to go. Can we talk more tomorrow?" With the conversation so short, it was easy to believe he was bored with me already.

I hesitated in disbelief that it was over and felt a sense of dread that we would never connect again. It was too good to be true. "Of course," I replied, hoping this wouldn't be the last time I would hear his voice. I was clinging to a shred of faith that I might see him again.

After dropping Callie off at the airport the next day, I headed back home, but realized my mind was less concerned with my friend's departure and more riddled with questions about the coming weeks. There were a few days of summer left until school started. *Another new school,* I thought. It's difficult to take a step back and attempt to count how many schools I attended in the various cities within the states of California, Louisiana, Arkansas, Illinois, and Texas. It's true; my mother emphasized the importance of education, despite not having one herself, and we knew how much she wanted us to go to college. She often proclaimed that both my sister and I could be president someday if we wanted to. We kept good grades, but school wasn't always easy to focus on with what seemed to be an ever-changing home life. More often, the social side of adjusting to yet another new school took precedence over academics.

I often felt reserved, especially in new environments, so initially I would keep to myself. The older I got, the less daunting it was to make new friends. In the early years, when tension would rise in a new school, my sister would fight on my behalf. Later, when she would transition into higher grades, I was on my own. By then, I didn't start trouble, but when it found me, I knew what to do. Like my father, when push came to literal shove, I too could be bold. If I'm being honest, however, the person who taught me, through example, to defend myself was my mother. In her words, she "didn't raise no cowards."

I'll never forget a heated exchange my freshman year in high school. It was how most arguments started—with stupidity. I was minding my business, eating in the cafeteria with friends, when I felt something cold and wet running down my back. I turned, touching my wet shirt, and looked behind me. A purple bottle of Gatorade was still spinning on the floor after hitting its mark. Luckily, I was wearing black, so I mostly brushed it off, but my eyes met the gaze of a guy I'd never met before. Granted, it was only my fourth day at this school, so there were literally a thousand kids I'd never met before.

Meeting my eyes, he said in a deep, intimidating voice, "What are you looking at?"

"Nothing," I said loud enough to be heard, but not loud enough to be antagonizing. I could hear him and his table laugh as I turned back and fielded questions from my concerned friends. "It's fine," I said.

I looked back over my shoulder as I recounted the details, when our eyes connected again and he asked for the second time, "What are you looking at?"

"Nothing." I repeated.

So much for not being antagonizing. He stood up from the table, grumbling some choice words as he took three long strides to our table. *Well, here we go.*

If there's one thing I've learned from neighborhood fights, you never stay seated. So, I took a deep sigh of annoyance, stood, and turned around to face him. *Ugh. He's a lot taller than I thought. This isn't going to go so well.*

"I said, what are you looking at?" he yelled in my face with a lot more intensity in his voice. He was twice my width, if not more, and his height towered over me. We were so close if I reached my arms around his waist, I would have been hugging him.

Expressionless and with an even tone, I repeated my answer for now the third time, "Nothing." I had no desire to get into a fight that day, but I also wasn't a coward.

"That's what I thought," he said with some attitude. Just then, the bell rang and everyone around us grabbed their things. At first, he didn't move for what felt like forever, although I'm sure it was a mere few seconds. He shook his head and, while maintaining eye contact, walked a couple of steps backwards, saying, "I'll deal with you later." *Great.*

Later never happened. He was a senior on the varsity football team, and it showed. Once he found out I was a "Diecedue," he left me alone. I didn't have to worry about anyone wanting to fight me, at least for a little while. I was reserved, but bold.

Between my mom and me, our best count is fifteen schools, three of which were high schools. While we may forget one or two, it's still entertaining (and sobering) to run down memory lane. Some schools I wished I had stayed at longer, while others I was so happy to move on from. For this reason, I didn't always mind the change.

When the first day of school arrived, in San Antonio, the realization that I was starting over—again—hit me hard. In my mind, there were basically two options: 1) I could either go "all in" and dive into school clubs and activities, making new friends and new memories in San Antonio; or 2) I could retreat. Well, I retreated. If I'm being honest, I always had a habit of choosing option two. I regretted my decision to move away from all my friends in Chicago and the familiar surroundings I had enjoyed for years. In my heart, I think I had hoped for a glamorous transition to Texas, but I was still the same girl. I realized with the beginning of another school, I was tired of starting over. Not to mention I still couldn't shake being the girl too uncomfortable to come out of her shell in a new environment, so I mostly stayed to myself.

As I walked into the house after school, I turned the air conditioner on full blast to combat the blistering temperatures outside. Callie was gone, and it was back to reality for me.

With everyone out of the house, the day seemed to drag on as I waited for Tomas to call. By the afternoon, I was second guessing everything about our conversation. Bounding down the stairs, a doubt crossed my mind every time my feet touched a wooden step. *Did he say he would call? Did he say a specific time? Was the entire thing just a fever dream?* Suddenly, as I was sitting down at the kitchen table, the phone rang.

"Hello?" I answered.

"Hey Christina. It's Tomas." There it was again, that beautiful voice. And just like that, all was right in the world. I tried and failed to sound cool and relaxed with a far too high-pitched, "Oh, hi Tomas. How are you?" as I paced around the kitchen.

"I'm great. I just want to see if you would like to go out with me tonight. Maybe we can go see a movie?" That's hilarious. I could've sworn I had heard Green-Eyed-Boy-Of-My-Dreams ask me out on a date.

"Hello? Christina? If you're not free tonight, uh, we could do another time…"

Wow! He was serious. This was real. Now my sense of humor turned to a sense of flying, as I could hardly contain my excitement. I continued pacing, my feet barely touching the tile as we spoke. "Tonight? That sounds great. Let me see if that will work. Can I call you back?" I asked.

"Sure. Call me back and let me know. Talk to you later," Tomas said.

I hung up the phone and squealed with excitement. I dialed my mom, immediately planning in my head how I was going to get her to agree. All the odds were against me. With my mom being so protective, "dating" had always been out of the question. Not to mention, he was in college. How was I going to get her to say "yes"?

Before I could get a full script together in my head, I heard my mom's voice chirping a quick greeting on the other end of the line. "Mom, I met a guy. He's a friend of James', and he goes to our school. He's a senior and wants to know if I can go to the movies." Huge lie, and I've never been a good liar. My mom knew that. So, I held my breath as I heard my mom respond.

"On a date? Oh, no! That's not going to work. I don't even know who this guy is. Do you like him? I'm going to have to meet him first. You can have him come to the house. Otherwise, no. The answer is no." She was as solid as an oak tree on this. There was absolutely zero point in arguing with her. I thought moving to San Antonio would have loosened her up a bit, but sadly, I was wrong.

Dipping my head in disappointment, yet not fully surprised at her answer, I replied, "Okay, I'll call him." As I hung up the phone, I realized my mission now was to strategize how I could get Tomas to think it was a good idea to come to my house and meet my mom.

Refusing to give up, I decided on a different route. I called Tomas, and he answered after two rings.

I smiled and said, "Hi Tomas. Listen, it looks like my cousin is coming over to my house tonight. We're going to watch a movie and swim. Would you want to come over and join us?" There was a long pause, and I thought to myself, *he's not going to want to hang out with us. He's way too cool for this.*

After a beat, I heard the line crackle back to life as he answered, "Yeah, sure. That sounds good." Relieved and excited, I breathlessly whispered, "Perfect. So how about seven thirty or so, you know, whenever you're free? We'll be here at the house."

I hung up the phone and nearly missed the corner of the couch as I plopped down in utter disbelief. I could not believe he said "yes," and he was coming over! A moment before seven thirty, the front door swung open. It was James, my partner in crime through this whole ordeal, coming to see me through the first "date." Sensing my nervousness, he chuckled and said, "You must be out of your mind right now! This should be fun."

I escorted James into the kitchen, where everyone was gathered. "James!" my mom exclaimed. "I love seeing your handsome face! Come, sit down. Are you hungry?" As James got settled, I motioned to him that I was going upstairs to finish getting ready. Before I could put the finishing touches on my lipstick, I heard the doorbell ring. It was Tomas; I knew it in my gut.

I quickly finished up and headed toward the stairwell. As I was nearing the stairs, I could already hear Tomas speaking to my mom, and the sound of it was making me melt. But that was nothing compared to when I saw him. As I came around the corner, I caught a glimpse of him; basketball shorts and coordinated Jordans... yes, please! Smiling from the bottom of the stairs, he looked up at me as I tiptoed my way down. Our eyes stayed connected the entire way. I had been waiting for this moment for nearly a month, and I was ready for it.

"Hello." I can still remember the look on his face to this day. A bit shocked, a bit smoldering, I thought.

If my exterior could convey at least a mirage of confidence, internally I still couldn't believe he was in my house, and this was happening. My mom quickly evaluated this young man and the interaction she had just witnessed and barked an order at me. "Christina, go see if your sister needs help. Tomas, come with me and I'll show you around."

As she showed him around the house, I tried to listen to the conversation, but it was impossible. At one point, Tomas was released from her grasp, and I was able to pull him into the other room. Smiling from ear to ear, Tomas looked at me like he hung on my every word. It made me feel awful about what I was planning to tell him. "So, I didn't tell my mom you were in college. I told her you were a senior in high school."

He laughed a little and said, "It's all right. She already knows."

Shocked, I felt my heart filling with a sense of dread. I knew I was toast. *She's going to kill me*, I thought to myself.

"She knows?!" I asked him incredulously.

"Yeah, she took one look at me and said there's no way I was your age. I couldn't lie to her." Ugh. I could hear the chorus to Meatloaf's song "I Would Do Anything for Love" in my head.

I feared the worst, and it was true. She was going to kill me. Well, my only option was to enjoy the evening while I was still alive and breathing. Carpe diem and all that.

I took Tomas into the family room where James was, and we plopped down onto the couch to watch a movie. Though we were sitting a respectable several feet away from each other, I was sure James could hear the buzzing of tension between us as the scenes played out on the screen. When the credits rolled, we stood, stretched our growing teenage limbs, and headed to the pool as planned.

If I thought the tension was high before, it had kicked up about five gears.

When we walked outside to the deck, my sister came with us. No need to ask. I already knew she was "on assignment" from my mom. Slowly, I took off my shorts and tank top with my bathing suit hiding underneath and waded into the pool where James had already jumped in. The pool had become our constant summer hangout, and James had discovered that the second-floor balcony was the perfect launching pad for his epic cannonball.

As I turned around, unbeknownst to me, Tomas had already taken off his shirt and began to walk into the pool. I thought back to when Tomas had mentioned he had transferred from another Texas university, where he was on the basketball team. Yup, that body was not one of a high school student; it belonged to a man. He had basketball written all over him with his broad shoulders, muscular arms, and chiseled abdomen that made me blush. I caught myself giggling and quickly stopped.

Tomas swam to where it was deeper, and our eyes connected. The whole night, I felt like I was under his spell. He had this way of looking at me with those green eyes where I couldn't help but hold his gaze, and everything else would fade into the background. It had to be magic. I couldn't explain it any other way. This look, with no words, told me, "I'm totally into you." That evening had me reeling. I was in love. I knew it from the moment the doorbell rang.

His beautiful eyes, tan skin, and amazing body were nothing to complain about, but our connection was truly what made me feel like there was no one else but us. This is what it's supposed to be like, I thought. If he proposes marriage tonight, I'm saying "Yes!" As Tomas said his goodbyes at the end of the evening, I knew in my heart of hearts this was just the beginning.

* * *

I truly believe what drew me to Tomas, besides his good looks, was the fact that he felt safe. He felt solid, like someone you knew would drop everything for a friend in need. Tomas wasn't just a "glass half full" kind of person, but a "glass so full I can't help but spread my joy to others" kind of guy. That was contagious. He wasn't just attractive; he was going to help me attract the life I wanted.

I've asked Tomas about those first few moments of our relationship, from the quinceañera to the dip in the pool. It's rather hilarious to see how our stories differ and yet bob along this same line of knowing there was something special there.

I had read him correctly in that, the moment the words "sixteen years old" came out of my mouth, he had pulled back, at least as much as he could. He later confessed that meeting me was one of the first times he had ever introduced himself to anyone as Tomas. To everyone who knew him up until that point in his life, he was just "Tee." For whatever reason, he chose to use his full name with me, and he wouldn't find out until years later how it had captivated me.

Tomas says he felt a magnetic pull to me from the beginning, and thought my a cappella performance was indicative of a big, outgoing personality. Why else would a girl have the guts to do that? But as he got to know me better, he discovered I was far more insecure than I had let on at that moment. Rather than deter him, however, he saw it as a challenge to bring out the best in me. To hold a mirror up to my self-deprecating nature and show me I was, in fact, amazing. To say that he was mature beyond his years is an understatement. What I saw as flaws, he saw as an opportunity to love me.

And while he had been looking for me, I completely misread his lengthy conversation with Callie before I could get him on the phone for the first time. To hear him tell it, he was eager to get me on the phone, but didn't want to be rude to my friend. So he stayed on the line with Callie and let her ask him an assortment of weird questions. It was comforting to know that he had felt the same way about me from the moment our eyes met. That much was mutual and totally in sync.

Over the next several months, as our mostly platonic friendship grew, Tomas started coming over more and more often. Although my mom enjoyed his presence, she was nowhere near ready to accept us dating. A college boy? Nope. I was still in high school, and in her eyes, that would never work. For a woman who had experienced so much, she was never letting me out of her sight alone with a boy—and I couldn't blame her.

That didn't deter Tomas. He began leaving "friendly" notes on my car or sent a card in the mail, even stopping by to visit the family. Tomas would bring us all together, encouraging a game of Monopoly. When he secured a property in the game by auction, he would loudly proclaim, "Sold! To the Puerto Rican in the pink shirt!" And that color looked so good on him. He was energetic and funny. Everyone in my family became used to Tomas being around and enjoyed his company.

Enter the hopeless romantic of the family—Ms. Anna. Since our time with her in Florida, so many years earlier, we had fondly grown to call her Nanna. Although she had stayed in New Orleans during our time in Chicago, Nanna joined us in San Antonio to help with the transition. Something to note about Nanna—she couldn't resist watching a love story unfold. A huge smile would spread across her face anytime Tomas entered the room, and her eyes would immediately dart to me, giving me an equally megawatt smile. My mom worked most of the time during the day, which left Nanna in charge to play matchmaker.

Muttering her insistence, Nanna would push Tomas and I out of the door to take Santina's six-month-old son in his stroller for walks. Conveniently placed securely in the stroller with a fresh diaper on and a pacifier in his mouth, she would glide chubby little Michael up to our usual spot on the couch, saying, "Here, take the baby. He needs some air." Nanna would give us a knowing smile, fully aware she had created an opportunity for us to be alone and get to know each other.

"Christina, where do you see yourself in five years?" Tomas asked me as we rounded the corner, pushing my nephew's stroller through the neighborhood. I looked down at the baby in front of me and thought to myself, *I don't want one of you, yet, that's for sure.*

"Five years? I'm just trying to make it through the semester at another new school." I laughed as I tried thinking of a serious answer. "Well, I've dreamed of being a foreign exchange student, so maybe I'll do some traveling after I graduate. Why? Do you want to run away with me? I hear Italy's nice this time of year." I half joked.

"Sure, as long as our next stop is Egypt." I would later learn Tomas was fascinated with the pyramids and Egyptian history since learning more about it in middle school. This is how most of our conversations would go. Tomas would ask a serious question; I would make a joke and he would return one. We balanced each other out. He would get me to think about my future, and I would help him remember we were still young and carefree.

Our first real "date" was planned by Nanna; a family night at the movie theater to watch the 1995 romantic drama, *A Walk in the Clouds*. By this time, Tomas had seamlessly worked his way into the fold of my family. So, when Nanna purchased tickets, she casually invited Tomas to join us, and strategically sat in the aisle, followed by my sister, Tomas, and then me.

With enough space to feel as though we were free, Tomas quietly propped his right elbow up on the armrest, tucking his left hand under his arm and reaching out to hold my hand. I did the same, holding his hand for the entire movie. I was in L-O-V-E LOVE. Even with the small amount of time I had spent with Tomas, I knew I could be in his company for the rest of my life, and all my years would be blessed.

As time went by, my mother got to know Tomas more, and she became a little more relaxed with us being together on short supervised or public excursions. Tomas would take me with his family to a football or a basketball game or other social functions where we might not find ourselves entirely alone.

When we were together, we talked about everything under the sun. Our past, our every day, and of course, what we both dreamed about for the future. It was easy to get to know each other, as our relationship wasn't clouded by being physical. We both respected my mother's insistence on being "just friends" while I was still in high school. But after a while, I wanted to kiss this boy more than anything, and based on how he was always looking at me, I was convinced he wanted to kiss me, too.

One fall evening, Tomas brought me home to Buda to visit his mom, Renne. As we were leaving, he suddenly stopped me under the front porch. With only a moment's notice, he leaned over, slid his arm around me and kissed me. Every fiber inside of me ignited. Short, sweet, perfect. It would be the first of many secret kisses we would share over those next few months. "Secret" only because we were under strict orders from my mother and the law to remain purely platonic. We just adjusted the definition of that word slightly. Friends… who kissed.

With the extra freedom, I felt like I was living a real-life fairy tale with Tomas. I recall one afternoon Tomas stopped by my house with everything needed for a skating adventure: in-line skates, helmets, knee pads, elbow pads, and hand guards. I looked at him half in disbelief and half fully in-love with everything he did to create special time together. Although I grew up with traditional roller skating, I had never in-line skated before. That afternoon he patiently taught me, while I kept falling into his arms and laughing away the next hour. I eventually got the hang of it, but we later found ourselves heading down a small neighborhood hill. Close to falling, I jumped the curb and fell onto the grass of a neighboring yard. Tomas tumbled next to me as we rolled around laughing at ourselves. And in perfect love story fashion, he leaned over and gently kissed me before helping me up. With each day that passed and each moment we were together, I couldn't see myself with anyone but him, and I knew from what we shared, he felt the same about me.

During the fall semester of Tomas' sophomore year of college, he was invited to church by a fellow student named Rafael. Tomas enjoyed it so much, he started attending regularly and studied the Bible with this friend. Tomas slowly began making changes in his life, taking it seriously. We didn't attend the same church and, although I had always considered my faith to be strong, it seemed superficial compared to how strong Tomas' faith was becoming. Though it had barely taken off, it was apparent that our relationship could not only jeopardize his goals of becoming more spiritual but could also be a bit dangerous considering our age difference. He was twenty, and I was only sixteen, so he was advised by his peers in the church that it would be best to end the relationship before it went any further.

One afternoon, Tomas called and asked me to stop by before basketball practice. He coached basketball for a local high school, but he'd never asked me to swing by the gym before. I pulled into the parking lot to find him sitting outside on a picnic table under a tree near the basketball court. He seemed stoic, which was unusual and immediately concerning. The typical enthusiastic, bigger than life Tomas had been replaced by a more somber, quieter version, and I had no idea why.

"Hi," he nearly whispered, as I got closer to him.

"Hi," I returned, not having anything more in me to break the ice. I could feel there was something wrong; I just wasn't totally sure what was going on in his mind.

He gave me a soft kiss on the cheek as he gestured for me to sit across from him.

"Thanks for meeting me. I'm not really sure what to say. Christina, I really like you, but I think the best thing for both of us is to just be friends."

As I stared back at him, I tried to process what he was saying.

"I got some advice, and I think we are just in two different places in life right now. Before we get closer, it may be best if we don't see each other." I could hear the uncertainty in his voice. Maybe he believed it in his mind, but I could hear that his heart felt conflicted.

Just as I could feel the burn in my eyes and the inevitable tears welling up, we were interrupted by a couple of the kids from his basketball team walking towards us. Tomas excused himself, promising to return shortly. As he stood up from the table, I looked away in the other direction, trying to avoid anyone seeing me wipe away the tears from my eyes. *Pull it together Christina.*

By the time Tomas returned, I had done just that. I wouldn't let him see me vulnerable. I wouldn't let him know he'd hurt me.

"I understand and agree it's for the best," I said, tipping my chin up in defiance, in an attempt to save my pride, since it's not what I felt in the least. Before I lost the emotional fight within me, I stood as I told him, "I should really get going."

Tomas stood from the table and offered a single extended open arm for a side hug. *Great. A side hug.*

I couldn't say goodbye quickly enough. Getting in my car and driving away, I tried to convince myself of the lie I had told him: *It's for the best.*

Best for who? I wasn't sure. All I knew was that in only six months, I had moved to a new city, moved homes four times in that new city, and enrolled in what would be my third high school before

I even completed junior year. As if that wasn't enough, I'd also begun and ended a relationship with the person I thought I'd eventually marry. While I tried my best to act unfazed by it all, it was a bit more than I could process. I had left everything familiar to me back in Chicago. It was hard to maintain friendships when I was always moving, but Tomas helped fill the space during my initial transition to San Antonio.

Now, without him, I felt I wasn't tethered to anything or anyone. It felt like another abandonment in my life. A rejection. A reminder of that old feeling of "not enough." I'd always worried that Tomas was too good to be true, and now he was. I didn't know what was wrong with me. What I did know was I could no longer hold on to the past.

Chapter Seven

Run.

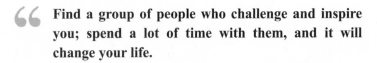 **Find a group of people who challenge and inspire you; spend a lot of time with them, and it will change your life.**

— Amy Poehler

Not too long after Tomas and I officially agreed to be friends, he called me to tell me about going on what he referred to as "casual and friendly double dates" with other girls in his church. At first, I was content to listen, happy for any reason to talk to him. But the more it appeared he was moving on, the more it affected me, though I pretended it didn't. I hated hearing anything about him dating anyone else.

I knew many of his new outings were just friendly dates, but it was complete torture to listen to all the details. Finally, I summoned the courage to tell him I couldn't hear about his dating in the church any longer; truthfully, it hurt too much, knowing we couldn't be together. Like I had most evenings, since Tomas and I stopped seeing each other, I was singing my heart out to *Beyond Justice to Mercy* by Susan Ashton when my mom entered my bedroom.

"Hey baby, I'm heading out. But just a thought before I leave. Maybe it's not the best idea you keep talking to Tomas. You don't seem like yourself, and as much as I love hearing you sing, this song is a little sad. Don't you think so?"

I looked at my mom, slightly shocked. I hadn't realized my private pain wasn't so private. "But we're just friends."

"I know you're just friends, but because you're friends and you keep talking, it's like nothing has changed. I think if you really want to move on, you can't just 'close the chapter' on the relationship. You're going to have to shut the book, put it on the shelf, and pick a new one. Just something for you to think about, sweet pea."

As my mom turned and left my bedroom, I digested everything she had said to me. As much as I wanted to keep Tomas in my life, it was becoming clear it wasn't the healthiest thing for me. I knew if I didn't act on this moment of conviction, I might not call him at all. So, I went out into the hallway, paced up and down to double check there were no unwelcome ears around, and dialed Tomas' number.

"Hey, I was just thinking about you!" Tomas' cheery voice rang through the phone line. It was an extra dagger to the heart that I was about to cut off the last tie to him.

"Hey," I answered back, not sure how to jump right into it. I decided to rip off the bandage and say what was really on my mind. "So, I don't think we should talk anymore."

"What? Why?"

"It hurts too much to keep talking like nothing has changed. I don't think you should call me anymore. I really need to move on."

There was a long pause before I heard Tomas sigh and speak up once more.

"I don't know if I understand why we can't just be friends, but I want to support you. If you think this is for the best, I'll respect your decision."

"It's too hard to be friends," I exhaled. A weight I didn't know was on my shoulders suddenly lifted. Gathering strength to finish the job, I continued on, "I'll see you around, Tomas."

"Umm, yeah, see you around Christina." Tomas said with a faint sadness in his tone. I wondered if the realization that it was really over was sinking in. I wasn't trying to hurt him, but what my mom said to me had resonated. The only way to move on from my feelings for Tomas was to separate myself from him completely.

Tomas liked this idea just about as much as I liked his suggestion to be "just friends," so it didn't last very long. Occasionally, he would still call me to catch up. But it wasn't like it used to be. During one of our conversations I mentioned needing a job, and Tomas suggested I work in the place where he had begun the prior year as a telemarketer. I quickly signed on and began training.

Since the company we were now both working for was quite large, Tomas and I rarely ran into each other. The few times we had seen each other, it was usually as everyone was leaving the office for the evening.

Within my training group, I met a young man about Tomas' age with similar features—specifically green eyes. We quickly became friends… okay, friends who flirted with each other. One evening, after walking me to my car, the two of us lingered a while, chatting. Most of the employees had exited the parking lot when, suddenly, a car drove up to us. As the window rolled down, I saw a smiling Tomas. We exchanged some quick and awkward hellos and good-byes, then Tomas drove off. *Weird.*

I arrived home to a furious mother. "Where have you been, and why were you out talking with some boy in an empty parking lot?" *What? How did she know?* After a brief but intense exchange, I realized Tomas had called my house asking for me. When my mom mentioned I was still at work, Tomas volunteered, "Oh, really? Work ended a while ago… she must still be talking to that guy in the parking lot." He knew exactly what he had done, filling my mom in on that privileged bit of information. I was in deep trouble, and if I had anything to say about it, soon Tomas would be too. It seemed that if he couldn't have me, nobody else could either. *Hmm... I guess he's not as over me as I thought.*

Time passed, and life without Tomas became the norm. I felt the distance between us, but the sharp edges of pain were dulling. Before time completely softened my broken heart, my mother thought my life could use some positive influences. So, she encouraged me to attend Tomas' church. While she didn't believe Tomas and I should spend hours chatting on the phone, she felt the church he and his family attended was made up of good people who formed a strong community. Something she knew was missing in my life. And as much I would have loved to argue with her, I couldn't disagree. Over the next year, I studied the Bible, as he had, and quickly became an active member of his church.

While Tomas was in the college group, I wasn't since I was still a senior in high school. There were lovely people in my group, but many of them were much younger than I was, so it was rough staying with the younger teens while Tomas was in the "big kids' club." I comforted myself with the idea that, as soon as I had "done my time" and graduated, we could pick up right where we left off. No more age issues, right?

Over the next few months, I saw Tomas at events or various functions at church. Although we were friendly, we didn't really spend a lot of time together, and it felt as though we were growing further apart. I could see the writing on the wall: I would eventually have to let him go in my heart. There would never be a "Tomas & Christina." He was moving on with his life, and I needed to follow suit. But how?

* * *

In the spring, military recruiters began visiting my high school campus. In fact, a friend who had graduated a year before me enlisted in the Air Force. When he was out of boot camp and into his training, I would hear the stories and could easily picture my life in some exotic location, far away from my life at home. My interest in signing up grew.

Coincidentally, both Tomas' dad and stepmom, Tom and Kim, were actively serving in the Army. Because we all attended the same church, I could continue my friendship with them. So, one day I approached them with my idea of enlisting in the military. Luckily for me, they could not have been more supportive.

I began asking them about life in the Army, and we talked about the physical fitness aspect of boot camp. They both agreed that if I put in the hard work, preparing for the mile, push-ups and sit-ups, prior to going to boot camp, I would be in a much better place to handle the other challenges. So that's what I did. Tom and Kim had a fitness gym set up in their garage and were certified in training. They willingly offered to get me started on my journey when I expressed interest.

It was self-inflicted pain. Both physically and emotionally. Although Tomas lived with roommates in an apartment across town, he would return to his parent's home to visit or do laundry. Occasionally I would run into Tomas while training and although I would never admit it then, I'm sure it was written all over my face when I would see him. I still loved him, but knew I needed to move on. So that's what I did. I focused on the future. The training made me feel physically stronger, but also more connected to my decision as I pictured what my life would be like dressed in a uniform.

As my senior year wound down, Tomas and I were definitively "just friends," and that status became even more clear to me when I was told by a friend that his heart had moved on with a girl named Jasmine. She was his age, attended our church, and they had been hanging out more and more regularly for weeks.

Jasmine was beautiful, sweet and completely devoted to her faith, which was exactly the type of girl I imagined Tomas would marry. I heard that old familiar chorus of *you're not good enough* ringing through my mind, leaving me awake in the middle of the night and wondering how I had ended up here. Although Jasmine and Tomas weren't officially boyfriend and girlfriend, I knew it was only a matter of time.

Before they were formally a couple, I knew I needed an exit strategy. I didn't want to stay around to watch it unfold in front of me; I knew it would break my heart. At home, I wasn't totally happy. My inner child, who had moved more times than she could count, was yearning to be on her own and out exploring what the world had to offer. The main problem was I didn't have the means to do it. The Army seemed like the solution to my problems.

I recall a sit-down conversation with Kim's soul sister Katherine, who also served in the Army, just before my official swearing-in ceremony. I remember her asking me point-blank, "Why do you want to join the Army?" As I began explaining to her what I wanted to experience and how it could help me go to college, she abruptly cut me off and said, "No! You're joining the army to serve your country."

I never forgot that conversation with her. The things my recruiter had explained along the way were the "perks" like travel, having college paid for, and more. But I needed to understand that they were that— just perks. The more important thing to remember was that I was committing my life to serving my country, no matter what that entailed. The question was, is that what I really wanted? I felt strongly, at the time, that the answer was "yes." In reality, though, the idea of military life, for me, was more like responsibly running away and starting over. I had seen my father and my mother use their deployment to Italy and subsequent return to New Jersey as jumping-off points for new identities. Why couldn't the same be true for me?

I anxiously waited for the day I was scheduled to report to the Military Entrance Processing Station (MEPS). This is where all recruits are put through a battery of tests, including aptitude and physical examinations. By the end of it all, and if I passed the exams, I would raise my right hand at the swearing-in ceremony, pledging to defend the U.S. Constitution and obey all orders, among other things. After the ceremony, the only thing left to do would be to graduate from high school before I could be shipped off to boot camp.

When the day finally arrived, I felt more than ready. With all the physical training Tom and Kim provided, I felt extremely confident. Even though I knew it would still be a couple of months until basic training, I was excited to make my decision to join the military official. I got a good night's sleep, set my alarm, and arrived fifteen minutes before my scheduled 5:00 a.m. report time. This was totally outside of my personality, but perhaps the military was transforming me already.

I was assigned to a small group of girls, and we stayed together throughout the day as we completed a series of tests, including my favorite, the duck waddle. Modest me, dressed only in my undergarments, bent at the knees in a squat, walking from one end of the room to the other. *I guess I need to get used to this.* The day flew by until we were all sitting on a bench after completing our physicals, and my name was called along with another girl.

Eventually, I was unceremoniously summoned into the captain's office and, as he gestured for me to sit across from him, he opened a file to look over the information. Without looking up from his paper, he declared, "You tested positive for syphilis." I must have stared at him in response with the most puzzled expression, so he repeated himself, "You tested positive for syphilis, so you won't be swearing in today. I'm sorry."

I couldn't even repeat the name. I had no idea what it was, so I asked him quizzically, "What's that?" I was certain I learned this in health class, but I had quickly discarded it as useless information. After all, I'd barely kissed a boy, much less slept with one.

Slightly annoyed, he responded gruffly, "It's a sexually transmitted infection."

"I've never had sex. How could I have that?" I'll never forget his comment back to me, mostly because it replayed in my mind as I tried to figure out the meaning of it.

"Well honey, I can't tell you how many girls have sat across from me in the seat where you are sitting now and told me they were a virgin, only to be holding a baby nine months later."

Unbelievable, he thinks I'm lying. Standing abruptly, the captain handed me some documents and dismissed me, saying, "Do what you need to do."

It felt like I was being pranked as I took the papers out of his hands, standing up to leave, still stunned at the conversation. *That was it? What just happened?* I left the room, noticing my group was no longer seated on the bench. Quickly, I made my way to the exit. I looked over to see them in a back room huddled together, reciting the same oath I'd been planning to say when I woke up that morning. All the training I had done, all the preparing. I couldn't help but feel it was all for nothing and was being taken away.

I called my mom, explaining the disappointment of not having been sworn in, trying to explain as best I could what had just taken place. My mom respected my decision to wait until I was married before having sex, so I didn't need to explain to her any further. She immediately booked an appointment with the doctor.

Not long after I left the MEPS, the city health department also came knocking at the door of our home asking for confirmation of my diagnosis. Of course, two examinations and two tests later, both came out negative. *What a mess.*

Either way, I had cleared my sexual health status. With all the drama behind me, I was ready to forget the whole thing and finally complete the elusive swearing-in ceremony.

Truthfully, though it seems ridiculous in hindsight, the whole ordeal was incredibly upsetting. I had never been to a gynecologist before, so the multiple tests felt intrusive, not to mention very overwhelming. As many women have discovered before and after me, I received the most condescending looks when telling the nurse or doctor I was a virgin who was trying to prove I didn't have syphilis. No different from the captain who gave me my results.

I tried to put my pride aside, since the only thing that mattered was that I needed to make it official with the Army. I spoke with my recruiter after the results were received, and I was booked again for 5:00 a.m. the next morning. Unlike the first visit to MEPS, I stayed up late the night before, and my parents asked if they could speak with me.

My step dad called me into my parents' bedroom, and before I could get settled, he began, "Your mom and I have been talking, and we think you should consider waiting to enlist."

"Why? I'm swearing in—in just a few hours." I responded, completely taken by surprise.

"With everything you've just been through, it gave us the time and the opportunity to think about how you might be better off going to college first, then entering as an Officer. Like I did." I imagine they didn't take me very seriously the first time around and were given the extra time to consider what it meant if I enlisted.

"What do you mean, 'enter as an Officer'?"

"Well, entering as an Officer means you join with your college degree and receive the benefits that come with it." My step dad saw there wasn't much fight left in me, so he continued, "Time never hurts, Christina. If you still feel like joining is the right call when you graduate college-*great*. You can join then, as an Officer."

"I've done all this training. I'm ready now." But even as the words left my mouth, I considered what he was proposing.

Realizing I may not be ready to give up the idea all together, my mom interjected, "Christina, all we are suggesting is that you wait a little longer. If you feel the same even in a year, and you decide to enlist, we'll still support you."

Since the idea of the Army had first become a topic, they had never voiced any concern, only support. After all, my father was in the Navy, my grandfather was in the Navy, and my stepdad was also in the Navy, serving as a Captain for over thirty years. That's why I was so surprised when they asked me if I would wait.

I had just gone through months of training, a false positive health result, a humiliating conversation with a Captain accusing me of lying, a home visit from the city health department, multiple exams courtesy of two separate gynecologists and now this.

"Yes. I'll wait." I replied, feeling resigned. It wasn't any one person's fault, but I was done. I honestly felt indifferent about the whole decision at that point. So, I agreed to wait.

I woke up a few hours later at four thirty in the morning and went to meet the recruiter to tell her face-to-face I would not be swearing in. I believed I owed her the courtesy.

This recruiter didn't take my withdrawal very lightly, but after a longer conversation over breakfast, I stood by my decision. I would wait until I completed college to join the Army as an Officer.

It wasn't an easy choice, especially because I had envisioned my new life already. It took me some time to come to grips with what I had given up, even if it was temporary. I've always been someone who, when I set my mind to something, I stop at nothing until I've achieved it-regardless of how hard it might be. So, the idea of quitting when I was so close didn't sit well with me. Deciding to stop my journey here was accepting that I would be disappointing myself more than anyone else.

I didn't realize it then, but I would never end up serving in the military. It's funny the twists and turns life takes to lead us from where we think we're supposed to go to where we're truly meant to be. Thanks to one false positive, my life was set on a completely different path.

* * *

Though my post-high school dreams were shattered, my senior prom was still rapidly approaching and, of course, no boy held my attention after meeting Tomas. His affections had turned to Jasmine, but they still weren't a couple. I accepted the fact we would never be together. Nevertheless, I imagined my last special event in high school to be shared with Tomas and no one else. I wanted to go with someone who I could connect with. Maybe that was my idea of closure?

I scheduled some time with my friend, Karen, whose relationship with her husband, Peter, I admired. She knew my intentions, and I trusted she would give me her unbiased opinion. I wasn't ready for Tomas to possibly reject my request, either. After speaking with Karen, who agreed it was a good idea, I called Tomas and asked him to go with me to prom.

Trying as best as I could to ignore my nerves, I picked up the phone and dialed. With each passing ring, I couldn't help but feel more and more stupid. I paced back and forth in my bedroom until I'd had enough. I hung up the phone. *What were you thinking?* I mentally reprimanded myself. *Why would Tomas want to go to a High School prom? He's twenty-one. Forget it. I'm not going.*

My downward spiral was abruptly cut short by the phone ringing. *Was he calling back?!*

Panic leapt in my throat as I ran back to my phone and debated whether to answer. Finally, I picked up and could barely squeak out a "Hello?"

"Hey Christina! You just called? What's up?" Tomas' ever-joyful voice sang through the line.

Immediately second guessing if I even wanted to go through with my original plan or not, I seriously contemplated claiming I mis-dialed. But my heart won out. I decided to go for it, feeling my voice shake as I said, "Hey! Yeah, um, is there any chance you're free on May 9? Wait. I should probably tell you why I'm asking that, right?" Cue the nervous giggle. "Well, would you maybe want to go to my prom with me?" Before he had a chance to consider my proposal, I continued, "I totally get if you can't or don't want to but-"

"No, I think that'd be fun. I love dancing!" Tomas interrupted enthusiastically.

Honestly, in that moment, talking to Tomas, I felt a sliver of shame for the first time. Here I was, the little high school girl asking the big college boy on an important date—like it was a favor, and maybe he had known I was going to ask him. It wasn't anything he said or did; in fact, he agreed without hesitation. I'm sure the thoughts in my mind had everything to do with my own insecurities screaming at me.

With my date secured, I forcibly shook off the notion that he was going out of a sense of pity, and my mission to look drop-dead gorgeous began. If this would be my last evening out with him, I'd make sure it would be one for the books. I was resigned to the fact that Tomas and I would not be a couple, but I still wanted him to know what he was missing and, ultimately, have a fantastic evening.

When Tomas arrived to escort me to prom, I walked out to greet him, outfitted in a black, velvet off-the-shoulder gown with my short hair pulled back on one side. Although I felt beautiful, I couldn't help feeling a little self-conscious as Tomas followed me into the house. Years earlier, when Tomas and I first met, he had been my date for homecoming, and the memories of those happier times came flooding back to me as we sat on the couch, nervously waiting for my mother to find her camera.

After taking the traditional photos, we were off to the St. Anthony Hotel in downtown San Antonio, and it was just the two of us. It felt natural being with him. It always had. Tomas parked about a block and a half away from the venue and, as we walked to the hotel entrance, I placed my hand around the crook of his elbow since I was walking in heels. There was that familiar heat, that electric connection between us. Organically, it was crackling back to life with every minute that passed, whether I liked it or not.

We danced the night away, having the time of our lives. Out of breath and genuinely enjoying each other, we stepped off the dance floor to find a quiet corner of the ballroom with an empty table. The two of us huddled close enough to hear the other's thoughts, talking about everything from my discarded military plans to his next semester of classes. All I can remember from that evening is talking the night away, noticing the easy ebb and flow of our conversation and how much I had missed it. How much I missed him.

As we stepped out of the hotel and back onto the downtown street, I thanked him for coming with me. I realized then that this was one of the few times we had ever been alone for a significant length of time without a baby stroller in tow. Nanna would have been very pleased if she could have seen us at that moment. Except, in my mind, I was letting go of the idea that Tomas was my forever person, imagining his heart had already moved on. I accepted the idea he wasn't interested; he was accompanying me purely out of politeness and friendship.

Unbeknownst to me, my prom night would be a far more transcendental experience for Tomas than originally intended. As I was jabbering about my hopes and dreams, he saw me. All of me. The good, the bad, the insecure. He saw the woman I was becoming and how much I had matured in our brief time apart. With me, right there with him, he saw it clear as day. Our future, our strength as a couple together, and of course a stunning black dress with a girl who adored him inside it. This was the evening he chose me. He chose *us*.

After that night, Tomas went back and confided in Rafael, now one of his closest friends, that he was no longer interested in pursuing a relationship with Jasmine. His friends thought he had lost his mind when he told them he was going to marry me. They knew me as the young high schooler who came around the college group now and then. But Tomas knew I was so much more than that. I just wish he would have told me that night, too.

* * *

In June, I walked the high school graduation stage and enrolled at San Antonio College (SAC). My mother encouraged me to transition into college life by helping me move in with some friends. With Nicole in Chicago and Santina living in Oklahoma, both married with children of their own, my mother and Isaac were officially "empty nesters." I began studying psychology in the hopes of becoming a music therapist. I loved singing and the idea of helping others through the power of music intrigued me enough to dive in. The community I gained through church was a great encouragement for me when it came to music. Occasionally, I would be asked to sing a special song or even perform at a wedding. This opened my mind as I met so many talented musicians in our congregation alone. I learned so much. Being on stage, like when I was in dance, helped me become a little more comfortable in my skin.

Don't get me wrong, I was no recording artist. I never received formal training, so I wish I could say I never squeaked out the wrong note or even forgot the lyrics all together. And I wasn't the only "equipment malfunction." I recall one wedding when my singing partner didn't arrive on time, which left me attempting to sing a song solo, when it was written as a duet. I wasn't a confident and seasoned artist like Adele, who would stop midway, apologize to the crowd, and start over. But I received similar grace from an audience filled with people who loved me despite my imperfect performances and encouraged me to keep trying. With new goals and a new me, I was transforming right before everyone's eyes into a young woman with the self-confidence to create a plan.

As I began my freshman year, I continued to develop more friendships within my church community. One of those friendships, of course, was with Tomas and, although we were "just friends," I'd be lying if I said there wasn't *some* friendly flirting going on ever since that night at prom.

Like most college students, when I wasn't at school, working or studying, I spent most weekends hanging out, enjoying my youth.

One afternoon, while on campus studying in the student center, some friends came up and asked if I was interested in joining them downtown the following weekend.

"We can check out the Tower of the Americas, maybe walk around. Or just figure out something to do once we get there, you know, just hang out," Misha excitedly explained.

"Sure, I love the Tower. I don't have any plans. That sounds like fun!"

"Great, we'll pick you up at seven thirty. Oh, and don't forget a jacket. The observation deck at the Tower gets pretty windy."

"Thanks. See you Saturday!" I smiled as I returned to my book, appreciating the friendships I had made.

When Saturday finally came around, I found myself alone in my apartment, since all my roommates were already out for the evening. I was getting dressed, while giving all I had, singing along-side Mary J. Blige's unplugged version of "Sweet Thing." Just then, the phone rang.

"Hey, what are you up to?" Tomas' sister, Keisha, asked inquis-itively.

"I'm just getting ready to go out with Misha and some friends. You?"

"I'm hanging out here with my dad and Kim... oh and Tee (Tomas). We're about to make dinner."

"That's awesome," I said in a cheery voice, imagining what it would be like to be there, hanging out with Tomas. Attempting to switch my mind off of him, I asked, "Is your dad making his famous arroz con gandules?"

"I don't know, maybe. So, what are you wearing tonight?" Keisha asked, quickly changing the subject. *That's weird.*

Feeling like her question was a little out of the blue, I answered, "Uh, jeans and a blazer. Why?"

"I was just wondering. Didn't you say you were going down-town? Maybe it'd be fun to dress up a little." *Why?*

"Yeah, I think that's the plan, but I don't think we're doing anything fancy."

"Well, maybe you should think about dressing a little nicer. That's all I'm saying."

"Nicer? Keisha, I'm just going out with friends. I mean, I think what I'm wearing is okay?"

"I'm sure you'll pick something nice."

The entire conversation felt slightly off. Like I was missing something obvious, but I couldn't figure out what. So instead of thinking about it much longer, I picked up where Mary J. and I had left off.

Soon after, I heard a honk outside. I headed towards my front door and as I opened it, I saw Jacob behind the wheel, joined by our friends, Misha and Dan. I yelled out to the car, "I'll be right down, just grabbing my stuff!"

While we made the trip downtown, we all chatted about life, catching up on each other's most recent family get-togethers over Thanksgiving.

We pulled into the parking lot just near the Tower. Jacob popped the trunk of his car and, after shuffling a few things around, he pulled out two silk scarves. Handing one to Misha, and the second to me, he said, "Now, we're going to have you put these on." *Huh?* Dan could see the hesitation in my face, and with a little gentle encouragement, looked at me and said, "We're going to play a little game. Just go with it." Being blindfolded was not my idea of a "fun game." Not to mention, vulnerability has never exactly been my strong suit.

I trusted both Dan and Jacob, so I knew whatever they had up their sleeves would be fun. I just needed to let go of the fact that I would have to agree to be in darkness. Without my ability to see, I'd have to allow Dan to lead the way.

I looked at Misha, who gave me a sweet, encouraging smile. *Okay, let's do this.* Blinded, the boys led us in all sorts of directions. I could tell they were enjoying it with all the laughter.

I heard the *ping* of the elevator before I felt the shift of the floor under my feet, letting me know we'd entered the Tower's elevator. I heard someone whisper, "Oh! Look at those girls; they're blindfolded!" Once we stepped out of the elevator, I overheard someone say the observation deck was closed. *Uh oh.*

Apparently, the boys had planned for this, so Jacob and Dan pulled us aside and one of them said, "Stay here for a minute. We just have to set up Plan B." And with that, we were alone —blindfolded.

A few seconds later, Dan returned, walked me over, assisted me into a chair, and asked, "Would you wait one more minute? I just need to do a few more things." As I sat alone in the silence, I had no understanding of my surroundings, so I casually reached out my hand to see if I was seated at a table. When I felt nothing in front of me, I quickly retracted my hand, feeling a little embarrassed. *Hopefully, nobody saw that.*

After what felt like an hour later, though it was probably just a matter of minutes, I heard a voice.

"Take off your blindfold." This voice was different. It was deeper and felt like velvet running through my ears. *Great. I'm hearing Tomas. I can't get this guy out of my head.* "What?" I finally answered back, still confused by hearing Tomas' voice.

"Take off your blindfold," the voice repeated.

"Am I supposed to do that?" Not wanting to break any game rules, I needed to be sure.

I heard a small laugh, followed by, "Yeah, Christina, it's all right. Go ahead. Take it off."

I did as I was told and removed the blindfold. It took a second for my eyes to adjust to the light, but when they did, I felt just as confused as before.

Sitting across from me was Tomas.

Is this part of the game? I thought to myself. He had the strangest smile on his face, like he was proud of himself for pulling off the switch.

It wasn't until Tomas handed me a tiny, wooden, carved box that it sank in. Opening it revealed a little angel resting on some dried flowers and something handwritten by Tomas placed on the inside cover:

"LORD, you are my God; I will exalt you and praise your name, for in perfect faithfulness you have done wonderful things, *things planned long ago*." Isaiah 25:1 (NIV)

When I finished reading the scripture, I looked up at him. He smiled, taking my hand, and said, "Christina, we met so long ago and even then, I knew I wanted you in my life. I've watched you mature into a beautiful young woman, both inside and out."

Should he be saying this to me? I mean, we're good friends, sure, but this seemed like something more.

He smiled even bigger as he scooted his chair closer to me. Leaning in, he told me, "Christina, I'm grateful for our friendship, but I want more. And I hope you do, too. Will you be my girlfriend?"

I wanted to answer immediately, but paused, worried that my voice might crack from the emotion bubbling up. As my first tear broke free, I whispered, "Yes."

Tomas jumped up from his seat and took me up with him, wrapped his arms around me and pulled me in for a long, drawn-out hug. Releasing me, he stepped back and with both of my hands resting in his, he looked at me with that all-too-familiar smoldering gaze. I was completely and utterly lost in those green eyes.

"Christina. I love you."

Confessing my love to him didn't feel like much of a confession at all. The feelings I had for Tomas had never gone away. If anything, they'd only grown.

"I love you, too." I said.

I was exactly where I needed to be. We knew each other inside and out, never looking back once we finally became an official couple. With all the barriers gone, there seemed to be nothing but blue skies ahead.

* * *

As I began the second semester of my freshman year at SAC, Tomas and I were becoming even closer and were eventually asked to become leaders in the student ministry group. This gave us the opportunity to spend more time together. Our group of friends eventually realized that we were a forever kind of thing. It was refreshing to be a couple together without the awkward questions around age or status. We were Tomas and Christina and, after a while, it was hard to imagine us as anything other than an insepa-rable unit. As for my mom, once I stepped foot on a college campus, Tomas was in the clear as far as she was concerned. She saw his devotion to me and respected his willingness to wait.

As the semester flew by, I felt my sense of self growing stronger with each step. Despite everything I had been through in my childhood, I had survived. Even better, I had Tomas in my life, something I thought was lost.

Tomas had decided he wanted to become a teacher. He'd enjoyed his time coaching basketball and organizing various day and overnight camps. To this day, I've met no one else who can spin a basketball on their fingertips for as long as he can. He had also spent many years developing his leadership skills within our church, speaking and teaching. It was easy to picture him at the head of a classroom. His genuine enthusiasm would help him connect with students, making them feel like they could achieve anything. Everything made sense. Life was good.

When we weren't in school, studying for a test, or having a Bible study, we were driving teens in our group to and from their functions. During our free time, we would plan the sweetest dates. We spent time exploring the Texas Hill Country or in downtown San Antonio strolling the Riverwalk, as I had imagined so many years prior. We even created our own scavenger hunts for each other with friends, calling them "Mystery Dates." We didn't need elaborate plans to enjoy each other, though. Often, we would have the best time sipping coffee and exploring the new additions at our local bookstore. It didn't matter what we did; we appreciated the simplicity of life in each other's company. Not to mention the free dates were especially helpful since we were two broke college kids.

As Tomas neared graduation, he dreamed of our future as Mr. & Mrs. Martinez. I remember one late evening, while studying in the computer lab on campus, Tomas leaned over to me, and his voice suddenly took on a serious tone. "Would you say 'yes'?"

"What are you talking about?" I asked, completely oblivious to his train of thought.

"If I asked you to marry me. Would you say 'yes'?"

I instantly blushed, flashing back in my mind to the moment I met him in the ballroom of a quinceañera. There had been hundreds of little moments leading up to this big transforming one. Sitting across from me was the person who knew me more truly than anyone else. Yet, here he was, asking me in the simplest terms if I saw him, too.

"Yes," I said without hesitation, and kissed him gently. He smiled and returned to his studies, confident that all was right in the world. In college and in love, what could go wrong?

Chapter Eight

Darkness.

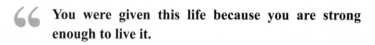

You were given this life because you are strong enough to live it.

— **Ain Eineziz**

June 9, 1998. It was your average summer day in San Antonio. At least that's what I thought when the morning sunshine broke through my bedroom window. Life was a breeze, and I couldn't have been happier. But I would replay every detail of this particular day in my mind over and over more than any other day in my entire life, including the day I met Tomas.

I was approaching my sophomore year at SAC, and my plate was full between church, family, and girlfriend duties. I woke up just after six thirty, late for an early morning bible study with Tomas and some of our friends. *Typical.*

I had stayed over at my parents' house the night before since there was a leak in my apartment. Had I slept at my apartment, I could have walked to the meeting. I was now halfway across town and pretty sure I was going to be more than fashionably late. At least I had a new outfit on.

I headed to a friend's apartment for the meeting and walked in as everyone was getting settled. After the meeting broke up, I gave Tomas a quick hug before he ran off for class. My head snapped back to the sound of folks shuffling out the door. I looked up to see Laura, one of my best friends, smirking as she walked towards me to give me a hard time. We first met at church and instantly connected, becoming fast friends that felt more like sisters. The kind of friendship where there is understanding in the absence of words. Though she was always a blast to be around, she wasn't afraid to tell me when I was off-track. She had a way of guiding me, almost like a big sister, that was loving and caring.

"Glad you could make it," she said sarcastically. I returned her sass with a similar look on my own face as she gave me a big hug.

"I'd rather show up late than ugly." I replied jokingly. "Oh, I'm just playing. You know I overslept."

As we left the meeting, I gave Laura a rundown of my hectic morning, coming from my parents' house, and she nodded with understanding as she walked me to my car.

"Come with me," Laura said. "I'm going to campus to invite people to International Day." I always enjoyed hanging out with Laura and chatting about life. If I wasn't with Tomas, working or at school, I was probably with Laura.

I agreed, and we fell in step together as we crossed the parking lot. Celebrating International Day was one of my favorite traditions with our church. This year, we were renting out the entire Majestic Theatre in downtown San Antonio for the event. If you've never stepped inside this theater, it's difficult to describe just how "majestic" it really is.

Each year, we would gather for a morning of musical performances while welcoming new members and connecting with our community. I was buzzing with excitement about performing that year. The church had become my avenue to sing, and I had never performed on a stage like the Majestic Theatre before.

As we walked and passed out flyers, our conversation inevitably shifted to Tomas.

"So, Tomas and I had an interesting conversation last week," I said to Laura.

"What do you mean?" Laura asked. "Interesting good? Or interesting bad?"

"Good, I think. He asked me if I would say 'yes' if he proposed to me." Eager to see her reaction, I waited for her response.

"Really?" Her face brightened with a smile. "Well, you love him, don't you?"

I answered without hesitation, "More than you know. I can't stop thinking about him." We both giggled as we neared my car.

"Well, we both know he'll be ready to get married once he graduates. If you're going to date someone older than you, you have to meet them where they are in life. So, eventually you'll need to, Christina. Think about it. If you love Tomas, then it's time to decide if you see a future with him." I gave her a big hug and opened my car door, cranking up the radio as soon as the engine came to life.

As I drove away, the only critical decision I was thinking of at that moment was what to have for lunch. Since I had skipped breakfast and it was getting closer to midday, I was starving. I pulled out of the parking lot and turned onto the access road. Ahead of me was a Whataburger restaurant. Jackpot!

I pulled into the drive-thru lane and ordered a kid's meal with a cookie—my usual order. As I pulled away with my lunch, I peeked in the bag to grab a couple of French fries and noticed two cookies, not one. This was turning out to be a great day. After I snacked on my lunch in the car, I headed out to conquer the rest of my day off from work.

As I drove on, Laura called, "Hey, why don't you join me for my wax appointment with Manijeh at one o'clock?" she said. "You know you're starting to look like Pancho Villa. It's time to get your upper lip done!"

Allow me to be honest. Being Sicilian meant dealing with a little hairiness. So, I regularly joined Laura when she made an appointment with Manijeh, her esthetician. Even more beautiful than she was on the outside, was the heart inside of her. Pure gold. Thanks to Laura, Manijeh had become a dear friend.

I knew Laura was only joking, so I laughed before agreeing. "Okay, fine, but only because you're right and, if you've noticed, I'll bet everyone else has."

As I hung up the phone, I received another call. This one was from the Marriott hotel where I was working, asking me to come in right away to cover someone's shift. As I thought about it, I heard my manager exhale with a stressed sigh as he explained, so I quickly responded. "I have an appointment and will need to go home and change, but I'll try to get there as soon as possible. Is that all right?" The overtime hours on my paycheck would be nice. I learned from a young age that a job equaled freedom for me. Though I had always contributed to household bills, the rest of my paycheck was for me. It was my independence. Knowing I had just committed to Laura, I didn't want to stand her up, but I knew I could make both work.

"That's no problem," my manager said. "Thank you, and I'll see you soon." I tossed my cell phone onto the passenger seat and was about to approach the interstate to head in Laura's direction when I realized I didn't have any money to pay Manijeh. I pictured in my mind the route to Laura and where I could cash my paycheck. Nothing came to mind, so I turned around and went back to the H-E-B grocery store, where I knew they could process my check. As I approached the light ahead, I noticed it was green. *Yes. Another stroke of good luck today,* I thought.

Having first learned to drive in Chicago, I knew not only how to drive in poor weather conditions like snow, but also to be aware of my surroundings. I kept my foot on the accelerator and just before I approached the intersection, I noticed a silver car next to me slowing down to come to a complete stop before turning right into the shopping center. Another larger blue vehicle attempted to exit from the same shopping center at the same time. I assumed the silver car beside me was waiting for the blue car to exit since it would be difficult for both cars to fit in the same entrance/exit.

Without warning, the blue car exiting from the parking lot pulled out directly in front of me. This happened so quickly, I had no time to react—not even enough time to move my foot from the accelerator to the brake. I didn't even think to brace for impact. It didn't feel real.

What happened next seemed to unfold in slow motion. I felt a gasp escape me and heard the crunch of metal hitting metal. We'd collided. I was thrown back in my seat in the next instant, ripped back seconds too late. Too late because I had already put my head through the windshield.

My car, whom I had affectionately named Elsie, had over 140,000 miles on her and was nearly as old as I was, but she was my trusted companion. I had always tried not to resent Elsie for being built without an air conditioner while I suffered through the Texas heat. But what I loved most about her was her size. She wasn't too big. I could stretch my arm out comfortably and roll up the passenger window in the rain. And yet she never felt too small. It was now, in this moment, that I realized I had never given any thought to how she might protect me in a crash.

As I recoiled from the shock of the impact, everything looked cloudy. I couldn't see. It felt as though I was in a room with all the lights turned off. I blinked and blinked but still couldn't see. Feeling alone, I started talking to myself out loud.

"Pull it together, Christina. Pull it *together*." I demanded of myself. I continued to blink hard to get the blur out of my eyes, even shaking my head, hoping it would disappear. But my head was heavy, and I was feeling disoriented. None of it felt real.

I reached for the passenger seat, feeling around for my phone. I had to call my family. I continued searching around the seat. Although I couldn't find my phone, I could feel the contents of my car spilled everywhere. Papers were scattered all over—my lipstick, even the extra Whataburger cookie. But still no phone. The smell of smoke suddenly invaded my senses and, feeling as though I was still sitting in the dark, I could feel myself growing scared.

Am I dead? I'm not ready to die...

The panic inside of me mounted. With my vision still blocked and silence all around me, I felt like I couldn't breathe. I felt stuck in my seat, unable to move. "Somebody, help me! I can't see!" I yelled out my window. My attention turned back to my phone. If I could find the phone, I could call for help; I knew that much. I needed help! Since it felt like no one was coming for me, I rooted myself on. So, I thought to myself...

You gotta do this.

You gotta do this.

With my motivating words as the only help I had, I reached further forward on the passenger floor, when suddenly, a gigantic bucket of water poured over my head. It was like a rushing water-fall. Only it wasn't water at all. I didn't know it then, but my entire head was covered in my own blood. I was losing a lot of it, and I was losing it fast.

As the warm liquid continued to pour down my face, I sat up and leaned back in my seat. I tried as best as I could to blow the blood out and off my lips, almost like I was whistling, forcefully trying to prevent any of the blood from entering my mouth. I was so confused. I felt even more panic take over. Why couldn't I move or see anything? I yelled out the window again, this time louder, a little shake in my voice but with more urgency. "Help!" Nothing. Silence.

One more try, Christina. No one is coming unless you try. You've got this.

I took a deep breath and leaned over the passenger seat to the floor once more. Finally, as I reached a little further than the first time, I felt the smooth plastic case of my cell phone. Thank goodness. Still having trouble with my vision, I tried blinking harder and focused on bringing the phone closer to my eyes. Nothing. I couldn't see anything. The phone design during that time included a speed dial feature and my stepdad was number two. Knowing Isaac was home, I pushed the number, and the phone rang. As I dialed the phone, someone came up to my driver's side door. I could only see a blur of white, making whoever it was appear angelic. I felt immediate relief and handed the phone over.

"Are you okay?" a shaky female voice asked.

"Please tell my dad what happened." I pleaded, handing over the blood-covered case.

The angel took my phone, and I could hear her talking in the distance. She had been in the car behind me and saw the accident happen. In a twist of fate, we later learned that both of us worked about eight miles away—she at a restaurant I frequented, explaining the "white blur" I'd seen coming from her long, white apron. While I worked at the Marriott directly behind the restaurant. Masochistically, I wondered; if I hadn't turned around, would this girl be in my place?

Knowing she was finally speaking with my stepdad, I could take my first deep breath, and I thought to myself, *Okay, you're okay. Family is coming. They're going to help figure this out.* My attention came back into focus as I faintly heard an ambulance siren and another person step up to Elsie's side. Overwhelmingly grateful to have at least one person now by my side, I was still clueless as to the severity of what was taking place, and no one was stepping up to be the first to mention the gaping hole now in my windshield.

"Hi, here, put this to your face," a faint voice said as he handed me a bundle of soft cloth. I held it to my face to stop all the bleeding. This second good Samaritan had run from the restaurant across the street, through two lanes of traffic, and literally took the shirt off his own back, giving it to me to stop the bleeding on my face.

"What's your name?" he asked.

Relieved to have someone by my side, I answered him, "Christina."

"Hi Christina, you're going to be all right. Is there anything you need?" he said. I felt hot. My skin was burning with a tingling sensation I couldn't place.

"I'm really thirsty," I replied. "And can you please help me move my seat back?" I could feel a dull ache and discomfort from my leg in its current position, and I desperately wanted to move back and stretch out. I could feel him try to reach under my leg to grab the bar to move it back, but he was struggling. Although I encouraged him to reach between my legs, he wouldn't. Looking back, I think I understand why. He was a gentleman, and maybe that maneuver in my shorts was a little too personal of a reach.

"We will get you something to drink." As I heard his footsteps walk away, I sat there helplessly, still not feeling like I could move or get out of the car. Nothing hurt, but I felt immobile. I was frozen in that moment, as if sitting extremely still would pause time and take me back to a reality where this had never happened.

"I've never been in a car accident," I mentioned off-handedly to the man returning protectively by my side.

"Really?" he asked, handing me a bottle of water. The tone in his voice suggested he was trying to keep me talking. Keep me conscious. The ambulance sirens grew closer still as he handed me the bottle, and I struggled to raise it to my blood-stained lips.

"Maybe this means I'll get a new car?" I said, half joking with a desire to fill in the silence. When the joke fell flat, I shifted my attention again, asking, "Is that an ambulance?" The sirens were so loud, they sounded like they were inside the car at this point.

"Yes, the paramedic is coming towards us now, and he'll take care of you," he said.

"Oh, I thought you were them. That's good. Thank you. I've never been in an ambulance either," I said to him, rambling on as if we were awkward strangers on a plane, not two people navigating a crisis. Without my sight, I was still confused about who I was talking to and what was going on amid the chaos. It's sad to think I would never know who this kind stranger was, so I could thank him.

The paramedic arrived, calm and controlled, as if he'd seen this type of thing a million times before. For all I knew, he probably had, but it sure didn't feel like a commonplace occurrence to me.

"Hi Christina, I'm Joe," the paramedic said. "Do you know what happened to you?" I recounted the incident in a quick summary. I don't remember exactly what all I said, but I'm sure I talked his ear off. I had to. It was the only way for me to get through that moment that felt so much like a dream.

"Can you tell me your full name?" he asked. I replied and answered his questions until I interrupted him with my own: "Am I going to ride in an ambulance? I've never been in an ambulance before."

Deftly avoiding my pointless questions, he didn't respond but instead asked, "Do you think you can get out of the car?" He was trying to assess my injuries as he slid a brace around my neck.

I sat with the question for a second and replied, "Maybe, but not everything is working. I don't think I can move a lot." I motioned to my left arm and right leg, which felt oddly detached from my body.

"That's all right. We can sit here and talk," he said. "Christina, do you have a copy of your insurance card?"

"Yes, it's in the glove compartment. You know, I'm going to get a new car after this. I really have been wanting one for a while now."

The paramedic agreed and continued to monitor my injuries. I heard the passenger door open and then the voice of my stepdad, Isaac.

"Christina, it's me. I'm here." Finally, a familiar voice.

Speaking more calmly than the moment warranted, I said, "They pulled out in front of me. I didn't have any time to stop."

Isaac, trying to match my calm, responded, "I know; it's okay. Can you tell me where your insurance card is? They're asking for it."

"It's in my glove compartment. So does this mean I get a new car?" I nonchalantly asked, figuring this was as good a time as any to seal the deal.

He didn't laugh but rather answered solemnly, "Sure. We'll see about that." I could hear him rumbling through my car, looking for the insurance card.

"I get to go in an ambulance. How cool is that?" I said to Isaac when he returned to me, still trying to lighten the mood for those around me.

In an almost morbid tone, I heard him say, "That's great, Christina." As we exchanged those words, I heard the *chuf-chuf-chuf* of a helicopter.

The paramedic interrupted our exchange with an explanation: "Christina, we're going to get you to the hospital by helicopter." *How exciting is this!* I immediately began thinking how I'd always wanted to ride in a helicopter, of course not remembering that I'd already ridden in one the day I came into this world.

With the trauma to my head and the blood loss, I needed to get to the hospital, and an ambulance wouldn't suffice. Rather than piece all that together, my immediate reaction was, "Wow! I have always wanted to do *that*!"

I can only imagine the look on the paramedic's face since I got little to no audible reaction while he focused on the job at hand and said, "I'm going to need your help. We're going to get you out of the car now."

I don't know how this is going to happen; I thought. *I can't really move.* I was stuck.

"Christina, your mom is on her way," Isaac interrupted, "but she's gotten lost. She may not make it before you leave, but we are going to meet you at the hospital, all right?"

My mind was being protected with a layer of shock and fog, so I didn't feel afraid in the moment, nor was I crying. In fact, I was eerily calm. My attention was focused solely on the task at hand as Joe and his team pulled me out of my car and onto a gurney.

As much as I could, I twisted and turned, feeling like a limp noodle. I felt horrible that these poor paramedics were going to have to haul my dead weight onto the gurney. Somehow, between my efforts and theirs, I was dragged up onto the flatbed. My tennis shoes were removed and placed on the ground, while all my other personal items remained inside the car.

Once secured, the paramedics pushed me quickly toward the helicopter. I remember hearing the crunch of glass as the wheels of the gurney rolled over the hot asphalt, shattered pieces everywhere.

My heart quickened to the pace of the helicopter blades whizzing above my head. "I'll meet you at the hospital. I love you." My stepdad's strained baritone faded out and was replaced by the unfamiliar sounds of the helicopter and medical devices. I was alone again. My vision was impaired as it was covered by a fresh cloth. I couldn't see any of my surroundings nor the people who helped me as my gurney sat secure in the belly of the helicopter.

"Hi Christina, I'm Joan. We're going to take you to University Hospital," the Life Flight Paramedic said in a sweet voice. All the while in the background, I could hear others stating my heart rate, blood pressure, and other medical jargon I couldn't make out. "There's a team waiting for you that is going to take good care of you. It will be a flurry of activity, but I don't want you to be concerned. They're going to fix you right up. After they wheel you inside, they will more than likely cut your clothes to remove them because of your injuries."

I interrupted her, exclaiming, "Wait! Cut my clothes? I just bought these shorts, and this is my favorite bra!"

I'm sure this wasn't the first time a patient had fixated on something illogical amid the crisis, so rather than laughing at my absurdity, she gently responded, "I'm very sorry. They're going to help you, but they don't want to hurt you. So, in order to do that, they'll have to cut them... and don't worry, with technology today, you won't even have a scar."

Wait.

Scar? I didn't understand. *What scar? Why would I have a scar?* I didn't know what injuries had happened to my face. *I'm not in any pain.*

Surrounded by darkness since my face was still covered, I felt like I lingered on all the words and sounds I could hear. The shock and fog crept back into my consciousness as I mulled over the meaning of her words in my head. Suddenly, we were on the roof of University Hospital, and as the summer heat rolled into the helicopter, I was oblivious to the fact that I would not leave this hospital as the same person as I was when entering it. Both physical and emotional scars would be to blame for my waiting transformation, but in that moment, I was buried deep in confusion.

"Okay Christina, here we go. We're going to take you inside," Joan said. Her well-meaning warmth made the time in the air fly by, but this was a bittersweet end to my exhilarating helicopter ride. I didn't expect the experience to involve my being blind-folded and covered in my own blood. The Texas sun warmed my skin as the trauma team got to work getting me inside the hospital.

"Christina, this is goodbye for now," Joan softly explained. How extraordinary the job of a first responder must be? To meet someone at the scene of one of the worst moments of their life, get them to safety and stability, and say goodbye forever.

I was pushed inside the hospital to a burst of cold air. Following the relative peace of the helicopter ride, everything seemed to pick up pace with a whirlwind of activity and a barrage of questions by people I could hear but could not see.

"What's your name?"

"How old are you?"

"What happened? Can you feel this? What hurts?"

Finally, a calmer voice cut through the chaos. "Christina, I'm Dr. H, and I'm going to take good care of you. We're going to get you all cleaned up." Her voice revealed the steady nature of someone who had seen injuries like mine before. I felt my heart seize at the thought of my clothes being cut off in front of these complete strangers, but it seemed they would remain intact, at least for the time being.

Not knowing how to properly introduce myself, I blurted out what had basically become my mantra at this point: "I'd never been in a helicopter before. That was my first time. I've never been in an accident before, either." I couldn't tell if the doctor was still there or if she had left, so I decided it would be best to keep quiet from that point on.

The next moments were filled with a flurry of people. Similar to the helicopter ride, I could hear voices calling out my vitals but, this time, they did so with a little more intensity. Without much warning, I felt the cold scissors against my skin. They quickly loosened and removed my shorts from my right thigh and then my left. It didn't take much to realize I was now undressed from the waist down. Next, I could feel the cool metal touch my side, going all the way up to the collar of my shirt and then the other side. Finally, I felt them on my chest and with a crunch, my bra was off.

I gasped and felt my eyes dart from side to side, desperately trying to process what was happening in my very lucid state of being.

For someone as reserved as I am, this was the worst-case scenario of my life. Not the dream where I was undressed and could eventually wake up, but the living nightmare where I was naked and fully aware. I could only think about how I was completely exposed on the table. My face might have gone through the windshield, but this... this was going to kill me. I couldn't see anyone. I could only hear movements, the shuffling of people, and hurried medical talk. So, like a toddler playing hide and seek, I pretended it wasn't really happening. Since I couldn't see them, they couldn't see me, right?

My attention was suddenly drawn to a warm sensation on my foot. *How did they know that would feel so nice? So comforting. Wow, they're really good at this.* Although I felt a dull ache, I hadn't realized I had broken my talus—the small bone that sits between the heel bone and the two bones of the lower leg, keeping the foot and leg connected. The warm sensation was from a chemical reaction as the splint hardened on my foot. Later, I would find out my wrist was broken as well. I'd never broken a bone in my life before, much less multiple in one fell swoop. The pain still hadn't set in yet, but it was absolutely about to.

I was so oblivious to my injuries, I remember saying out loud to the team surrounding me, "Thank you. That feels so much better."

128

Then a voice I hadn't heard before spoke. "Christina, we're going to do some tests to see if everything is okay." Thankfully, a "modesty" sheet was placed over me, and I was wheeled into another room. Then another; then another. Different scans were completed to check for internal bleeding, brain swelling, and other potential problems. After completing the last scan and the final poking of my body, it finally dawned on me why everyone was making such a big deal of my neck. All day long, every medical person I'd interacted with had been extremely concerned with my ability to move my body. They were checking for signs of paralysis. For the first time, tears began to stream, leaking outside of the bandage on my face as I connected the dots. Since I had been the happy accident victim from the moment I arrived at the hospital, my tears caught some attention.

"What's wrong?" the X-ray technician quickly asked, noticing I was holding my breath. Through my tears, I tried the best I could to explain myself. "I'm not paralyzed, and that's what you've been checking for, right?"

It had finally clicked. This was serious. No amount of humor or conversation could change that. It was dawning on me that so much more could have happened, and here I only had a hurt arm and leg with some scratches on my face. I wasn't aware of what my face really looked like and how I would need multiple surgeries to recon- struct it. Although I didn't have all the pieces, the severity of what I had been through was slowly coming together.

When all the tests were finally finished, I was parked in a quiet area, lying on a gurney with just my thoughts and the sound of my breathing. Never had I been surrounded by so much activity and attention, and yet so utterly alone.

By this time, my face was no longer held together by a t-shirt, but was entirely bandaged up except for my lips and chin. With my eyes still covered, I couldn't see anything, but thankfully, I was getting more and more used to the noises of people around me talking and walking by. A few moments passed, and a nurse came up to me to say, "Christina, your mom is here to see you before we wheel you into surgery."

Frantically, I tried to process what had been said to me. *Surgery? Why am I having surgery?* I felt fine, uncomfortable, but I didn't think I needed surgery.

My racing thoughts were interrupted when the nurse urgently said, "Christina, your mom is coming in with some of your family and your boyfriend."

My boyfriend?! No. I was naked underneath the sheet. What if he could see me? Knowing full well that hospital sheets are white and very thin, I pleaded with the nurse, "Please, tell me, can you see me underneath this?"

"No, dear, you're fine," she kindly answered. I didn't get the sense from her casual tone she understood my terror.

"No, really, I don't have any clothes on, and I'm worried you can see me through the sheet. I don't want anyone to see me!" I felt the panic rising, my entire body going ice cold at the thought of Tomas seeing me stark naked for the first time under these circumstances.

I heard footsteps pad away into the hallway, returning a few moments later as the sweet nurse came in with another sheet for my peace of mind.

"How about this, just in case?" she said gently. As I felt the weight of the added layer, I quietly thanked her and took a deep breath, unsure if I was prepared for what the next moments would bring. There was no escaping the reality of where I was or the state my body was in. As I struggled with regret for an accident I couldn't have predicted nor avoided, I realized it didn't matter. What had happened had happened.

In the hospital waiting area, my mom remembers walking through the emergency room automatic doors and finding my stepdad pacing. Tearing up as the fear and sympathy pains for me set in, she wrapped her arms around Isaac and asked with trepidation, "How bad is it?"

In a moment of honesty, he hurriedly confessed, "It's not good. It's not good at all. There was a lot of blood. She's alive, and it's going to be okay, but it's a lot." I know it must have been difficult for him to say those words, to break it to her at that moment that her baby was not okay. But I needed her to have a moment to absorb this information, process it, and be prepared to be by my side. I would need that desperately over the next several months.

And so, as soon as Isaac's words hit her ears, my mom's misty eyes turned to full-on sobs. I was the child who had caused her the least amount of heartache over the years; yet, here I was, now, causing her agony. Just then Tomas walked in, worried sick and unsure of what all had happened.

Tomas remembers arriving at the scene of the accident moments after the helicopter had taken off. Standing outside my car was Aaron, Tomas' friend. He had waited there for him, planning to drive with Tomas to the hospital. Aaron had been down the street from my parents' home when Isaac got the call from the waitress about my accident. My mom was out on an errand and, with only one vehicle between them, Isaac ran to ask Aaron to drive him to the scene.

I knew Aaron fairly well by this point. He was kind, energetic, and friendly. He wouldn't hurt a fly, so I imagine seeing blood from my face soaking through the stranger's shirt and my car demolished was overwhelming. He stood there in shock, looking at my car with the hole in the windshield and blood splattered everywhere.

While my stepdad was busy answering questions, Aaron watched in horror as the cloth I was holding to my face was removed by the paramedic, revealing the skin that was completely torn from my face and the destruction that lay underneath. Like a gruesome war movie, he watched the scene unfold and he would even say later it was an image that would stay burned in his mind forever.

When Tomas pulled onto the scene, Aaron met him at his car and told him, "She's already gone. They airlifted her to the hospital." Tomas looked at Aaron with disbelief in his eyes, as if he couldn't even process what was being said to him. Then his eyes shifted over to the car, flitting from Aaron's concerned face back to the wreckage that lay beyond him. Anticipating the panic that would no doubt take place if Tomas saw the damage up close, Aaron shifted his stance, blocking him from view. He then firmly instructed Tomas: "Don't. You shouldn't go to the car."

Puzzled, Tomas looked at Aaron with eyes that were quickly glazing over with even more shock. Sensing he needed to make some decisions quickly, Aaron stated, "Let's go. Let's go to the hospital." And with that, they were off.

Tomas would tell me that Aaron prayed with him the entire way to the hospital and, when they arrived, he looked over at my poor boyfriend and said, "She's okay. She's going to be fine." As Tomas entered the emergency room, his eyes darted around until they landed on the front desk receptionist. Taking long, anxious strides towards her, he asked if he could see me. She glanced down at the piles of paperwork and pulled up my name, but before she could direct Tomas to me, he looked over and noticed my mom and Isaac huddled together in a corner of the waiting area.

Without hesitation, Tomas said he walked over and gave my mom a big hug, emotions spilling over for both of them. Before they could say much, a nurse stepped through the double doors and said, "She's prepped for surgery. You can come see her now, but we would suggest going into the room one at a time, so it's not overwhelming." By this time, a small group of my friends and family had arrived and wordlessly agreed that my mom would be the first to see me. Her only prayer was that I would be alive and stay that way.

I can't imagine the apprehension that must have been flowing through my mother's veins as she took the steps down the hospital corridors to where I was waiting. She didn't know what to expect, or what kind of condition I would be in. But her mother's intuition always alerted her to when we needed her. Preparing herself, my mother wiped her eyes, cleared her throat, and passed through the doorway into my room.

"Oh my baby, how are you?" Rushing to my side, she explained, "I'm sorry I couldn't get to the accident. I was completely turned around. I'm so upset I wasn't there. Are you in pain?" Though her questions were a lot to take in, my mom's presence instantly soothed me.

My mom has always been the type of person you want by your side when you aren't feeling well. Maybe it's because she's been through so much herself, or maybe because she has learned to find the silver lining in her surroundings. Either way, she would never let us stay down. She was the person I both wanted and needed at that moment.

As my mom stepped out to speak with the doctor before my surgery, I felt Tomas enter. I was still cracking jokes with the nurses around me, but I slowly turned my face in Tomas' direction when I heard his voice. I tried to give him the best smile I could. I was going for "dazzling" but with bandages covering most of my face, I'm not sure I quite achieved that. Understandably, Tomas was unsure of what to say. He placed his hand on my non-broken foot and in his most cheerful voice said, "Hey!"

Not the most profound thing to say, but it did the trick. I felt the familiar warm and fuzzy sensation pass over me. He was here. Never one to let too many emotions linger, I busted out my newly minted joke of the day, "Hey guess what? I'm getting a new car!"

Little did I know that beyond my bandages, where I couldn't see him, Tomas looked over at my mom with a look of surprise. "Wow, she's on a roll," he said. "She's hilarious right now."

My mom nodded with a bittersweet smile. "That's what they say. She's been making jokes this whole time."

Through it all, Tomas stood there in disbelief. He couldn't understand how I could be so calm and positive in that moment or how I could be so aware of who was in the room. He thought I didn't know the full extent of what happened, which at the time was true. Or maybe that I was trying to make everyone feel good about the situation, even though it was scary. Also true. He was used to my downplaying what I really felt in other situations, so he wondered if this was no different.

I can't help it; I've always coped with difficult situations by being silly or adding in humor to lighten the mood. I'm not sure if it always worked, but it's what I did to deal with things. It's hard to be scared when you're being silly.

What I couldn't have known in those first few hours in the hospital was how long my recovery process would be. I really didn't even have a sense of what was wrong or why I needed surgery. I was still in the blissfully ignorant phase, otherwise known as an adrenaline rush, thinking it was fine. I didn't have to process what was happening to me. Surrounded by the people I loved, I felt safe.

In the end, it was probably a blessing in disguise that my face, including my eyes, were covered for everyone's first reaction to my condition. I have an uncanny ability to read faces, which I attribute as a trait I inherited from my mother. So, if I had detected even a hint of hesitation or pity in Tomas or anyone else's eyes, it would have killed me.

As I was being wheeled into surgery, only Tomas was left, letting go of my hand last and calling out that he would be waiting for me when I woke up.

Please God, I prayed silently, *keep me safe. Don't let me die.* I'd seen movies about people who were still awake under anesthesia, and I continued to pray that it wouldn't be my luck today. Surely, I'd had enough bad turns to last me the rest of the year at this point? I was brought back to my present surroundings by someone calmly explaining the impending surgery to me, hooking me up to monitors all the while. She asked me to count backwards from ten.

Nine... Eight... Seven...

I felt my mind get fuzzy around the edges and realized the anesthesia was kicking in. *Tomas*. That was my last thought before slipping into the best sleep of my life.

Chapter Nine

Tacos.

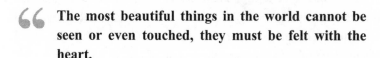

The most beautiful things in the world cannot be seen or even touched, they must be felt with the heart.

— **Helen Keller**

Silence and darkness. My first memories coming out of the anesthesia were of darkness. The surgery was done, but the bandages remained securely across my eyes. It felt claustrophobic all that time with my eyes closed, and in contrast, it heightened my other senses. I could hear every movement in the room and could feel even the slightest brush of fabric or air against my skin.

Suddenly, I felt someone tuck their hand under my shoulder, then some object being abruptly pulled from my throat and out of my mouth. Funny since I hadn't noticed the tube until the removal. As much as I fought to stay conscious to find out what was next, I felt the inevitable pull of narcotics dragging me back under. They weren't skimping on the good stuff. Before slipping back into a dream state, I felt the ridges the tube had left imprinted on my mouth, running my tongue over the odd bumps.

During that first hour, I remember someone holding my hand. I couldn't tell you if it was my mom or Tomas or a nurse, but I do remember being too tired to care. I was grateful for the companionship. Grateful to know that even in the darkness, I wasn't alone.

In those first few moments following surgery, I could hear someone rise from their seat and take a few slow footsteps as they slid a chair across the floor, the noise growing louder as it came closer to me. Following the squish of the recliner's cushion, I felt someone take my hand and kiss my forehead.

"Hello, sweet pea. How are you feeling? It's Mama. I'm here. Everything's gonna be okay."

It was her voice. The sound of it was all I needed to let go of the mountain of stress on my shoulders. But this hospital setting still didn't feel real. The world around me was still miserably cloaked in darkness, and the weights attached to my foot and arm were getting heavier with each passing minute. The hospital blanket alone felt like a strap holding me down, while my head felt like a mound of lead. I was tired, and I don't mean sleepy. This was an excruciating level of exhaustion I had never experienced before.

I tried to return my mother's greeting, grateful she was now by my side, and I wasn't alone anymore. Still in darkness with bandages over my eyes, the shift in the surrounding sounds led me to believe it was nighttime. The hustle and bustle in the hallway had been replaced by muffled sounds and soft whispers. When I finally answered my mom's question, I could only get out a murmur.

I had an overwhelming dryness in my mouth. My voice, when it emerged, felt hoarse. "Thirsty," was all I could make out to my mom. She grabbed a couple of ice chips and tentatively placed the first one in my mouth, unsure of how I would handle it. While she held her breath, I felt nothing but relief. It's incredible what a difference a tiny piece of ice can make.

Before the tears started, I slipped into the tough questions. "Mama, why is this happening to me?"

Answering truthfully, as she considered my condition, she said, "I don't know, baby, but it's in God's hands. I'm just happy you're alive and safe with me." We didn't talk about the specifics of my injuries that night or very much the entire hospital stay. I think my mom knew I needed her to be there and not overwhelm me with the enormity of it all.

A moment later, I felt my arm gently lift when my mother squeezed in next to me in the hospital bed. I was basking in the comfort of her presence next to me when she started humming quietly. "It's been a very long day for you. Try to get some sleep, baby." With her gentle hands moving through my hair, I drifted off to sleep and tried my best to rest through all the body spasms and painful aches. I still hadn't fully grasped the extent of my injuries and couldn't shake the feeling I was stuck in someone else's hellish dreamscape.

Prior to the accident, I had rarely ever taken over-the-counter pain relievers because I thought most pain was in your head. I quickly learned that was not always the case. As the days passed in the hospital, I became accustomed to the constantly rotating cocktail of morphine, codeine, and all my other options. I felt almost drunk in the beginning, or at least what I thought was feeling drunk, since I'd never tasted alcohol before. My mom recounts the stories of me speaking gibberish for hours on end, not able to fully understand what I was saying.

The first morning after my surgery, I woke up and was horrified when I realized there was a catheter attached to me under my hospital gown. *Ugh, when did* that *happen?!* There were all sorts of firsts taking place in those days, and all sorts of boundaries being crossed I hadn't been physically or emotionally prepared to tackle at only nineteen years old. The bandages covering my eyes made those first few days, post-surgery, feel like a lucid dream I couldn't snap out of.

That morning, I also woke up to a group of voices in the room talking loudly among themselves. My mom later explained it had been a group of medical students conversing with their teaching doctor. I had been flown to a teaching hospital because of the extent of my injuries and their Level I Trauma Center.

As I laid there, I could hear the students and doctor speaking, discussing my case as if I wasn't in the room. They were specifically focused on my arm and my leg, tossing around terms like "closed fracture" and "low risk of osteomyelitis." After several minutes, the doctor beside me finally paused to offer me a greeting. "Hello, I'm Dr. M, your orthopedic surgeon." I didn't know what his specialty of surgery meant since I had broken nothing before. This was the case with most of the specialty physicians who would visit me regularly over the course of the next few weeks.

Dr. M had a dry disposition with the absolute worst sense of humor. I imagine as a physician it has to be a difficult undertaking, maybe even awkward at times, to visit the room of a trauma patient. Especially ones like me, who were wrapped around in gauze like a mummy. Years later, this same doctor would tell me, in no uncertain terms, that my nose was crooked, as if I didn't already know that, and that he believed I had been... *wait for it*... brain damaged. I honestly couldn't argue with his professional suggestion. How can you put your head through a windshield, live to tell the story and not be a little brain damaged? Either way, I did my best to be respectful, as the future of my bones was in his hands.

My future was in many people's hands, and I disliked how much my condition forced me to ask for help. Besides requesting the occasional sip of water from my mom, I hated having to ask anyone else for favors and, to be completely honest, I lacked the energy to say anything at all. I couldn't see; I was exhausted; and I wasn't even capable of joining in on the free medical school lessons that were happening around me.

Finances, or the lack thereof, came into play the first morning when, after the student group had exited the room, someone entered from the hospital's billing department to get my information. I'm sure my mom was not aware of how much our current tab at the hospital was totaling, but rather focused on getting whatever medical help I needed. I remember after the admin left the room, my mom was shocked and incredibly grateful to find out I had taken it upon myself to sign up for a financial assistance program, coincidentally through the same hospital I had been flown to. Thankfully, this would cover a lot of my medical bills. As much as I needed my mom to take care of me in those early days, she had also raised me to take care of myself, and it was a very good thing she had.

Pity parties weren't an option in my family growing up. In the most desperate of times, my mom would snap out of it, switch gears, and attempt to change the mood by taking on the cheeriest of dispositions. In her most "Disney-*esque*" voice and with a song-like cadence to it, she would try to lift our spirits by jokingly singing the first line of *Let Me Entertain You* from the movie *Gypsy*.

In perfect Vivian fashion, she snapped right into character after the last of the shuffling feet exited. Because the room was becoming almost too quiet, she recognized her cue. She leaned in close to me and in a cheery falsetto asked, "Okay, what do you want for breakfast?" just as if we were considering what to order from room service at a five-star hotel. It was comically obvious that she was hoping to switch the subject from the weight of surgeries and hospital bills.

Throughout my childhood, it was like she had the never-ending job of making whatever negative situation we were going through seem as if it weren't a "situation" at all. As a child, I would see a convincing smile on her face and, by listening to her, you would genuinely think she was happy, without a concern in the world. However, the weight of everything we experienced was always on her shoulders. Always. After everything she had lived through, it was no wonder she had developed some coping mechanisms over the years.

I had little appetite during my recovery in the hospital. Frankly, I had no appetite at all. My mom was never one to take "no" for an answer, so she tried to entice me with comments like, "Well, how about some scrambled eggs and toast? Wait. They have pancakes. You love pancakes. Let's do that!"

I nodded my head and whispered, "Thank you." At this stage post-surgery, I couldn't move much nor feel very much, other than pain. I remained with little to no energy and, if it was somehow possible, would feel even more tired than the day before.

"Mama, I hurt so much everywhere."

"I know, baby, it's temporary. But you're a fighter, you've got this," my mom responded.

I picture my mom looking at my face, only imagining the pain as she said, "I'll ask the nurse if we can get you more medicine for the pain." Feeling like I had taken more medicine in the last few hours than in my entire life up to that point, I agreed, hoping it would help me.

Over the course of weeks and months, I learned that every hurt was different. But every pain called for the same remedy: medicine —so much of it, I was eventually connected to a pump which offered me more control over the pain relief. Some pain stung; some ached; some felt sore, burning, or pulsing. Some medicines gave me relief, while others caused me to violently lose my groceries. What mattered now wasn't putting on a brave face and showing how tough I was. It was making it through the day, hoping to finally feel less. Try as I might, my mom could still tell I was unsettled. My face was directed up at the ceiling, with tears pushing their way past the bandages and down my swollen face.

"Mom, has she come to see me?" I choked out.

"Who, honey?"

"The woman who hit me."

I wouldn't find out until later that the woman who was driving the other car was believed to have been taking medication that made her drowsy behind the wheel. I held no resentment for the decisions she made the day of the accident, nor did I feel anger towards her. It's called an "accident" for a reason. But at that moment, I wondered who she was, what she looked like and if she even knew or cared that I was alive. I never got any answers, though, since she never did visit me. Whether we like it or not, we will forever be bonded by this one moment in time on Thousand Oaks street. And yet, to this day, I have never spoken with her.

My mom weighed her next words carefully and said, "I haven't seen her sweet pea, but don't worry about it. You just focus on getting better." Our conversation was suddenly interrupted, and like many details surrounding my accident, we never did speak about the woman again.

"Good morning! I hear we have some yummy breakfast on the way, Christina." Said one of my nurses as she stepped in the room. "I'm Nancy, how about we get those bandages changed." Not knowing what was coming next, I could hear her setting some things down on the tray-table next to me. With that cue, I heard my mom rise from her seat and announce, "I'm going to step outside. I'll be right back." What I hadn't realized then was, she wasn't ready to see for herself what was hiding under my bandages.

As I heard my mother's footsteps fade away, the nurse said softly, "Okay, Christina. We're gonna do some quick wound care. I'm gonna use some saline solution to loosen the gauze we've already placed." She tilted my head back with my chin up high. Using a plastic syringe, she squirted some solution on my nose and the area over my eyes. Streams of saline ran down my right cheek as the nurse tried to catch as much as she could with a tissue. She leaned over my bed for a few minutes like that, dabbing my face and adding a little more, trying to loosen the dried bandage.

When it was soaked to her satisfaction, she spoke again, "You're going to feel a little pressure here." But there was no pressure, only pain—excruciating pain. She lifted the now soaked bandage off my face, but it felt like she was ripping my skin off along with it. At this point, I still couldn't see, but I could feel the symphony of pain playing across my face. Every gentle tug of the bandage built to an explosive crescendo, followed by the diminuendo of numbness before the sharp pain struck again. I would never guess she was removing only bandages covering what was *already* torn off skin. There was no skin to speak of, really, just flesh.

To say it was excruciating is truthfully an understatement. As she pulled the bandages off, I grasped the bedsheets with my working right hand, pressing my head back into the pillow, burying a guttural scream deep inside my belly. I gasped for air. *Breathe in, breathe out. Breathe in, breathe out,* I mentally chanted.

Why was I in so much pain? I kept thinking to myself how the flight medic in the helicopter had said, *"Don't worry. With technology these days, there's hardly going to be a scar."* I replayed that sentence repeatedly in my head, willing myself to comprehend how her optimism could line up with the torture I was currently experiencing. Even so, I couldn't make sense of it.

The nurse spoke up, interrupting my thoughts, and said, "I think the hard parts are almost over Christina. I'm just gonna put some gauze and a new bandage on your face and then we're done." Feeling the weight of the cold, wet, saline-soaked gauze being placed on top of the most tender areas of my face, I could hear her unfurl the roll of tape and the snip of scissors. Then, pausing for a second, her fingers gently secured a single T-shaped bandage in place.

"She did it!" The nurse happily told my mom as she reentered the room. "The hard part is over. Unfortunately, though, we're gonna have to do this every day, Christina, to prevent infection. I'm so sorry, but I'm gonna take good care of you, as will all the nurses. You're in good hands."

Just then, the sound of wheels squeaking and the smell of breakfast by my bedside invaded my already heightened senses. A sweet voice said, "Good morning, I have breakfast here for you." The woman's gentle footsteps passed in front of me as she placed what sounded like a food tray on the table nearest to me. "I've got eggs and pancakes here for you with a little side of butter and some syrup. You're all set. Is there anything else I can get for you?"

I moved my head silently in the general direction of where I imagined my mom was seated, and without skipping a beat, my mom spoke up, answering, "Nothing needed at this time. Thank you so much." Footsteps began to move across the floor, sounding further and further away. When the quiet had returned, my mom interrupted the silence and said, "Christina we've got to get you to eat."

"No, Mama, I can't. I don't feel like I can eat."

Replacing her soft request with a more serious tone, she answered back, "Baby girl, you have to eat something. The nurse said there are no restrictions on what you can eat, so what are you in the mood for? If you don't like the hospital food, let me know what sounds tasty, and I can go get it."

The problem wasn't the hospital food; it was food in general. I had no appetite, but it had been too long since my Whataburger kid's meal.

"I don't know, Mama. I'm sorry. Let me think about it." But instead of breakfast, lunch or dinner, the only thought in my mind was: *What am I doing here?* I was supposed to be prepping for the International Day concert. I was supposed to be a normal college student. I just wanted to be grabbing breakfast tacos with Tomas, not stuck here in a hospital bed in pain.

The sounds of clanking silverware interrupted my spiraling thoughts. "What are you doing?" I asked my mom.

"Well, if you're not going to eat these pancakes, then I will. I mean, we can't both starve!" My mom chuckled and said, "Who do you think you got your love of pancakes from?!"

I couldn't help it. Despite the doom and gloom filling my mind moments earlier, I chuckled. A slow rumble at first, then building to as full of a laugh as I could manage with all my wounds. I continued, only stopping to blurt out, "Ouch! Mama, don't make me laugh. I'm sore!" And with that, we both began to really laugh. It was a moment of levity in a very trying time. My mom and I had gotten through much worse together. We knew we could get through this. I believed to my core that my mom always told me the truth, even when it was something I didn't want to hear. So, if she was able to laugh and tell me everything would be okay, it would be.

Pancakes didn't sound good at all, so I racked my brain, trying to think of any favorite foods that might strike a chord with my appetite. Suddenly, I heard myself say, "Maybe some pickles?"

She laughed softly and repeated, "Pickles?" My mom continued to laugh, getting a kick out of my unusual request.

Now I know my body was craving the sodium in the pickles, packed with electrolytes, to replenish my dehydrated system. But back in the hospital room, my mom replied with that familiar singsong tone, "Okay! Pickles it is!" Stroking the top of my hand, she announced, "If my baby wants some pickles, I'll find you some pickles!"

We laughed some more as she continued to enjoy the pancakes. Just then there was a knock at the door, and a soft questioning "Hello?" rang through my hospital room. My mom quickly stood and walked towards the knock. I strained my ears to hear their conversation but could only catch unrecognizable hushed greetings before the now very familiar sounds of shuffling feet once again coming towards me. As the sounds of the steps became closer, they halted abruptly, and I heard an incredibly shocked gasp, like someone struggling to breathe. Instinctively, I turned my head towards the sound.

My mom caught up to this mystery visitor before they could say an actual word. She whispered to them, "Oh no, no, no. Let's go." And with that, the shuffling feet retreated towards the door until they disappeared completely. Suddenly panicked, and now desperate to hear exactly what was going on around me, I listened intently, trying to hear the conversation. I could only pick up my mom's voice in an intense but muffled whisper over the sounds of sobbing.

I was so confused. What had I missed? What was so awfully upsetting that it would make someone gasp in shock and cry out loud? That was the moment I realized how severe my condition was. Everyone, from the folks at the scene of the accident, to the flight medic in the helicopter, to the doctors, and even my family, had kept telling me it was totally *fine*. I was going to recover just *fine. "You're hardly going to have a scar,"* repeated in my head. But whatever this visitor had seen wasn't good. So, what was it, then? I was craving the truth far more than I was craving pickles.

I waited for my mom to finish this emotional encounter as I tried to decide whether I was going to bring it up when she returned. Did I want to know the reality of what was happening? I'd been self-conscious enough as a teenager. Did I really want to confront the very real horrors of my appearance in my fragile state? The earlier doctor visit hadn't clarified anything for me about my injuries.

Just then, my mother returned to my bedside without a word of the dramatic visit she'd just experienced. A few minutes later, I worked up the courage to ask what had happened. She brushed off my question and answered, "It was nothing." To this day, I do not know who that mystery visitor was. Maybe that's for the best.

Looking back, I can only imagine how it must have felt for each friend and family to visit me in the condition I was in. There's a hospital scene in the movie, *As Good As It Gets* where the characters visiting the patient can't hide their reactions and yell hysterically (comically so) at seeing the shape their friend is in. Thankfully, I know everyone, save that one poor visitor, was trying their best to ignore their own discomfort for my sake.

My mom, brilliant at creating distractions, fussed and fixed some monitors on my chest, adjusting where they were itching and worked to get me comfortable. Adept at navigating emotional landmines, she quickly changed the subject. "Does that feel better? You know, Laura is supposed to stop by later. And Tomas. They have some classes this morning, but they'll stop by after school."

Classes. I have classes, too, but I guess I'm not going back to campus any time soon. I wondered if I needed to tell my professors or the school. A sudden wash of apathy passed over me as I realized I didn't have the energy, nor the desire, to think about it. I did, however, wonder if my boss knew, so I spoke up. "Mom, I should probably tell work that I won't be coming in for a while."

"I already did. I called the hotel's front desk and told them. Your boss wanted to tell you they're all thinking about you and, as soon as you're better, you can go back to work."

I suppose that should've felt like a glimmer of hope—that my mom was already assuming I could get back to work at some point —but, at that moment, it just felt like an enormous mountain had been placed in front of me. I now had a recovery process looming ahead, though I didn't know how complicated or drawn out it would be. However, at the end of that process lay a humdrum daily life that I would give anything to return to over this mess. Back to work. Back to class. Back to a simple life I had taken for granted before.

This latest wave of sadness was fortuitously interrupted by the arrival of Peter. He and his wife, Karen, were real, kind, and genuine. They met at a fairly young age, just like Tomas and me. We saw so much of them in us. They had always been trusted mentors and confidantes.

With my eyes bandaged, I could picture him with his big, friendly smile walking over to me, and I heard the warmth behind his voice offering a very sincere, "Good morning!" As his footsteps neared, he continued, "Christina, did you do this for attention? Because you're going to *get a lot of it* from us!" This was typical Peter; he had a way of addressing any situation with sincerity yet lightheartedness. It was just what we needed.

My mother also must have felt a sense of respite from his warm and welcome arrival. She was sleeping overnight at the hospital in an upright chair, so Peter's visit in the daytime allowed her to break away and return home. This would become their daily routine.

Even if it was only for a handful of hours, Peter's time gave my mother a chance to get caught up on work, take a shower, and be refreshed. I'm sure she needed some space from the hospital, too. The room had to be full of sadness, uncertainty for the future, and the reality of what had happened. She and everyone else could see it. I, on the other hand, could not.

During my time at University Hospital, so many loved ones stopped by and visited. It was humbling to know my hospital windowsill was decorated with flowers, cards, and gifts. Many days were filled with Laura, Tomas, and Peter. The three of them never missed a visit.

Years ago, I had learned from Gary Chapman's best-selling book, *The 5 Love Languages,* that my love language was "quality time." This meant that, while the items piling up on the windowsill were incredibly kind and generous, what I really craved was being around those I loved most. That singular truth must have been circulated among friends, family and our church congregation because everyone contributed to the overflow of this "bucket" for the nearly three weeks I was in the hospital.

It seemed to be their goal to make me feel as if each of them had nothing better to do than hang out with me, although I'm certain that wasn't the case. I always imagined Peter and Karen were stretched thin with their obligations—running between events, and countless other responsibilities, besides being parents of young children. I knew the magnitude of what it meant to have so much time with them, and I appreciated every second of it.

After my first week in the hospital with one leg in a cast and the other leg exposed, Laura jokingly commented about me still looking like Pancho Villa since I had obviously missed my wax appointment the day of the accident. Only this time, the Sicilian hairiness had spread from my lip to my legs. Thankfully, only one leg was visible. She eventually purchased an electric cordless shaver to save me further embarrassment. What a friend.

Another beautiful friend, Susie, returning for another visit with her friend David, entered my hospital room one day with bags in tow. Never one to come empty-handed, she placed a large, soft, plush puppy dog under my arm cast, helping to keep it propped up. David stretched an oversized, colorful *Winnie The Pooh*-themed comforter he had purchased for me over my hospital bed.

"What?" she said to me after noticing my puzzled expression. "If you're planning on sticking around the hospital, and it looks like you are, your room could use some brightening up!" There were lots of moments like that—people showing me kindness for no other reason than they wanted to.

Walking in each morning, Peter would have his leather briefcase in one hand and a white paper bag filled with tacos in the other. I recall one morning about halfway through my stay I noticed Peter came in without a small, white paper bag. No tacos, just the briefcase.

We said our usual "good morning" and he couldn't help but notice that I had noticed he was without his tacos. He sat his brief-case in his usual corner on the chair. He opened his briefcase as he normally did, taking out his laptop. Looking back over at me, he reached in and grabbed something inside. As he lifted it to reveal the familiar white paper bag filled with tacos. Smiling at me, he said, "Looking for these?" We both got a good laugh at what had become our morning routine. It meant the world to me and kept me holding on.

Knowing Peter would care for me like his own family, my mother only left my hospital room if he was there. Because of this, Peter became the person "on duty" in the mornings when it was time for me to have the bandages on my nose changed. After the new bandages were placed, he would return at the perfect time for the obligatory nose cleaning. Without hesitation, Peter picked up the gauze and long swab from the nurse, letting her know, "It's okay. I've got it." Ever so gently, he swabbed away the remnants of blood inside my nose, chatting casually with me all the while.

"Peter, do you realize you're picking my nose right now?" I joked, half embarrassed and needing a good laugh. But honestly, who does that? Who is willing to step into the mess of nursing someone back to health for no other reason than they're a good friend? I didn't feel worthy of all the attention or deserving of all the tender, loving care—not just Peter, but from everyone.

I later learned that Peter stayed behind to gather my belongings from the car, a gruesome task that I wouldn't wish on anyone. Peter had received a call alerting him to me being in a car accident. Karen and Peter lived less than a mile from the scene of the accident. He told Karen that he planned to see if there was anything he could do to help. As he walked out of his home with his keys in his hand, he looked up at the sky, hearing a helicopter fly over him. Instantly, he thought to himself, it was far worse than he had imagined.

Even so, he would have no idea what he was about to drive into. As he was nearing the opposite side of the intersection, the congestion of cars trying to make their way around the scene was already in motion. As he pulled into the same parking lot where the helicopter landed, he watched as it was taking off. Peter placed his car in an empty parking spot and began walking towards my car, steam still coming from out of the car hood, and began taking it all in. Realizing everything I had was left behind inside my now totaled car, he sprung into action.

He first collected the contents of my school backpack, making sure to grab my wallet and driver's license. Peter bent inside the vehicle to retrieve the last of my belongings, careful to only take things that didn't reveal what had taken place. Although he didn't see me before I was taken to the hospital, looking at the large, open hole in the windshield, it didn't take very much for him to assess some of the damage. On the ground outside of my car, he noticed my shoes, discarded by the paramedics in their rush to get me to the hospital. He lifted a single sneaker, adding it to the backpack, and as he tilted it, blood poured out onto the pavement like tea from a kettle. If it wasn't clear how serious my injuries were by then, now he knew.

* * *

The hospital days seemed to run together seamlessly, one leading to the next as we fell into a familiar routine of meals on trays, nurses changing shifts, and medicines being doled out. It didn't occur to me to even ask when I could go home because, physically, that seemed impossible, in my mind anyway. As morbid as it sounds, you could tell just from how many machines and wires were hooked up to me, not to mention the bandages that disguised the disfigurement of my face, I was far from a full recovery.

One major improvement, however, was the day I finally had the bandages removed from my eyes. The nurses had been hyping up this moment as a major milestone, and I felt an odd sense of pressure to perform well. It didn't feel like it was time for a victory lap. I was still unsure of what my new reality would be.

As the nurse gingerly lifted the bandages from my eyes, I squinted as my sight adjusted to the brightness around me. Like the feeling of stepping out of a dark movie theater into a bright and shining San Antonio day, suddenly, the room I had been imagining was actually coming into focus. I saw, rather than felt, my stuffed animals and blankets. I saw, rather than smelled, the gorgeous flowers by the windowsill.

Fortunately, a silver lining of having my eyes bandaged for so long was that my first interactions post-removal with everyone were not so upsetting. After all, they'd all had up to this point to adjust to my appearance. I was comforted to see their faces for the first time and find only tenderness, not fear or pity.

The one person I was still nervous about seeing, though, was Tomas. "He has a certain look he gives me, Mama." I confessed. "If I look him in the eyes for the first time and it's gone, it will kill me." The time seemed to double as I waited for his visit. *I'll know in a second,* I thought to myself. I would instantly know if that look of desire he saved only for me was replaced with one of pity, or worse—repulsion. When the familiar sound of his voice finally rang through the hallway, I couldn't help but turn my head away from the door. *Maybe if I don't look up, I won't have to see the shift in his gaze?* So, like a middle schooler, I avoided his eyes, preferring to look at just about anything else in the room rather than face this cruel possibility.

He had never given me any reason to doubt him. It had been my own insecurities that were screaming he wouldn't want to stick around through something like this. The fact of the matter was we weren't married. We didn't have children. Though he was my serious boyfriend, we'd only been steadily dating for seven months. I couldn't deny that there was nothing requiring him to see me through the worst of this. Other guys might have slipped quietly away, but he never did.

Tomas pulled up a chair next to my bed and leaned over to get closer to me. Much to my surprise, as soon as Tomas managed to catch my eye, all my worries over his desire for me disappeared. There it was. The look. *My* look burning as bright as ever. To this day, I cannot explain how or why it remained, but it doesn't matter. *My* look was there. Rather than tear us apart, this mess only drew us closer together.

When it was time to change the bedsheets, some poor soul had the laborious task of getting me out of the bed. With only one "working" leg and one semi-functional arm full of needles, I'm sure it was a challenge. After lugging my dead weight off the bed, I was placed in a large wheelchair. I wish I could tell you it was a sweet ride. In reality, the chair resembled a life-size version of a child's pipe cleaner craft, made from PVC pipe and designed to be used in the shower. Unfortunately, with all my injuries, I never got the pleasure of taking one. After I was situated in the wheelchair with my beautiful catheter not far behind, Laura would roll me into the bathroom to help me freshen up while my mother tidied the room.

There must have been an instruction given or agreement made, without my knowledge, that I was to be strategically wheeled in backwards each time so I wouldn't see my face. I realized this after my first couple of trips to the bathroom. I had asked for a handheld mirror not long after my bandages were removed, but was firmly denied, saying it was best to let things heal. "Not yet, honey," my mother would say.

Perhaps I let it go because I lacked the stamina to fight under the fog of all the medication, or maybe I let it go because, frankly, I was a little scared to discover what the reflection would reveal. Whatever the reason, the curiosity never went away. I recall a couple of the bed changes, Laura would stroll me into the bathroom, and I was left alone so I could "have a moment" to myself, she would say.

Even if just for a few seconds, I would lean over to my left side, fighting past the discomfort from my arm cast, to try and catch a glimpse of myself in the mirror above the sink. When that didn't work, my eyes darted around the bathroom for anything that would offer a reflection.

After about ten days of being denied my reflection, I remember my eyes landing off to my right when I was in the bathroom alone. There I was suddenly confronted with the reflection of my face in the stainless-steel toilet paper holder. There it was—the moment I'd been equally avoiding and been denied for almost two weeks. The metal cover was tarnished with age, so its finish didn't offer the sharpest view. Peering down, I could see the white bandage along with the swelling, stitches, bruising, and what looked like hundreds of cuts all over my face. I was looking into the eyes of a person I'd never met before.

Scrambling to make sense of what I was seeing, my first reaction was remembering a movie I had seen years earlier that portrayed a domestic violence victim. My face looked like it had taken a literal beating. I guess in many ways, it had. As I began to comprehend my blurry likeness in that cold hospital bathroom, again I felt like things were moving in slow motion. My inner voice begged me to look away, but I just stared. It was so surreal. *That's me. I am her. That face is mine.* Though only seconds had passed, hearing Laura walking back towards the bathroom snapped me back to the present moment, as I shifted my weight away and pretended that I was fine. Everyone had told me not to look. Maybe I should have listened.

There was one nurse who worked in the ICU that I really connected with. Many people who have been through a traumatic event have a story about at least one healthcare professional who bonds with them through the tragedy. Nurse Lori knew when I needed to "suck it up and get over it," but she could also tell what my tolerance for pain was. We instantly became very familiar with each other and built a rapport of trust that could fight through the pain.

One day, Lori came in with the latest issue of a popular fashion magazine… but with a bit of a twist. She had taken a marker and strategically criss-crossed tiny, black marks over the beautiful models' cheeks and forehead. A "T"-shaped bandage was fashioned over the forehead, just like the one I had on my face at that very moment. The model had short dark hair, just like me, and the resemblance made me chuckle. She placed the magazine gently in my lap and said with a smile, "Well, what do you know? She looks just like you." Had it been anyone else, it might have felt like a cruel joke, but I knew the banter we shared and the sweet spirit behind her actions.

Laughing and getting a kick out of my self-portrait, I said "Thank you," not wanting her to think I was upset in any way because I was far from it. On the contrary, it felt like a gentle nudge that I, too, could still find a way to feel beautiful. I could come to terms with my appearance and still feel good about myself. Or at least Lori seemed to think so. And maybe that was enough for now.

The sound of silence in the evenings at the hospital was almost piercing compared to the busy, visitor-filled days. My mother would help me bear the discomfort of the night, stroking my hair, and offering soft whispers of hope. It became clear when it was time for my mom to take a break. Karen would insist on taking over, sleeping upright in the same chair my mother would in order to get some rest. On the first morning after Karen had spent the night, a nurse came in early, ready to change my bandages as usual. Since most of our time together was at night, Karen had missed out on my ever-so-awesome daily routine. She hadn't realized that everyone would normally leave the room during the procedure, nor that she would be the first to see what truth was under my bandage.

Unlike the others who exited the room on cue, she insisted on sitting with me and offering comfort. When the nurse lifted the gauze and revealed my face, Karen nodded to me, taking in the damage and trauma that was revealed. Softly, and with self-assured confidence, she whispered, "It's okay. You're going to be okay." Her simple words were enough to assure me that whatever was beneath the bandage would not break me. I would survive this. Despite having little ones of her own at home, Karen sat with me during the evenings and talked, offering me peace and the promise that God was not to blame for this tragedy. Yes, amidst all the struggles and despair, there were moments of joy and laughter as well.

* * *

One afternoon, Tomas stepped into my hospital room and announced, "We're going on a date!" He helped me tenderly into the wheelchair and proudly wheeled me away from the ICU, down the elevator, and into the hospital cafeteria, of all places. Quite the hot spot for dates, as you can imagine. We sat together—Tomas in his hard plastic hospital chair and me in my wheelchair.

Tomas placed the bag he was holding on the table and gave me a sly grin.

"Let me tell you how special you are." As he reached his hand into the bag, pulling out some rocky road flavored ice cream, he continued, "The Chicago Bulls are playing tonight."

"And..." I said, waiting for the punchline.

He placed a napkin and a spoon on the table in front of me. "It's Game Six. Of the NBA Finals." Giving me an extra big Tomas smile. "Do you know what that means?" *Not really.*

"That you're missing it?" I said, feeling a little stupid, not knowing where he was going.

He put his hand back in the bag and presented a box of Red Hots cinnamon candy—the thing he loves most when he's not feeling good. "It means I love you. More than anything. The only place I want to be right now is here with you."

If only he knew. The game he missed ended up being Michael Jordan's final game with the Chicago Bulls. It would go down as the most intense and highest watched basketball game in NBA history. One person not watching the game, though, was Tomas. Because he chose me.

We continued to chat about everything we could. Everything but the long road to recovery that still awaited me. The T-shaped bandage across my nose and cheeks allowed my lips to chatter away, but in a momentary pause between topics, I felt Tomas brush closer to me. His lips touched mine for just a moment, and I felt myself blush.

His wasn't a kiss of urgency, but rather a tender reminder he was still here. He still wanted me, despite the scrapes and bruises, and even with our uncertain future looming ahead like a dark thundercloud on the horizon.

My journey back to a "normal" life was far from over, but that kiss was a desperately needed reminder that my life would, indeed, have joy again someday. I just didn't know how far away that someday was.

Chapter Ten

Reflection.

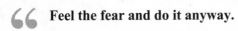 **Feel the fear and do it anyway.**

— **Susan Jeffers, PhD**

"He'll do it? Really?! That's amazing! Let me tell Christina." I could hear my mom outside the hospital room, excusing herself from a gathering of nurses to come rushing into my room. "Christina, they found a surgeon willing to try."

As the weeks wore on, we heard a lot of debate among my doctors and medical team surrounding what to do with my face. My mom would be huddled near the door with specialists in plastics and trauma, discussing possibly transferring me to another hospital because the doctors at this hospital didn't offer an option we were willing to accept. And by "we," I mean everyone else. I'm not sure if it was because I was heavily medicated or if it was my lack of experience with medical emergencies, but I could never fully grasp what they were saying, even when they spoke directly to me.

The collision had done several things to my face. First, the top of my forehead was opened, leaving it and my cheeks with severe cuts, scrapes, and embedded remnants of glass. Some of these could be stitched, while others needed to heal naturally to avoid creating any additional scarring. This challenge was minor compared to the main one the doctors faced. Across my eyebrows, the skin had been completely torn off from one end to the other. The same had occurred with the right side of my nose, leaving only the nostril behind.

Originally, the doctors had hoped that my skin would scab over on its own, but after dressing and re-dressing the wound, it didn't look like that was going to happen. A skin graft was our next best option, but it would be a challenge because there were very few plastic surgeons in the hospital who were willing to take on my case. Most declined, I imagine not wanting to potentially mar their track records with a facial deformity that was almost certain.

This was what my life had come to. I was feeling like a lost cause. *Was I a lost cause?*

The original plastic surgeon assigned to me was nearing his retirement and had suggested I just go home and heal. By "heal," he meant changing bandages daily on two gaping wounds over the next two years, pray I avoided any infection and just "wait and see." In one of the rare moments I was left alone in my room, the Doctor's last words to me landed like a lead balloon: "Well, you know, beauty is in the eye of the beholder."

What? What does beauty have to do with anything? My mind went back to days earlier when my mystery visitor had gasped in shock, unable to continue with her visit. Did she see the same thing the doctor was seeing now? Until that point, I had been surrounded by friends and family who were always so optimistic. The doctor had left me shaken.

When my mom learned of his response to my predicament, she was livid. So livid, in fact, that she marched straight to him and demanded to know if he had a daughter. The surgeon fumbled and managed only a half-answer before my mother retorted, "I didn't think so." She then gave him a piece of her mind, hoping he retired the very next day. No one, male or female, should ever be made to feel like they're beyond help.

But now, after more than two long weeks of daily bandage changes and debates on what to do with my face, the hospital had finally found a surgeon willing to try. He was a young hot shot who was willing to take the risk, and we were more than willing to let him. Anything was better than the alternative of "wait and see." This surgery would be another thorough scrubbing of my face to remove any remaining glass and debris, close the one plus inch gap across the bridge of my nose, and more importantly, reconstruct the side of my nose using skin grafted from my neck. *At least it wasn't my butt,* I thought to myself.

At the end of the reconstructive surgery, and assuming all went well, I would leave the hospital with two temporary pins in my left wrist and two permanent screws in my right ankle. I was wheeled into the operating room once more and, as the anesthesia kicked in, I thought of home. I was so close I could feel it.

The morning of my surgery, Lori came in and asked if I had any special music I'd like to play during surgery. I remembered in the bag of things Peter had retrieved from my car and brought to me, was a well-loved CD. Lori got it into the operating room so when I was rolled in, I could hear the sounds of Sarah McLachlan's *Surfacing* album. Listening to the lyrics of the song "I Love You" put my mind at ease as I drifted off to sleep and into the hands of my surgeons.

I woke up to the cacophony of noises exclusively made in a buzzing hospital. Based on the commotion and the surrounding movement, I imagined myself in a hospital hallway, the hustle and bustle of busy nurses surrounding me as I tried to gather my thoughts.

Lying on the hospital bed, seemingly paralyzed and only able to move my eyes underneath my eyelids, I noticed a deep ache in my leg. The immense pressure was causing a rapidly accelerating panic to pump through my body. I couldn't move. I couldn't talk.

How could I alert someone to what was happening to me? Ironically, nothing was preventing me from speaking; I just couldn't muster a sound. Whatever force was stopping my voice was invisible.

I felt like I was losing my mind between the darkness, the pressure on my leg, and this newfound inability to speak. Grasping for anything to bring me back to reality, I reached out from under the thin sheet and began shaking my hand, feeling it thump against the side of the mattress. My stiff fingers began to tap out a rhythm, weirdly grounding me as pain and confusion were relentlessly coursing through my body.

Like a virus running through my body, fear and anxiety had started in my head, stolen my voice, pulsed through my hands, and finally, burned their way through my legs. How long would this feeling last, and why couldn't I wake up from this living nightmare?

Mercifully, the tapping of my fingers against the firm mattress caught the attention of a nearby nurse. Within a few seconds, she came to my side and leaned down close to my ear. With the calm yet self-assured demeanor only a nurse carries, she spoke just loudly enough to wake me from my internal torment.

"Are you all right, honey? Is there anything you need?" As quickly as her response reached my ears, I immediately made the connection with my own voice.

Feeling like someone else was pushing their words through my cotton-filled mouth, I answered, "There's just something on my leg. Can you please take it off?"

I imagine she must've leaned over in that moment with a slight frown of confusion before she took off the thin hospital sheet which had been draped over my ankle. With just that slight movement, I experienced immediate relief. What felt like three hundred pounds of weight was lifted away and gone. Apparently, even the nonexistent weight of the sheet was too much for my injury to handle.

Sighing with relief, I gratefully thanked her. It felt like she had saved me. The deep ache of my broken bone, now fitted with metal screws, left that part of my body feeling as though it had been detached. Like it no longer wanted to be there. I couldn't blame it; I didn't want to be there either.

It was all a little disorienting. Lying in a rolling hospital bed, I was moved from one place to another without warning. Perhaps they assumed I was asleep or, maybe, that I was still under the effects of anesthesia? But I was awake enough to be aware of the non-stop movement. Like a game of "red light, green light," with a constant stop and go. I could feel the vibration of the rolling wheels beneath me each time I was moved and the shift in noise that came with the switch of environments. Move, stop. *Wait*. Move, stop. *Wait*. Move.

I woke up the next morning groggy from surgery and remembering little from the evening prior. The nurses had dutifully returned me to my assigned room, and I was in and out of sleep throughout the night. With my mom by my side, the next morning I was unceremoniously woken up by someone from the hospital staff telling me I needed to get up and walk. *Walk? How am I supposed to do that?*

To say I felt like I was in a fog was an understatement. Cognitively, I couldn't put together what was being asked of me. I just kept repeating their words in my mind. My bed was already positioned upright, so I was halfway there, right? I felt someone hold up my foot, still in its cast, and then grab my left ankle to help swivel me so I was sitting with my legs dangling off the bed.

If I thought my head felt heavy immediately after hitting the windshield, at this moment it felt like Planet Earth was resting on my neck instead of a human head. I couldn't even sit up straight, so I hunched over and allowed my head to lower until my chin rested on my chest.

I felt a hand on my back as someone new said to me, "Now, I need you to stand up and walk with me." It was the physical therapist coming for post-surgery therapy. But my body wasn't prepared to meet his request just yet. Like a robot, I had grown accustomed to obeying every demand. I just couldn't fathom in this moment how I was going to physically do this. A wave of emotion crashed over

160

me. Closing my eyes, I began to cry. I don't mean the sweet silent cry, but an out loud sob. I couldn't stop, and I couldn't keep quiet.

My mother stood to the side, watching all this unfold. She knew this must be hard for me because I wasn't one to shed tears easily and almost never loud enough for anyone to hear. She wanted so badly to intervene, but knew she couldn't.

I think I startled the therapist with the amount of emotions I was showing. He walked out of the room and a nurse returned. She rubbed my back and quietly whispered, "We can wait until tomorrow. Lie down, Christina, and rest." I felt as if weeks' worth of emotions were releasing all at once as I was helped to recline, and my legs were hoisted back to their resting position. As I laid back down and, without my permission, tears continued to stream down my face. I was so mad at those tears. Traitors.

I couldn't do this anymore. I had complied with every test and every request, endured every pain and every ache. This was a never-ending marathon race, going in circles; it was exhausting. I wanted out. I couldn't do another lap. *Take me out, Coach.* Not even one more single lap.

I slept most of that first day after surgery. No visitors, no laughing and passing the time. Just a dim, silent room like the first night I had arrived where the day quickly turned into night. The irony of returning to the same place where we first began my healing journey was not lost on any of us.

The next morning, I woke up already dreading the promise of that awful "walk." Based on the previous day, my mother knew there was no way she was going to be strong enough to push me. After all, I was her baby. If I said I was willing to fight, she would believe me, but if I said I couldn't, she would also believe me. Unbeknownst to me, she had called in her cavalry: Peter, followed by Tomas and Laura. Everyone arrived just as they had day after day, so I honestly thought nothing of it. Seeing and interacting with them every day had become such a routine for me, and I felt myself relax into the comfort of our new normal.

My mom kissed me on the forehead and looked me in the eye as she said, "Sweet pea, I'll be back in just a little bit. I love you." As she walked out the door, a therapist arrived with a pair of crutches in her hand. Except these weren't your ordinary set. One of them was outfitted with a padded forearm support that featured a strap and a handpiece. I learned later it's called a gutter crutch, but in that moment, I just called it torture.

Still in pain from surgery but a little more coherent, I looked at the therapist, confused by the contraption she was presenting. What crazy person in the medical supply department thought this was going to work? I was expected to place my arm, which had just undergone surgery and was fitted with a partial cast and crutch around like no big deal? *Someone better be ready to catch me when I stumble and fall.*

Like the previous day, my legs were lifted and swiveled over to the side of the bed. My right foot, now outfitted with screws, felt like weights had been attached to it. It was like my mind and my body were conspiring against me in a revolt and I was too weak to fight against them. I sat there on the edge of the bed imagining my body working in full unison as it had done once before I entered the hospital. Although my head still felt heavy and everything hurt, I was not getting out of this. Even I knew that.

The crutches were placed in front of me, and I was helped to stand. This was the first time in over two weeks that I had been truly standing upright. That, in itself, was such a weird feeling. I immediately felt lightheaded and nauseous, but I threw my right arm over the crutch anyway, until it settled in under the sleeve of my hospital gown and placed my injured arm on the spaceship crutch.

I slowly shifted the weight of my body down over the top of the crutches and looked up at the therapist with an expression that said, "I'm not sure how I'm going to do this, but let's get this over with." With Peter behind me pushing my IV pole, and Tomas and Laura on either side of me, I took a step forward. My head was still faced down as it was too heavy to stand up straight, so I focused mostly on the floor.

In less than two strides, I was breathing heavily, feeling like there was no way I could walk from my hospital bed to the door. With my cavalry cheering me on, I felt faint by the time I reached the doorway of my room. Just as I was about to turn around, I paused to catch my breath and took in all the hustle and bustle of the hallway that I hadn't seen from this view before. It's an odd feeling when you realize the world has been speeding on without you while you've been stuck in a crisis cocoon.

The physical therapist in front of me spoke and snapped my attention back to the task at hand. "Christina, you need to go up the steps, across the platform and down the steps. Once you do that, you can rest." As she gave these instructions, she pointed to a two-sided physical therapy staircase that had somehow appeared with impeccable timing. To my fuzzy post-surgery mind, it was a beast, a monstrosity in the middle of the hospital hallway.

Throughout my hospital stay, I kept my emotions in check. "I'm fine," had become my daily answer, accompanied by a smile on my face. But *this*, this was too much. I had nothing left to give; no jokes to tell. Even my coping mechanisms were having trouble coping. It was like the universe had sent this physical therapist my way just to torture me. I had barely made it out of bed and to the door. *How am I supposed to make it back?* So, more tears. It was just going to be that kind of day.

Before I could express any of my doubt out loud, my cavalry began cheering me on again. "Come on Christina, you've got this. Come on. You can do it. Just one step and then another."

I'd like to say I sucked it up and made it all the way to the beast like a warrior, but nope. I cried all the way there. I placed the two crutches on the first step and fought through the shaking to pull any strength I could to lift myself up the first step, feeling the extreme heaviness of my entire body. Then it was time to tackle the second one. Shaking like a leaf, I attempted to lift myself onto the platform but wasn't getting anywhere. I could feel Laura and Tomas' hands on either side of me helping to lift me. Tears streamed down my face as I felt like everything was drawn out and exaggerated. I felt so much pain pulse over my entire body and there was no amount of medicine that was going to help take the pain away.

With slow shuffles, I struggled to get to the other side of the platform. I felt unsteady and unsure as I lowered the crutches and took a step down, picturing myself falling forward and flat on my already beat up face. *Almost there*, I thought, as I repeated the move for the final step down. I could feel the sweat all over my body as I turned back towards my bed. What I wouldn't have given to be back in that bed I'd been stuck in for weeks.

I couldn't believe it. I had done it, but I knew full well that if I hadn't had the cheering, the motivation to keep pushing, I wouldn't have been able to do it. It may seem like nothing to a person of sound mind and body, but *my* body was beat down at that moment. Not only from the accident, but the surgeries that followed.

This, coupled with trying to wrap my mangled limbs around crutches, seemed like trying to accomplish something that was just not possible. It felt like the hardest thing I could accomplish, and Peter, Laura, and Tomas were at my side the whole way through. I had conquered one more mountain; home couldn't be that far away.

Chapter Eleven

Steps.

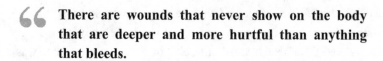

> There are wounds that never show on the body that are deeper and more hurtful than anything that bleeds.

— **Laurell K. Hamilton,** *Mistral's Kiss*

R *eady or not here I come.* Nineteen days, forty-two minutes, and twenty-three seconds after I landed on the roof of University Hospital in a helicopter, I was discharged through the hospital's automatic sliding doors and into Peter's sport utility vehicle. I was grateful for the incredible care I received, but was too relieved to be going home to have any fear or trepidation over leaving the security blanket of nurses and staff to take care of me. I may have been naïve, but there was a part of my spirit that thought if I could just get out of the hospital, everything would be fine. Everything would go back to the way it was before. At least, that's what I desperately hoped for.

Prior to being released, my room had been packed with friends and family who were eager to celebrate that my departure day had finally arrived. I was helped into a wheelchair with my brand-spanking-new crutches, which I had already decided were the bane of my existence. Not only were they impossible to use, but they hurt far more than they helped. Despite having my crutches at the ready, a wheelchair is what I was required to exit the hospital in and my new way of getting around for the next six months. I rolled out with my mom, Laura, Tomas, and Peter by my side. As the last of my things were placed in the caravan of cars that saw me off, my mom got into Laura's vehicle while Tomas got into the backseat of Peter's SUV to ride with me.

Leaving the hospital, it hadn't crossed my mind that, sometime, I would need to revisit the site of my collision. If I had thought about that horrible intersection, it was in the moments of questioning while I was in the hospital and looking backwards with regret. I hadn't yet processed that because it was so close to my parents' home, passing by the crash site would be unavoidable. As we weaved through the sizzling streets of San Antonio, Peter was purposefully occupying me with conversation. He kept me distracted, talking about things I had missed while I was recovering. I was oblivious that we were driving in the exact direction I had been on June 9. The realization didn't strike until he made a right turn onto Thousand Oaks and, just a few blocks ahead, I could see the intersection looming in the distance. I vividly remember looking at him with a quick panic and then, without registering my gut reaction, clasping the handle above the door with my working arm.

Riding in Peter's SUV gave me a higher view of everything around me, including the road. I looked back over at him again and nervously laughed. "I didn't even realize where we were," I sheepishly explained.

He smiled very kindly and quickly reassured me, "It's okay; you're safe. I just thought it was best for you to embrace it now and not be afraid of this patch of pavement." He felt strongly that avoiding it would give it too much power over me. He switched the conversation to the day of the accident, asking me a few specific questions. As I answered him and we neared the exact location of the accident, he switched lanes, placing his vehicle squarely in the left lane where I was driving that day.

Despite my best efforts to put on a brave face, I started to feel the tears involuntarily well up in my eyes. Never had I felt upset with Peter, not even mildly annoyed, but right then I didn't feel ready to be back in the place where my entire life changed in the flash of an instant. I couldn't help but think to myself, *Why?! Why do I have to do this right now? Can he turn around? I just want a moment to think about this.* As we came up to the exact spot where the car had pulled out in front of mine, I felt my body inhale deeply and held it like you would at the peak of a roller coaster track just before you make the descent.

In fact, this entire car ride had felt like a roller coaster. I had gone from the elation of leaving the hospital to the horror of reliving the worst day of my life. And I had certainly not signed up for this ride! I closed my eyes in a slow blink as we rolled over the point of impact. Instead of a prayer or moment of peace, in my mind I privately said just one single word: *Boom.* Opening my eyes, I looked at Peter. Nothing had happened. I was fine.

As much as it pains me to admit it, he was right. Living down the street from this intersection, I would eventually cross it hundreds of times after that day with Peter and Tomas in the car with me. And from that day forward, I never felt the need to avoid it or take another route. Daring fate, sometimes, I would even purposely switch lanes into the left lane. Of course, I didn't close my eyes but, for years, I would silently say *boom* in my mind each time I passed the specific spot where the accident occurred.

Declaring that word in my mind each time was like paying homage to a younger me who had a piece of me die that day. It felt like acknowledging a metamorphosis from who I had been pre-accident: carefree, in love, and independent to a girl who once again felt broken, uncertain, and completely dependent on others. I thought I had finally turned a corner and let go of those feelings of not being enough, but uncertainty had reared its ugly head in my life once more.

This trip through this intersection was the first of many times I would shed a version of myself to evolve into the next phase of life, whether good or bad. *Boom*. Life changes in an instant.

As my pulse settled, I felt relief and appreciation for Peter because even I could see that he had done the right thing. I needed to embrace the intersection, and I refused to be stuck in that tragic moment of my life forever.

Just a few minutes later, we pulled up to my house and, as I hobbled through the front door, I paused in the front entryway. A large mirror was hanging to the right of the front door. A mirror! One I had walked past thousands of times. You couldn't miss it as you passed, and it was too late for anyone to move it out of my sight. Time slowed to a crawl as I turned and took in the first real look at myself in almost three weeks. Unlike the cloudy stainless steel toilet paper holder in the hospital, this reflection was crystal-clear. It was more of a brief glance than a full-blown gaze, but I saw my face for the first time, or rather the face of whoever that stranger was looking back at me.

Logically, I knew the image was me, but my brain couldn't quite make the full connection. This was someone else. I could hardly recognize my eyes. With the new folds and scars, the surrounding skin had changed so much. The skin graft from my second surgery included a post-surgical bandage that looked like half a lemon that might be served at an upscale restaurant—the kind that is wrapped in yellow cheesecloth with a string wrapped around it at the top. It was sewn onto my nose with thick black surgical thread, hardly discrete and clearly going to leave a mark. Still very swollen, the image wasn't me. In no way, shape, or form did I look like the "Christina" I was used to seeing in the mirror for the past nineteen years.

My initial shock turned to awe at how anyone had managed to act like I looked fine these past three weeks. It was incomprehensible. Before I could linger on my loved ones' acting skills, I was pushed past the front door by the oncoming rush of friends and family and into the hallway. My mom rolled up with a shiny new wheelchair for me to sit in and, tired as I was with my aching limbs and cotton-stuffed head, it was a relief to sit.

I was pushed away from the hallway, which would have led me to my room, and towards the back end of the house where there was a sitting room instead. I remember glancing, if ever so briefly, over my shoulder and wishing I could just walk back to my room like a normal college kid, flop down on the bed and start listening to my favorite music. So many freedoms had been taken away that I had completely taken for granted. It hurt to think about these losses too much.

Anticipating my arrival, my parents had removed all the seating from said sitting room and replaced it with a hospital bed since I needed to always lie upright. However, the framed photos my mom always cherished and proudly showcased for anyone who came over to visit still adorned the walls. Knowing that I was already tired, my mom helped me into the bed so I could rest. She unpacked all the items we had brought back from the hospital, puttering around the room. She then set to work using the flowers, stuffed animals, and cards to decorate my new space and add a little brightness.

As she walked away to fix a snack, I laid there looking at the family photos and observed the ones that included me with newly jaded eyes. *Why wasn't I grateful for what I had back then? Why couldn't I have liked myself for who I was? Now it's too late, and I'm going to look like this forever.*

My mother set to work greeting our visitors and explaining that I wouldn't have the energy for lengthy visits, but they were welcome to stop by any time. I never spoke of how seeing those photos had awakened me from my hospital-induced stupor. Until that time, I had been pretending that everything would be fine as soon as I got home. Now it was sinking in that things would not and could not ever be the same. But Mom's picture wall gave her so much joy. I was certain if my mom knew how much pain I was in looking at them, she would have taken them all down. Instead, those photos and I remained roommates for six more months.

* * *

Of all the mountains I had overcome, using the wheelchair proved to be on the list of the most frustrating and challenging. I was like a turtle spinning with one fin, trying to push myself with one working arm and the other in a cast. I was also strictly forbidden from hopping around on one foot for fear I would fall and end up back in the hospital. All I could hear was my mom's classic "I can't afford for you to get hurt." To solve this conundrum, we replaced the difficult wheelchair with a small, armless office chair that easily glided over the tightly looped, carpeted floors while we were at home. I lovingly referred to it as the "Fun Chair" since it gave me the ability to move around quickly without anyone's help. It also provided a slight adrenaline rush since it spun around and rolled especially fast over tiled floors.

My mom and Isaac owned their own business during this time, and my mom was a large part of the daily operation. I knew the sacrifices she was making to stay with me day in and day out, and it broke my heart. Although I desperately wanted to tell her, "It's all right. Go to work." I selfishly knew I didn't have that freedom. I needed someone to help me. I needed the comfort of my mother. I needed *her*.

Slowly but surely, I fell into a rhythm with my new homebound life. Once I was helped onto the Fun Chair for the day, I could move from room to room easily. I became adept at lifting my right, casted leg in front of me and using my working left foot to scoot all around the house. It gave me the slightest sense of independence, and I was grateful for it. Granted, I still needed help to go to the bathroom and shower. When those needs arose, I would call my mom to help me out of bed and into the bathroom, but I quickly felt bad having to wake her so early. She'd spent so many weeks sleeping fitfully in hospital chairs, and now, here I was waking her at the crack of dawn every morning like I was a toddler all over again. The guilt was so strong; I started secretly hopping to the bathroom.

Mastering this ability reminded me I could sneak around in the early morning without waking my mom, allowing me some free time without someone hovering or worrying over my every movement. Having lived on my own prior to the accident, I was accustomed to having time to myself. I believed there was no way I could live independently in my state, but if I could carve out even an hour of alone time in the mornings, that time would recharge my batteries and give me the energy I needed to get through the day.

Soon after returning home, the "half lemon" bandage was removed from my nose, revealing the area of skin that had been grafted from my neck. This was always a great topic of conversation during the early days, when it was quite noticeable that I had undergone a skin graft. Even after the redness somewhat faded, for years the subject came up when I least expected it.

"Were you burned?" Or, "Where was the skin grafted from?" a well-meaning visitor or even stranger would ask. I didn't mind talking about it, I always preferred it over staring. Sometimes, they were trying to make conversation and, other times, their morbid curiosity made them blurt out the question.

I would plaster on a carefree smile and jokingly reply, "Oh, you know, from my butt." And then tap on my nose with my finger, as if to suggest I was slapping my rear end.

When the doctors had initially explained that they would take a section of skin from my neck, I mentioned to the surgeon that I had a couple of moles in that area and not so jokingly suggested he could take those during the process. Just my luck, though, after the stitches were removed and the surgical tape was gone, the moles were still there. The least he could have done was take a portion and place the mole strategically a la Marilyn Monroe or Cindy Crawford.

Before long, my mom decided some pampering was in order. Even as a young, broke college student, I somehow managed to always have enough funds to keep my nails professionally manicured. However, like so many aspects of normalcy in my life, the accident had totally thrown me off my routine. My once beautiful manicure was replaced with blood-stained, acrylic nails.

During my time in the hospital, a lovely friend, Raquel, noticed the shabby shape of my nails and cuticles on her first visit. Without saying a word, the following day she popped up in my hospital room with a little more confidence and ease. Having seen me the day before, the shock of her first visit had worn off. Raquel sat down a bag chock-full of every shade of nail polish under the sun and urgently said, "Okay, let's get your nails looking nice!" She picked a beautiful crimson with no mention that the shade served a dual purpose: 1) Looking fabulous. 2) Masking the blood that had stained my nails.

Raquel's kindness caused a ball of emotion to form in my throat. She didn't ask for permission. Raquel didn't worry if it would embarrass me. She had seen a need of mine that she could meet, and she did. It was a meaningful gesture, and the very essence of "the little things" that not only counted then, but that I have kept in my heart and still remember many years later.

So, upon returning home, my mom thought one of our first outings should be to the nail salon. In a twist of fate, the salon I frequented happened to be in the same shopping center that I was airlifted from that hot afternoon. My mom helped me into my wheelchair, wheeled me up onto the sidewalk and jostled my body along the ridges of the ramp. We had barely entered the salon when the manager called out to us, "Hel-*oh no!* What happened?" He rushed over and waited for one of us to answer his pending question.

"Well, she was in an accident. In fact, the accident was right out here," my mom answered, as she pointed through the window, beyond the nail salon parking lot, to the busy intersection across the street.

"That was you?! Wow, I remember that day. First, we heard a loud crash and saw the ambulance; then we watched the helicopter land right in the middle of the parking lot. We thought someone died. We knew something bad had to have happened."

"Yes, that was Christina. A car pulled out in front of her." My mother replied, as she squeezed my shoulder tenderly. "It's been a rough recovery."

It's an odd thing with tragedy. Folks often launch into their perspective on an accident or event without ever considering whether or not the person is in a good headspace to hear that information. They feel connected to the story and want to connect with you, the main character, but they forget that there is a real human with real emotions tied to the story. I'm sure I'm guilty of this, too. With that being said, I appreciated his intention in wanting to connect with me. Even if it was overwhelming to hear his side of my story.

The nail salon manager then turned to look at me with a slight look of pity on his face, "Don't worry Christina, we are going to take good care of you."

My mom shoved my wheelchair into motion once more and followed him towards the back of the salon where a nail tech was sitting, waiting patiently for us to arrive.

As the manager removed the chair from my spot, he said, "This manicure is going to be the best you've ever had!"

My mom was relieved to see the salon was planning to take great care of me, and explained she was going to run across the street to the grocery store while I settled in.

Just as both my hands were soaking in a soapy dish, I heard the moan of someone crying behind me. At first, I didn't give it much attention, but as it continued to get closer, I couldn't help but turn my head. Maybe someone was hurt and not being attended to? I wasn't necessarily in the capacity to help, but maybe I could try?

With my arms stretched out in front of me and my hands still dipped in soapy water, I gingerly turned my head to the right and peeked over my shoulder to see what the matter was. An older woman was walking with her arm around what looked like her adult daughter. With even just a quick glance, I could tell she was in good hands as her mom or caretaker was holding her close. They seemed to be walking her to the back of the salon, possibly away from whatever had obviously upset her.

Turning back to the nail tech and hoping whatever had caused her grief would dissipate quickly, he looked up at me and stated matter-of-factly: "She looked at your face, and you made her cry."

I felt a shock run through my body. I was in disbelief. Surely, he didn't say what I thought he said, right? I was convinced I misunderstood him, so I questioned, "I'm sorry, what did you say?"

Oblivious to my hurt and embarrassment, he repeated his original comment exactly as I heard it the first time, rattling it off as if he was explaining it to a passerby—not the human being at the center of the issue.

Trapped in my wheelchair, I felt no boldness to draw from. I didn't stand up for myself - I couldn't. All my life I had been taught to fight back, and now, suddenly, a piece of myself had been stripped away. Heartbroken, I could only shake my head as I looked down and muttered under my breath, "No."

I just wanted to reject this reality. I wanted to wake up from this nightmare. It was all I could do to hold back the tears and not lose my mind. Right then, his comments took me from blissful ignorance about how I looked, to feeling as if I looked like a monster. Enough like one, as it now seemed, to make someone cry in horror. The nail tech never said another word the rest of the experience, and neither did I. Cuticles clipped and polish dried, he rolled me back to the front and I sat there alone, waiting for my mom to rescue me.

I remember thinking, *Why do I have to live like this? No one will think I'm beautiful. No one will love me with this face. I can't do this.* I couldn't see the end of the tunnel.

Even though it was probably only a couple of minutes, it felt like an eternity had passed when my mom finally walked through the salon door. It didn't take her more than a second to figure out something had gone wrong. Her face dropping and tone going serious, she pressed, "What's the matter, sweet pea?"

She frantically searched my face and looked around the salon, trying to pick up any clues to what could have happened. Not wanting to make a scene and wishing this whole incident would just go away, I replied with a half-truth: "I'm fine, I'm just tired." This was my new go-to answer/ lie since no one usually argued with it.

She looked back at me once more, and with a slightly confused look on her face, she reluctantly grabbed the back of my wheelchair to push me out the door. We remained in silence, loading up into the car, but as we pulled out of the parking lot and into the intersection that had started this entire mess, my mother more sternly pressed, asking, "What's wrong? What happened?"

I could sense her regret for leaving me alone. Since the day of my accident, my mom had become accustomed to folks not having the most appropriate responses, especially in the early days inside the hospital. This was probably the reason she'd only leave my side if Peter or Karen were there to watch over me. But she couldn't save me from it all, much less stay by my side every second of every day. As I collected my thoughts, I started to recount what had happened and what the nail tech had said.

With all her force, my mom yelled out, "He said *what*?!"

The last words of my story were met by an angry silence from my mom. Even as we were pulling into our driveway, the silence continued. The first noise to break up the monotony was the slam of the trunk as my mom retrieved my wheelchair.

As usual, she did everything for me, setting the chair just inside the front entry and returning to the car. She gingerly helped me out of the vehicle and, with my arm resting on her shoulder, I hopped over until I could plop down into the seat and be wheeled into the house. Once inside, I transferred to the Fun Chair, though it was feeling less than fun with the day's turn of events.

I swiveled in the chair, turning back to face the front door as my mom quickly brought in some groceries. Rather than take them all the way to the kitchen in her normal routine, she dropped them at the front door. She straightened, making eye contact with me before she finally spoke. "I'll be right back."

Without another word, she closed the door behind her and left me at home, alone. Since returning from the hospital, she had never left me alone. I stared at the back of the door, barely processing that she was gone.

I swiveled around in the Fun Chair and, with my left foot leading the way, I made my way to the couch. In the hospital and for weeks after, I felt like a toddler who needed a nap every day, without fail. It was strange that, ever since the accident, even small bursts of activity exhausted me. I never considered how much energy my body needed for healing. I carefully moved myself on to the couch and turned on the TV, attempting to numb my feelings with whatever was on the screen.

My mother walked back in the door less than thirty minutes later. After she dropped me off, she had sped right back to the nail salon and given all of them, not just the culprit, a piece of her fiery mind. She had been in disbelief, as I was, that someone could have said those things. Though we'd shared our fair share of trying moments, it was not the first time my mom had fought for me. I couldn't blame my mom for the mistakes of her past. She was here for me now, and that had to be what mattered most. This was certainly a moment she got right, and I would always remember.

The unfortunate part was what had transpired that day would not be the last time I would experience it. I've never minded someone asking me about my scars; in fact, I invite it. It's nice to feel like someone cares or is interested enough to ask rather than just stare. However, not everyone exudes grace in their curiosity. Grown adults I have met for the first time have made comments like, "What happened to your face?" Or more commonly, because it's now the most noticeable at first glance, "What happened to your nose?"

One of the most damaging is perhaps the shortest question asked of me: "Are you going to fix it?"

What a cutting statement to make to someone, even now, all these years later. How could I "fix" anything? My scars and I were inseparable, literally.

* * *

One early morning, after I successfully made a round trip to the restroom undetected, I sat on my hospital bed. Later, I ventured towards the family room fireplace. There, above the mantle, hung a large, mirrored clock. *How hard could it be?* It was just on the other side of the sitting room. I felt confident I could make it without tiring or falling. Within just the first few hops, I made it to the brick fireplace wall. A few more hops and I was on the other side of the fireplace where the mantle was. Holding onto the mantle with one hand, I got on the tippy toes of my one good foot and straightened to make myself a little taller.

With a little effort, I could see my face close up for a long stretch of time since everyone was sleeping. I repeated this process maybe twice before I was caught. But those two occasions were enough for me to look in the mirror and inspect every new detail on my face. With all the ointments on my freshly minted scars, it made everything feel like it was in high definition: the angry redness, the peeling scabs, the paper-thin canyons where cuts had been, the outline of stitches now long removed, the hole in my cheek, and the folds in my forehead where the surgeon had done his best to put everything back together where it was supposed to be. I could barely trust what I was seeing in the mirror.

As hard as I'm sure the surgeon tried, nothing was how it was supposed to be and, looking at my face, it didn't take a rocket scientist to understand it would never be the same. It was impossible. Again, the words of the flight medic came back to haunt me. *With technology today, you're not even going to have a scar.*

It's hard to put into words the feeling of looking at your own reflection in a mirror, but never seeing the image you are expecting. It felt like I was wearing a mask I couldn't take off. There really isn't an easy way to describe it, perhaps because it doesn't make any sense seeing a face in the mirror that was, in my mind, not my own. I don't mean to sound overly dramatic or elicit sympathy here. I just want to be honest that I in no way loved what I saw in the mirror in those early days, even when I tried my best to hide it. It was as if fate had seen my years of wishing for skinnier thighs, perfect teeth, and a different face. Life threw me the most ironic curveball of all. At least I got one thing I'd asked for. Looking at me in the mirror was a brand-new face. If I thought I wasn't pretty before, well, look at me now.

* * *

My mom remembers one moment in the hospital when I asked her, "Why didn't I die?" I don't remember that exact moment, probably because I was a little too wrapped up in pain medication to be fully coherent half the time. But I do remember that when I arrived home, a dark cloud really settled in and took hold of my heart. I was sick of seeing that reflection in the mirror. I was guilt-ridden that I hadn't appreciated my health before and all the things which were RIGHT with not just my appearance, but my whole life. At that moment, staring at my "new" face in the mirror, I didn't want to live, looking the way I did. Apparently, for at least the second time since the accident, the thought creeped its way into my brain: *Wouldn't it have been easier if I had just died?*

These scars were going to be more permanent than any blemish I could have ever scrubbed away. More than the bump on my nose I despised. In my mind, God was punishing me for not loving the person He created and, while there was still a small voice inside me that knew that wasn't true, nothing else was making much sense in my life. *What am I still doing here? If I could barely look at myself in the mirror, who could possibly love me like this?*

But here's the thing about dark places. Sometimes, we don't get out of them by pulling ourselves out. Sometimes, it's just a simple step that keeps us around one more day. Then one more. Then another. Sometimes, it's just piecing together a string of "barely making it through" days until we get to a day that's *okay*. Which leads to days that are *good*. And then, eventually, when you least expect it, you find your way to *great* days.

I didn't know that at the time. I could just see ahead to tomorrow when I had promised my mom I would go to church. So, I would stick around just long enough to go to church. Then I'd remember a promise I made to a friend to go shopping with her. One more day. By then, I had agreed to go to the movies with Tomas on Tuesday, so that would give me a reason to make it two more days. Did everyone know how they helped me get to my next tomorrow?

Sometimes, a decision to live doesn't look like a bold strike of lightning. Sometimes, it looks like a string of saying *yes* for almost imperceptible reasons why, until you can find a big why.

* * *

If you or someone you know is in a mental health crisis, connect with a community, organization or call/text 988 for the Suicide and Crisis Lifeline. You are worth it.

Chapter Twelve

Lemon.

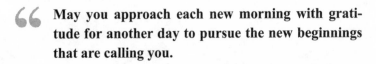

" **May you approach each new morning with gratitude for another day to pursue the new beginnings
that are calling you.**

— **Morgan Harper Nichols**

How do you restart a life? How do you go from being
homebound for months to deciding it's time to venture
out into the wide, wide world again? It felt as though the
accident had slammed its metal fist onto the pause button of my life,
and I would have to wrestle it away to press play once more. My
friends and family were there amidst the pause, but they couldn't
keep me on figurative life support forever. Eventually, I would need
to resume "normal" life and find out exactly what that would look
like along the way.

After sneaking a peek in the clock mirror, I began to make slight
comments to my mom about how my face looked. She could tell
right away I had found a mirror and spent time inspecting myself.
All the weeks prior, she'd been able to make sure I'd avoided one

because the restroom closest to my hospital bed was separate from the vanity. She didn't need to know how I'd discovered my appearance; all she knew was she needed to act. And that meant it was time to get back out into the world again.

When it came to venturing out in public, there was a distinct difference when seeing people I knew and seeing those I'd never met before. After the accident, when I would go out and run into a familiar face, my friend was running into a face that vaguely resembled a girl they used to know. The smile on their face couldn't hide the look in their eyes, which was almost always full of shock and disbelief. This would, of course, set off an emotional trigger inside of me. I would then immediately have to put on a strong face that I was fine, and everything was normal.

I'd try harder to strike up a "normal" conversation to help with the awkward moments but, emotionally, it was like reverting to my childhood. It was hard to not believe the emotional scars within me saying I was less than and very different. I never wanted to be different; I wanted to be like everyone else. This scenario rang true on the day our church held its annual International Day. This was the event I had been helping promote with Laura on the day of my accident.

After leaving the hospital, I had visited with a lot of people I knew, particularly in small groups, but on this special occasion, I would see everyone in our congregation for the very first time. When I woke up that morning, I was excited and eager to be with everyone again, but as we approached the front entrance of the Majestic Theatre, I realized not being part of the event as I had imagined was more disappointing than I had expected.

Several times since I moved to San Antonio, I had the pleasure of sitting in the audience at this beautiful performing arts venue. Each time, I would imagine my not-so-confident-self taking the stage and belting my heart out in song to hundreds of people. I was far from a performing artist and lacked much of the talent to get me there; however, my opportunity to sing at the event had slipped through my fingers with the accident. I didn't need to be Celine

Dion, standing across the piano from David Foster. I just wanted to feel as special as her for a single moment, and then I would be happy to continue being not-so-special Christina.

I had been so excited to sing in front of that large of a crowd for the first time and, now that the day had finally arrived, my life was completely inside out. It felt as though the accident was now taking something else away from me. Much like my childhood, everything around me seemed to be in pieces, not knowing what tomorrow would look like.

Tomas was standing at the entrance awaiting my arrival, and he couldn't seem more excited when our car pulled up. He whisked me into my wheelchair and strode towards the entrance of the theater with the same confidence he had when he walked into that quinceañera all those years ago. How had I gotten so lucky to meet my person at such a young age? How was it that he loved me as much as I loved him?

From the moment I was helped from the car and into the venue, each gracious smile and "hello" served as a reminder that I had lost a great opportunity. I couldn't quietly sneak in or hide from anyone. If the wheelchair that I was riding in didn't make me stick out like a sore thumb, the glistening on my face from all the gooey medication certainly would. I had longed for this day to pretend for a moment I was a shining star, and now I was forced to experience it as a sob story that had been circulating in our community since the day of the accident.

One member of our congregation, around my age, sat down and chatted with me for a while, asking me about the accident and all I had been through. She told me how she had also been in an accident. I listened intently as she explained she hadn't been wearing her seatbelt, and she hit the windshield, too, but was left with only a scar between her eyebrows. I looked at her in disbelief, trying hard to find the scar she was referring to on her face. After seeing a tiny, thin, crooked whisper of a scar, I stopped listening to what she was saying and began to feel angry.

*How did she only have this little scar on her face and, unlike me,
she wasn't even wearing her seatbelt? Why did she not have to go
through all that I had?* If only I had saved enough money to get a
new car. If only I had made any other decision that day to keep me
away from that intersection at that exact moment. But if we could
predict life, would it still be worth living? If we knew the anguish
that lay in wait for us, would we still step into the fray? And even if
we could control future outcomes or change past ones, would it be
worth it? I had survived the chapters of my story up to this point,
including this tragedy, and could tell the tale. There had to be a
reason. There had to have been some purpose in my going through
that windshield that hot afternoon and not dying in the middle of the
street.

I interrupted my own thoughts, realizing I was growing quite
emotional, and the service hadn't even started yet. This conversation needed to end. I politely interrupted her by saying I needed to
visit the restroom.

"I'll take you!" She offered.

It was very kind of her, but not the outcome I was hoping for.
Before either of us could say anything more, my mom returned and
asked, "Take you where?"

I looked at my mother as if she was my angel there to save me
and quickly answered, "To the restroom." This happened a lot
during the first few months of my recovery. There would be no cue,
nothing terribly obvious, but somehow my mom knew when I
needed her.

Taking one look at me and then turning back to the girl, my
mother grabbed hold of the wheelchair and said, "Oh, you are so
sweet, but I've got it." As my mom turned the wheelchair, I smiled
at the girl and agreed to "talk later." Of course, as kind as her offer
was, in my mind, later could never happen.

On the inside, I was quietly defeated after leaving the
International Day event. I didn't talk about it because I didn't want
anyone to know I was upset, like the journal I would never keep so
that no one could ever know the thoughts in my head. I could never

share this dream of performing at the Majestic or I would risk someone saying I was ridiculous. Worse, I'd risk someone saying I didn't have enough talent or asking what the big deal was about performing there, anyway.

I still didn't know why, but as the curtain closed on the event and I was driven home that afternoon, I realized the only path forward for me was to accept what was. This was my present. This was my reality. And it was time I stepped into the light. There were just a few more demons I needed to face first.

* * *

Once I was home, going to my room, closing the door, and crying was out of the question. My bed was still set up outside of my mom's bedroom in the sitting room so she would hear me. With all my injuries, I tired easily, so no one ever argued with me if I said I wanted to lie down. When I went to sleep, my mom often used this as a time to finish her tasks and, on this day, she left to go grocery shopping. As I laid down with my troubled thoughts and pretended to sleep, the house became silent.

When I realized my mother had given me a rare moment alone, instead of lying down, I got into my Fun Chair and wheeled over to the garage. Choosing a different type of torture this time besides the mirror, I opened the door leading into the garage and stood on one leg to hop over to my poor car. Resting my hand over the crumpled metal of the front hood, I ran my fingers across the car, feeling all the damage resulting from one tragic instant. So fragile, so easy to destroy. Just like me, nothing was in its original place or as it had once been.

Using the side of the car, I pivoted myself around the side mirror to hop over on one foot. As I reached the passenger door, I opened it and gingerly sat inside the vehicle. It was bittersweet to look around and feel the rush of memories flood my mind. This little car had taken me everywhere. The near perfect, light gray cloth seats were now stained with blood on both the driver and passenger sides, and it was everywhere. I looked over at the driver's side and noticed that the steering wheel was almost touching the floor. The steering wheel had snapped with the force of the collision and was now hanging ominously. *I guess that explains why my left wrist broke upon impact.*

Morbidly curious, I leaned over a little more to get a good look at the basketball-sized hole in the driver's side windshield where my head had gone through. The shattered edges of the glass stained with blood, still barely holding on to dried skin and what had once been my eyebrows and eyelashes. I vividly remember in that moment being able to still see the eyelashes coated with my mascara, stuck to the crackled pieces of glass after all this time. Feeling short of breath, I sat back in the seat as I looked around me, still shocked at the sight of so much blood covering my once spotless car. Wedged in between the seats was the rearview mirror, which was broken off during impact. I looked at the fallen mirror as God's way of protecting me from what I might have seen had my vision not been blurred and I'd caught a glimpse of myself. Looking down at the floor, I noticed the two lucky Whataburger cookies and the paper sleeves that had once held them. The irony.

I turned to look in the backseat and noticed the little stuffed animal I used to keep resting on my dashboard. There was the blood-soaked white T-shirt used to cover my bleeding face, given to me by a stranger who had been walking across the street just moments before the collision, picking it up, I inspected it, trying to piece together what had happened. The car was an entire mess, much like the inside of my mind. Elsie. I had loved her. Of course, like any young adult, I had coveted a newer, shinier model, but she was my very own and for so many years she had been my trusted companion. But not anymore. She had failed me.

* * *

My mom and Tomas had become extremely close, leaning on one another in their times of need after my accident. She would keep him updated on my progress when he couldn't be there, and he came by constantly to give her as much reprieve as he could.

One afternoon, my mom received a phone call from Tomas. I could hear her talking in the background and could tell that she was smiling by the tone of her voice.

After she hung up the phone, she walked over to me and demurely said, "Tomas wants to see you. He's working tonight." Despite his intense class schedule, Tomas had also gotten a job at Jim's Restaurant so he could earn a little extra money as a server. Jim's was, and is to this day, a San Antonio staple with several locations sprinkled all around town, usually off a highway thoroughfare.

After my experience at the nail salon, I questioned whether I should go out looking the way I did. Sure, my experience being surrounded by my community at the Majestic Theatre was encouraging, but I felt it was the exception, not the rule. Outings which included seeing strangers were only reminders of what I looked like. So, there were days when I didn't feel like going anywhere or seeing anyone. There were days I was just in a bad mood. *Why would I subject myself to humiliation?*

With the intensity of a stubborn little child, I said, "No. I am absolutely not going to Jim's like this." Gesturing up and down at my lackluster outfit and still mangled body, I looked back at my mom to see a stern look in her eyes—the one that would never take no for an answer. The only problem with that? She was now raising a headstrong daughter who didn't take no for an answer, either.

We began the dangerous dance of a mother arguing with her adult daughter, both vying to see whose stubborn streak would win and both utterly convinced it would be her own. But just a few minutes in, I had quickly spiraled from polite "no's" to crying and yelling, begging my mom not to make me go. Sensing her moment, my mom went in for the final blow: "Well, I already told him you were coming, and he's very excited. I'm not going to disappoint him. He's working really hard."

I'm pretty sure I screamed.

"We don't have time for this, Christina," my mom victoriously declared. "Get up. Tomas is waiting. He thinks we are already on our way. Get up. GET. UP."

I looked at the wall of photographs in the sitting room, spotting a photo of Tomas standing next to a beautiful girl at a formal dance. *That beautiful girl is gone.* She was never coming back. I wished so badly that I could still be that girl for Tomas and twirl into the restaurant like a scene from a *Lifetime* movie. *Carefree and confident, I'd breeze up to his side, peck him on the cheek, and slide into a booth to admire his hard work until his shift was over. Then we'd float off to the movies or take a stroll on the Riverwalk because life was easy for that girl. Truly, she thought she had it rough, but she had no idea.*

Idiot.

Why couldn't my family understand? I didn't want to see anyone, looking the way I did. I was tired of people. I didn't want anyone to look at me. But no one understood this. I wanted to scream to the world and everyone around me... JUST GO AWAY. But I didn't. As much as I wanted to fight back, I knew what was expected of me and chose to listen to my mother instead. So, I sat up from the bed and allowed her to help me to the car as she always did. I didn't say another word. I couldn't manage a smile right then. The best I could do was forcibly remove the frown that kept creeping its way onto my face.

I didn't want to be wrong for being upset, so I kept up the facade that none of it bothered me. Maybe if I pretended it didn't, eventually it wouldn't? All I wanted was to be alone with the thoughts brewing inside my head.

Thirty minutes later, we pulled up to the restaurant with its large glass windows. Through them, I could see Tomas smiling and pouring coffee for guests at their table. I felt heartsick that my own feelings for Tomas hadn't changed, but secretly, I was still waiting for the other shoe to drop when it came to him. Just as I had been coming into my own, building up my confidence and finding a life-long love, my dreams had been shattered across a windshield. He had given me no sign that he was going anywhere, and yet I constantly felt it had to be just around the corner.

He was handsome, a green-eyed prince, still just as perfect as before. It took everything in me to hold back the tears. I felt so full of shame for how I looked.

Makeup had long been replaced with glossy, shiny ointments all over my face to aid in the healing of the countless cuts from the windshield. Two large, horizontal stitched up lacerations, swollen and raised, shined a deep crimson red across my brows and eyes. The "cherry on top" was a freshly placed, oval-shaped skin graft draped over my nose, leaving a four-inch scar on my neck from where the skin graft had been taken. With Halloween around the corner, I was channeling Frankenstein with small strips of vertical tape, seemingly holding my neck together.

I remember both Mom and Isaac had come along for this, and they both helped me out of the car. There I was, with a gigantic cast on one leg, another on my arm, and my hair pulled back with a clumsy headband to keep my hair away from my face. They opened the door with smiles.

From the front seat of the car, I twisted into the wheelchair and kept my head down, feverishly trying not to make eye contact. I would have preferred melting into the pavement over feeling the looks of pity that I imagined were already peering from the diner booths as I rolled up the ramp and inside to the hostess stand. It was that eerie feeling of eyes on you. Not just quick glances, but long stares that refused to break. This was something I hadn't experienced before. I could forget there was anything wrong with my face. It was only those looks that reminded me I looked different. It was one thing to be inside my home feeling ugly, but an entirely different experience to read others' perceptions of my appearance.

During those first few outings, I felt so much shame. I hated the experience of depending on everyone for everything and the guilt of feeling like a burden only amplified my feelings that it would have been better if I had not survived the accident. That wasn't the truth, and deep down I knew that, but it was what kept replaying in my head. Lies have a way of taking hold of you like a hug you never wanted but can't release yourself from. Within a blink, I was once again arriving at this very dark place inside of me.

Oblivious or perhaps choosing to push past my sour mood, my mother greeted the hostess with a very cheerful and excited, "Hello!" Speaking softly, I could hear her discreetly requesting a table that could accommodate my wheelchair. Embarrassed, I watched as a whole commotion was made when a chair was loudly removed from the table, in front of all the guests, to allow space for my wheelchair.

Thinking back, as much as I was self-absorbed in that moment, that was probably one of the first "normal" things my mom and Isaac had done in weeks. A casual dinner out at a restaurant can easily be taken for granted, but not this time. My family had big smiles on their faces, like we had arrived at Disney's Cinderella Castle and miraculously won the last reservation of the day. I hardly had the chance to glance over the menu when a warm baritone voice interrupted my grumbling stomach.

"Can I get you all something to drink?" Tomas was grinning his signature megawatt smile. He was clearly so happy at that moment, as was everyone else at my table. I didn't want to disappoint the group, so I did my best to put on a cheerful face.

Before I had time to answer, Tomas began filling my mug with coffee, anticipating exactly what I would want. He didn't stop there, though. Tomas stirred in some sugar and *just* enough creamer to deliver my perfect cup. I smiled as he scooted it closer to me.

"Just the way you like it," Tomas said with a wink. *Those stinkin' green eyes get me every time.*

It was true. He had learned how to make me a perfect cup of coffee, as if he was taking notes to memorize what made me, *me*. It was the little things. Spending an afternoon together feeding the pigeons downtown near the Alamo, playing a game and enjoying his competitive spirit, or like this night, being in his company. It wasn't an extravagant experience when I fell in love with Tomas, but the every day, fairy-tale-like experiences just like this one.

As the evening grew later, we slowly found a rhythm to the ebb and flow of conversation that I had so enjoyed pre-accident. Tomas would pop in and out as his shift allowed, refilling our drinks and chatting as much as he could until his shift ended. Then he joined us at the table. The time passed, and the food came and went. I found it became easier and easier to focus, not on myself, but on the easy banter floating back and forth between all of us. By the time we stepped back outside, the San Antonio night had enveloped the restaurant, bringing a surprisingly fun night to a close. As it turned out, going out to eat and being exposed to the unpredictability of the public eye hadn't been the death of me after all. It was the start of something.

I imagine my experience that night was similar to someone's first roller coaster ride. At first, you're sure it's a bad idea and you're never going to get on, but eventually you give in to your friend's begging. You give it a try. Everything inside of you is screaming for fear of what will take place, but once you let go, you realize it wasn't the end of you. So, you get back in line, standing in anticipation once more, and do the whole thing all over again.

I begged my mother to leave me home and not go to Jim's where I thought I'd be humiliated, again, by how I looked. Once it was over, I realized it caused me no pain at all and how much joy that bit of "normalcy" added to my life. Sure, I had to get past the curious stares from other people, but the joy I would experience from living was well worth it. Although I knew it was going to be a challenge for me, it was then that I refused this slow, emotional death. No more sitting at home, hiding from the world. I wanted to choose life. It wouldn't be easy and there would certainly be days I'd regress, but I was going to get on the roller coaster, anyway.

* * *

Later that evening when we returned home, and without asking "permission," I scooted directly to the garage where my car sat. Everyone knew where I was going. My action was so shocking, it prevented my family from trying to stop me. I knew in a matter of days, the car would be picked up and demolished, so this was my last chance. The strangest feeling came over me when I flicked on the light switch in the garage: gratitude. The first time I saw Elsie after the accident, I couldn't get over how badly she was injured and in turn how badly I was injured. I resented her for not protecting me the way she should have. Now, with the crumpled mess of steel and glass in front of me, waiting to be wheeled off for her final moments, I realized the sacrifice she had made.

She didn't *fail* me. She *saved* me.

Without a hint of air conditioning in the Texas heat, or more importantly, without all the technology and safety features a newer car would have afforded, she still saved my life. Elsie took the real beating during the accident, for me, to the point of death. I was provided life—a life with scars, sure, but life, nonetheless. I couldn't help but feel gratitude for the grace I was given.

I felt like the woman Elizabeth Edwards described in her book, *Resilience: The New Afterword*: "She stood in the storm, and when the wind did not blow her away, she adjusted her sails."[1]

With new enthusiasm for what each day offered, my mom helped me out of the house any chance she could. Even if it was the simple task of going to the gas station. I wouldn't get out of the car, since that would include getting my wheelchair out. That beast of a contraption was a chore in and of itself. So more often than not, I went along just for the ride. Truthfully, my mother's entire intention was just to create activity to keep a conversation going. The goal was just to get my mind off my "situation," not to go on a scenic tour of San Antonio's greatest filling stations.

And so, life found a new rhythm. If not my family, friends were showing up at my home, ready to take me out. I enjoyed our congregation as we all enjoyed being together, whether for a church service or a social function. And there was almost always a wedding to attend.

I was asked to sing a duet in one of the upcoming weddings. Shocked, I asked, "Are you sure, because I'm not getting out of the wheelchair any time soon?" I didn't feel I looked the part to sing the romantic song, "Endless Love," a version made popular by Mariah Carey and Luther Vandross. The bride-to-be assured me she felt confident about it and in my heart, I wanted to sing more than anything. Looking forward to this was something I could hold on to. Over the next month, my duet partner would stop by the house, and we would practice the song until we felt comfortable with it. Magically, scars didn't inhibit my ability to sing. Instead, like music therapy, it allowed me to forget injuries, even if it was for just a little while.

When the day arrived, I announced to my mom I would not be wearing any of the gooey medicine on my face. She met my polite protest with a willingness to help so I could avoid any unnecessary time in the mirror. I wore a long floral dress to cover the cast on my leg. When we arrived at the wedding ceremony that day, I had a plan. I was wheeled onto the stage and stood, using a cane to balance on one leg and my trusted wheelchair behind me, just in case I lost my balance. For four minutes and twenty-one seconds, I felt like the old Christina, whoever she was. Since the accident, this was the most alive I had felt. I didn't think of the injuries, what my face looked like, or what anyone thought of me. I was "in the moment" and couldn't help but let my mind think of Tomas, my green-eyed prince who was sitting in the audience and who I still wanted to be with for the rest of my life.

Life was starting to no longer feel like a prison. Instead, it felt like a comforting nest filled with people who were now fully acclimated to my appearance. It was this community that gave me unending support, and I felt uplifted by their constant presence in my life.

Though, emotionally, it was getting easier to leave the house; it didn't mean I wouldn't inevitably notice others looking at my face like the first evening out. I didn't blame them. I had a face criss-crossed with angry red scars where there had once been only smooth, sun-kissed skin. Often, I would find myself caught up in the moment, engrossed in a conversation, when I would catch someone staring for just a moment too long. No matter how high I was floating on social interaction, it was always a jarring jolt back down to reality. From inside my head, I looked how I had always looked, but it only took a double take or a curious stare from a child to harshly remind me I had changed.

* * *

Though I was keeping myself busy, my college education was still looming in the backdrop with a gray and unclear question mark as the rest of my life slowly regained momentum. To fill up my day, just short of three months after the accident, I re-enrolled in classes at SAC, naively thinking I could pick up where I had left off.

The campus of SAC is just a few miles from downtown, surrounded by mid-century bungalows and quirky local restaurants. My mom pulled into the entrance, navigating through the student vehicles to an open spot along the curb. *Here we go.*

Trunk slam. Door open. Heave up. Spin around. Sit down. My arm was still in a cast, but I believed I could scoot around in my wheelchair. I wanted my mom to push me into my first college class just as much as I wanted to get into another car accident. In my mind, I had the use of my fingertips from my arm in the cast and one good, solid, working hand. What could go wrong? I was deter-mined; I could manage this by myself. She waved as she pulled away with the promise that she would return after my classes finished.

Wheeling myself towards the building, I glanced to my left and right in search of a wheelchair ramp. No luck. It wasn't until I made it to the side of the building that I finally found a handicapped accessible entrance. The wheelchair I was in was designed to be pushed, not self-directed, and certainly not with restricted use of arms and hands. While pushing myself up a ramp, the wheelchair would inevitably turn to the left from the uneven force of my push, causing me to crash into the side rail. This happened over and over again until, finally, I was at the top. Anyone who witnessed my efforts getting up the ramp that day was treated to a free comedy show.

If navigating the ramp was a molehill, the simple act of opening the building's door was my Everest. The luxury of an automated door, operated by a push button, wasn't available during that time so I struggled to open doors by myself. My elevated right foot, still in its cast, would block me while I attempted to open and hold the door with my free arm, simultaneously using my working foot to scoot myself over the door's threshold. Helping to guide this was my ever "useful" four fingers and thumb sticking out of my cast. The result was the door banging me and the chair or pinning me between the threshold, but I eventually made it in or out. I know, quite the visual, huh? It was a relief when someone would hold the door or, even better, see the struggle and give the chair the final push over the threshold.

I searched the printed directory for my classroom, then hunted for an elevator I could wheel myself into without bumping into other students, taking the quicker way to their floor.

By the time I wheeled myself into my classroom, the professor had already begun taking attendance, glancing up from his clipboard to ask my name. "Christina," I replied sheepishly. I resigned myself to a corner of the room, balancing my notebook on my lap and trying to focus as the initial lesson got underway.

After my first class, half the day was finished, and it was time for a lunch break. I headed to the student center. It was energizing when I ran into friends. They were gracious as they helped push me through the food line, even offering to hold my drink for me. We sat and chatted as if nothing had changed, talking about life or a class that day. When lunch finished, the group broke up to get to their classes. I followed, saying our goodbyes as we all headed to our next class.

By the time I found the building for my next class, I realized I was alone. Everyone else had easily slipped into their seats, leaving the sidewalks mostly bare. I reached into my backpack and pulled out my phone to call my mom. I was done—not just for the day, but entirely.

It wasn't the ramp. It wasn't even the door, but the mountain in its entirety. It was too much, too soon. Just thinking about it now brings me frustration at my ignorance to think I could go back to "normal" life so soon after the accident. Even though I felt mentally ready to go back, physically I was far from it, which caused me to feel emotionally defeated before the day ended. My mother knew it and didn't fight it. She would make other plans for me. She knew I needed a "win"; it was just a matter of finding it.

Chapter Thirteen

Curious.

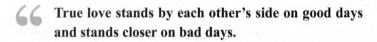

> **True love stands by each other's side on good days and stands closer on bad days.**
>
> — **Unknown**

My mom approached her friend, Trudy, our church administrator, to see if there was anything I could do around the church. Trudy was a kind and beautiful person who always appeared very organized. She was highly intelligent, efficient at her job, and did not need someone like me to "assist" her. Nevertheless, she agreed to my mother's proposal of letting me join her in the church office to help where I could. Because Trudy was a friend, and someone I respected, I didn't protest my mom's insistence. She was also smart enough to present it to me as a role I was helping to fill. Whether or not that was true, I felt needed.

I think everyone agreed, including Trudy. If I could just get out of the house and keep my mind busy, things would improve. The following week, she began picking me up early in the morning.

Thinking back, I remember her going through the whole hassle of loading my heavy wheelchair into her trunk before driving me to the church office each day.

Those days helping Trudy were filled with various office tasks like entering data into the computer, filing or sorting. The office was small, so it was easy to hobble around. Since my leg still needed to be elevated, I did most of my work spread out on the floor. My mother's instincts were right; I didn't have time to think about my troubles with Trudy keeping me preoccupied. Plus, I genuinely enjoyed her company. She took the time to teach me, so I felt useful, even valued. For months without fail, Trudy picked me up every single morning, no matter what mood I was in.

I'll admit there were days I was certainly not in the mood. Not because of Trudy, or any one thing. You better believe no one indulged me on the days I felt too tired or too weak to get out of bed. Those days were over. My mom would stand by my bed and sternly say, "Trudy is waiting. You're going to make her late. She came all the way over here to pick you up." And by "all the way" she meant one mile since Trudy lived right around the corner. My mother always had a knack for layering on just the right amount of guilt.

The tough love my mom offered and the respect I had for her authority pushed me and kept me focused on getting from one day to the next. On a rough morning, she would pull the covers off me and start moving me out of the bed. "Now go brush your teeth," she'd order. Looking back now at some photographs from that time, brushing my teeth appeared to be about all I did.

My job with Trudy wasn't the only part of my new routine I looked forward to. Tomas and I developed a more regular habit of going out with groups. I'm grateful we were surrounded by friends who didn't mind taking a bit longer for my needs or making sure wherever we went could handle my wheelchair. I might not have been able to stay out as long as before, but I could manage a half-day trip to Six Flags, or a movie night at someone's house. They made sure I knew I wasn't a burden. The smiles constantly on their faces made it clear they would much rather have me in this state than not at all.

As more time passed since that fateful day in June, we all tried our best to let it go by not speaking of it. For me, it felt like if I didn't feed the memory and breathe life into it, I would remove its power. I would learn later that this wasn't always the truth. But as a family, we all did our best to push forward.

* * *

By the fall of 1998, my casts were removed, and after being the passenger of many gracious drivers, I was ready to take back the wheel. Accidents remind you that each of us is fragile and has an expiration date. After the accident, I had this ongoing sense that I wouldn't live long... like I had escaped something I wasn't supposed to. This made me eager to live each day like it was the last.

I think I shocked everyone by my readiness to drive again. There were too many times I was almost in an accident while in the passenger's seat, so I couldn't wait to be back in control. My cousin Janet was visiting from New Orleans and ended up joining me on my first time behind the wheel since the accident. Lucky for me, Janet was always up for an adventure; so, one hour after getting my cast removed, I grabbed the keys to my mom's van. We were so excited you would have thought we were stealing the car. We had nowhere to go, so we settled on the corner store 1.7 miles from my parent's home. From the parking lot, I could see the intersection where the accident happened. Peter was right; there was no escaping it. Though it was a short drive, you can guarantee my hands remained at the ten and two o'clock positions the entire way. But I was so ready to get in the car. It was time; I needed to reclaim this piece of my independence again. This piece of who I was.

After six months in a cast and with no physical therapy, I did my best to build the strength of my wrist, and I limped around on my ankle until they both "cooperated." In hindsight, it seems silly that I didn't seek physical therapy, but at barely nineteen, I was more focused on getting back to normal. Without a wheelchair, I gained another inch of independence. Slowly, surely, I was coming back to myself.

I still needed help from time to time, so I didn't move out of my mom's house, but eventually moved out of the sitting room and into my old bedroom. Staying at home meant I could hide from others, like roommates, some complications which still lingered from the accident. This included trouble with sleeping and nightmares. It was common for my dreams to involve me laying in shattered glass, or being covered in blood, unable to breathe. Often, I would start mumbling loud enough for my mom to hear in the next room. It was like I was reliving my accident in my dreams, and my body was releasing the fear I wouldn't allow myself to feel when I was awake. It was mortifying to think of asking my old roommates to deal with this had I tried to move back in.

As much as I loved helping Trudy, when I was offered the opportunity to return to Marriott the following year, I was eager to go and enjoyed being welcomed back to my earlier job with open arms. I hadn't forgotten their kind gestures throughout my recovery, especially their sending word to all the Marriott hotels across the country, following my accident, and asking for prayers for my recovery. Hotel locations from all over sent flowers, balloons, and more to my hospital room. I was a simple front desk associate, but the company went above and beyond to show me and my family that they cared. They sent so much, in fact, that we were able to spread joy by delivering them to neighboring patients. I was proud to work for Marriott and even more so after the accident, knowing firsthand the kindness they showed their employees.

Tomas and I continued to date and grow closer. I felt like I was adding to my "normal" bucket daily, which kept me distracted from my scars and made me feel more whole. I understood if I didn't spend too much time in the mirror, I wouldn't get so caught up in my scars and could live almost as if they didn't exist. If they don't exist, I'm not ugly. I didn't want to be gorgeous, I just wanted to be enough. I no longer looked to my left and right at the other girls around me and pined for the things they had. With every fiber of my being, I knew I was lucky just to be breathing. Who cared if another girl had thinner thighs or a prettier smile? It seemed inconsequential to waste time thinking about it anymore, especially after everything I'd been through.

Truthfully, I was grateful for so many things in that time. The more days that passed after the accident, the more I could see that life was worth living. I became more aware that my circumstances were nothing compared to what others had endured. By my side was my family and my friends. And, of course, Tomas.

* * *

By the time the first anniversary of my accident came around, I felt like I had aged ten years. After getting dressed that morning, I went to find my mom. I'm sure it hadn't occurred to her what day it was.

"Christina, what's the matter?" She asked, concerned.

"I just want you to know, Mama, I'm happy I survived. I know when everything was happening, I said I wish I had died, but I want you to know I don't feel the same way."

"It's really been a year, hasn't it?"

We sat for a moment, soaking in all that had transpired in the last 365 days before I spoke again. "I want to be happy today. Thank you for all that you did to help me through one of the hardest things I have ever experienced. I can't imagine what this past year was like for you. I really needed you, and you never left me."

"Hello. Is anyone home?" came a smooth baritone from the front door, a flushed Tomas bounding into the living room just a moment later. "Come on, I've got something fun planned for us."

In true Tomas fashion, he had surprises up his sleeve when he knew I would need them most. We stepped out into the warm San Antonio summer onto my parents' back patio. I didn't take for granted how sweet it was to just be walking by his side, no crutches or wheelchair.

Already set up on the table was a breakfast picnic of sorts for us to enjoy. He remembered what day it was, and he was eager to "celebrate" it.

"I can't believe you're graduating in December." I said to Tomas, as we took our seats.

"You know I'm hoping for the two-for-one special, right?" He said with a smirk.

"The what?" I asked, genuinely confused.

"The two-for-one special. I graduate in December on a Saturday. I want to, uh, get married the same weekend. Two for one."

Excuse me? This was the first time he had put a timeframe on his desire to be married. The shock I was feeling on the inside must have made its way out because the next thing I knew, Tomas had his arm around me.

"Hey," Tomas said nervously, "Are you alright? You look a little pale. Not exactly the reaction I was hoping for."

"I'm sorry," I said, "I just have so much going on in my head right now. I wasn't expecting you to say that. Are you sure you're ready?"

A bit confused, Tomas asked, "Ready for what? Marrying you?"

"Well, yeah. I mean the last year was a lot, and I don't know how my injuries will affect me long term."

"Christina, look at me." He didn't have to tell me twice. Looking into his green eyes was one of my favorite past-times. "I was sure that I wanted to marry you the night I met you. I was sure the night we went to prom together. And I was sure on this day a year ago. Nothing is ever going to change that."

Tomas didn't wait for me to respond, instead continuing, "Christina, you are so loved. By me, by your family, by everyone around you. You have been the strongest person through all of this, and you are more beautiful to me now than you ever have been."

Though I had felt for years Tomas was my soulmate, in my mind, I kept feeling I was way too young to get married. Maybe it was because I imagined that when the day came for me to take on the role of "wife," I would be more like my Aunt Kathy when she married my Uncle Steve, back in Chicago—strong, established, and fiercely independent. At this moment, I was still feeling a bit shaky in my maturity, so I worried I wasn't quite ready. It wasn't Tomas' fault at all; he was perfect for me. It was an internal struggle to believe that, yes, even in this decision, I could trust I'd be able to rise to the occasion.

Remembering what Laura had told me just the previous year on the same day, I was more than aware that I had chosen to date a guy who was older, and he was ready. In my heart of hearts, I felt strongly that there was no one else I wanted to spend the rest of my life with, regardless of the difference in our ages. It was just a matter of making it official.

* * *

Over Labor Day weekend, our church took part in a state-wide conference in Dallas, Texas. One evening that weekend, I remember my mother asked me what I was planning to wear to dinner. This seems to be a common theme in my life. Though I thought it was odd that she was taking such an interest in what her twenty-year-old daughter was wearing, I was even more surprised when she insisted we needed a last-minute shopping trip.

It was not completely out of the ordinary for any mom to be casually critical of her daughter's appearance, but I thought she was acting odd and, also, a bit excited. I knew something was up; I just didn't know what, for sure. Before I could put much more thought into it, we pulled into the parking lot of a clothing store in the area. Searching among the racks, I picked a simple royal blue button-down shirt to go with some jeans I had brought with me.

That evening, after dinner, Tomas and I walked along the outside courtyard of the conference hotel. He held my hand as we chatted about his plans to become a schoolteacher. The evening was truly magical. A beautiful September Texas night. The wind was blowing just enough to offer a slight breeze. The courtyard we strolled through was romantically lit along the sidewalk with lights hanging from the trees. The garden was lush and green, full of flowers holding on to the last of the summer heat. You could hear the rustling of the leaves as the wind scattered them from one end of the enclosure to the other.

As we walked down the path, I realized the direction we had taken was leading us slightly off the main sidewalk to a more private sitting area. I didn't think much of it until we came to a stop. Looking down, I noticed a boombox on the ground behind a bench. I thought perhaps someone had misplaced it until Tomas pulled out a remote control from his pocket. He turned and pointed the remote at the radio, which began to play "Kiss of Life" by Sade.

Catching on, I laughed nervously as he smiled at me. The confident Tomas I was used to was shockingly absent at that moment. In his place was a boy, full of jitters, as he tried to form the words. As he poured out his feelings for me, he dropped to one knee and officially asked, "Christina, will you marry me?"

I still couldn't believe he wanted to be with me for the rest of his life. Me. Forever. Despite my scars, my youth, all the things that had tried to get in our way before this moment. It was a "yes" four years in the making. From the moment our eyes met, I was only his.

We left our cozy proposal spot to celebrate with everyone we loved. Like the days in the hospital, we gathered with my family and friends, including Laura, Peter, and Karen, all of whom had stayed with me during my darkest moments, now celebrating with me in the most magical one. We hugged and laughed and toasted our futures. No matter the time that passed or the miles between us, a bond was formed that would never be broken. For a girl who hadn't always been able to say she had that, it meant the world.

* * *

Upon our return to San Antonio, we met several times with Peter and Karen for pre-marital counseling. It was a great way to establish and set up expectations for one another and our family moving forward. By the time we entered this counseling, I had known

Tomas for four years and steadily dated him for two. Our time with Peter and Karen provided Tomas and me with some nuggets of wisdom we have continued to hold on to even until today. These included effective ways to argue, like trying to avoid using the word "always" or "never"; and how only one person can have a bad day at a time, meaning the other must rise to the occasion and be the balance for the two of you. We were encouraged to be open with each other, expressing our needs and communicating... a lot. And perhaps most powerful was this counsel: when you feel there is something you want changed in your partner, be mindful of the opportunity to improve yourself in that area as well.

One night, just before our session was about to start, we were all sitting down when Tomas excused himself. I was oblivious to any trouble until Peter spoke up to say, "Your future husband is throwing up with some sort of stomach bug in the bathroom." Beyond the gross factor, I remember pausing, thinking to myself, *Who?* It was the first time I could remember anyone referring to Tomas as my husband. *I could get used to this.*

With only 104 days between Labor Day and our chosen date of December 19, every decision for the wedding had to be made quickly. I was busy working full time with Marriott, and mom recognized early on that I only cared about three things: the groom, my dress, and the photographer. While she would gladly handle all the other minute details, I was insistent about those three. The first two were easy: Tomas couldn't have been more of a sure thing, and I picked the second dress I tried on at an affordable $200.

The dreaded photographer decision, on the other hand, was enough to suck all the excitement out of the engagement entirely. I was horribly conflicted, visualizing fitting into the mold of a bride who wants to feel beautiful on her wedding day. That wasn't me. How could it be, with the ribbons of red scars still crisscrossing my face?

As much as I had thought I was over my insecurities surrounding my accident, all the feelings rushed to the surface like a flash flood. How could I possibly be gushed over as the "blushing bride" on my wedding day with a face like mine? Lucky for me, I didn't have time to obsess over my flaws. Even if I considered premarital plastic surgery, there was not enough time or funds to make any changes. *I am who I am.* In hindsight, it was a good thing. I clearly still had a lot of heavy lifting to do mentally before cosmetic surgery, or in my case, reconstructive surgery would be a solution to my problems.

When my sisters and friends got married, we would always go through their wedding day photo proofs together. While flipping through a wedding photo book, there was always someone with a half-closed eye, or a double chin. For most people, the photographer seemed to be the last item on the wedding budget or didn't exist at all. I would hear a variation of this all the time: "I'm planning to have a friend take our photos." *What?!* I felt I had enough ugly to deal with on my face already; I couldn't bear the idea of being candidly photographed on my wedding day. All I wanted was to be photographed on "my good side," whatever that meant. When I flipped through my wedding album, I just wanted to feel beautiful. I needed a professional. More than that, I needed the most talented, fairy-tale-come-true professional who could connect with me and see I was more than my scars. Little did I know, she would fall right into my lap.

Working at Marriott, where we were constantly hosting wedding guests in room blocks, I met a lot of brides-to-be. I began religiously asking which photographers they were planning to use. One name kept coming up time and time again.

While looking for something in my room, one evening, I came across a photo of Tomas' family. In the bottom corner, a silvery embossed signature read: Elizabeth Homan Artistic Images. It was the same photographer everyone kept mentioning. Taking it as a sign, I looked up her information to call, only to realize her studio was located right down the street from my mother's house. This was now fate smacking me in the forehead, so I immediately booked an appointment.

On the day of my meeting with Elizabeth, I woke up late as per usual and scrambled to get dressed, arriving about fifteen minutes late. When I finally pulled into a parking spot in front of her office, I was surprised that the studio was a quaint little home nestled in front of a picturesque hill country view. The front porch had some rocking chairs and a solid oak front door with iron and glass tossing shadows across the stone floor. It was warm and inviting, putting my anxious mind at ease. Walking inside, every photo I came across was like artwork in a gallery. I instantly thought, *this is who I want to take my photographs with* and I hadn't even met her yet.

It took all of five seconds from the time Elizabeth opened the door and shook my hand to realize that she was a special person, not just talented. She sat patiently and listened to me ramble on about my concerns and my fears of hating the experience of being photographed on one of the most important days of my life. Smiling softly, she listened intently, then took a deep breath.

"Christina, I promise you, you will love the way you look in these photographs. We will take all the time you need, and we will get it right." That was all it took. Elizabeth was more than true to her word, proving it repeatedly in our engagement photos, our wedding photos, and every family photo shoot we've had since. I know there is zero chance I would have such fond memories of my wedding day had she not been a part of it.

With the weight of that decision off my shoulders, the "Big Three" were decided, and the rest of the planning could easily pick up steam.

That, of course, brought up the subject of who would walk me down the aisle and how we would address my stepdad, Isaac, and my father on the invitations. At the time of my wedding, my father was not in my life to be part of the celebration, like he had for my sister. Until that point, I had only received a single birthday card from him on my eighteenth birthday, which only included a signature and a promise of a "longer letter" to follow. It never did follow. I genuinely felt like the privilege of walking me down the aisle should go to Isaac, my stepfather, but I was sad to know my biological father wouldn't at least witness this moment in my life. His name was included on the invitation, but that was the extent of his involvement on the big day.

When the day came, our strategic plan from Elizabeth, my godsend of a photographer, was for everyone, including the wedding party and family, to meet at the reception venue and take our photographs before the ceremony. This would afford plenty of time for me to get comfortable in front of the camera. Laura met me there early, and we had some time to take in the calm before all the fun would begin. She had always been there for me through the good times and the bad—my accident, my recovery, and now my moment to be in the spotlight, however reluctant I might be. She was much more than a friend at this point. Laura had become family and someone who, no matter how much time might eventually pass between visits or what paths life might take us on, would always be bonded to me.

The entire morning was a flurry of activity between hair, makeup, photos and, before I knew it, Elizabeth was guiding me out for Tomas' and my first look. I remember feeling so relieved to have this private moment with him before the pressure of the ceremony set in. When we finally made eye contact, I didn't feel nervous, but rather like I was meant to be there in that moment with him. I thought about the love letters I'd find when I least expected them; on a napkin or the back of a deposit slip. The notebook Tomas and I had passed between us whenever we would see each other, like a record of our love story. The silly photos we would take; the teddy bear he gave me when we first met; the ticket stub from that first movie together. It had all led to this day.

Although there was only enough time for a few minutes of chatting and mushiness, both of us expressed how we were so ready to begin our lives with each other.

Tomas didn't get nervous until the ceremony was about to begin, whereas I felt a surreal sense of calm the whole day through. I imagined I would be a bundle of insecurities, but I was just happy. Happy to be marrying the man of my dreams. Happy to be surrounded by people who saw my scars and could not have cared less. How lucky was I?

My mother had jokingly said she hoped we would find a church with an extremely long aisle so she could take her time letting the day's occasion sink in as I walked down it. My mom got her wish; the aisle was indeed quite long. I had enough time to let Celine Dion's song, "The Power of Love," move all of us before I made it to the altar. As I stood in the foyer, I could hear the music inside the sanctuary swell as I looped my arm through Isaac's. With the doors held closed until the perfect moment, they swung open just as Celine sang out.

I did take my time that day, walking slowly, breathing in every single moment. Proudly standing at the front of the church, I met the eyes of my mother. I felt such gratitude towards her. She had fought through so much in her own life and then the years follow-ing, raising us. She had shown me how to fight through the pain and walking down the aisle felt like proof of that.

There were only smiling faces around me; I was without a nervous feeling in my body. It felt so natural to be in that moment. I didn't feel like the girl who grew up poor or with a chaotic childhood. I didn't feel like the girl who was in an accident with all the scars on her face or even the ugly bride as I had once imagined.

I felt like the girl who had found her Prince Charming, on her own terms, of course. Not because she needed a fairy-tale ending or needed him to feel beautiful, but because she did feel beautiful. He was willing to walk by my side, and I was ready to start a life with him. A little bruised inside, sure, and even with a few scars. However, leading up to that day and holding his gaze as I walked down the aisle, I knew I was approaching the man I was meant to marry.

This man loved me for exactly who I was and the way I was. In fact, my scars made me even more confident that he loved me for me, and not for the way I looked. Peter officiated, and I took in all that he said as if we were the only three people in the building.

Before I knew it, Tomas and I locked eyes, said "I do," and it was official.

With that, we were announced as Mr. & Mrs. Martinez, walking back down the aisle to Lauryn Hill belting out, "Can't Take My Eyes Off of You." It was fitting because I truly hadn't taken my sights off Tomas since the day he walked through the doors of the quinceañera, and his green eyes met mine.

Our wedding day was perfectly magical and there was absolutely nothing that could take away from it or ruin it. I remember when we were taking photographs someone came up to me, hesitant to tell me the flowers were late, and they wouldn't arrive in time for the photos. I smiled and truthfully responded, "It's no problem." Every time little hiccups like that happened throughout the day, it really didn't bother me. I already had everything I had ever imagined. I married Tomas. And that's all that mattered.

"The Night I Knew"

Black suit.
Shiny shoes.
Fresh haircut.
I had no idea that this very night would lead to
"I do."

Cold night.
Long walk.
Arm and arm, interlocked.
I felt an intense emotion that made me
feel every inch of my heart.

Sitting.
Talking.
Smiling and talking.
I knew that night I wanted to spend every
Second, every minute, of every hour,

Talking to this woman forever.

This was the night I knew.
I wanted to be married to you.

By: Tomas Martinez
December 19, 1999

* * *

The morning after the wedding, we sailed off on our honeymoon and enjoyed the beginning of life as a couple. Being married seemed completely natural, as if we were made to be together. It was surreal waking up to Tomas and feeling like our whole life was in front of us.

When we returned home, the future was wide open. Tomas had a teaching position waiting for him at a San Antonio Title One elementary school not far from where he had grown up while his father was stationed during his Army years. With his career path and income secure, Tomas asked if I wanted to return to school, and I thought it would be the perfect time. I signed up for the Spring semester and began looking for a flexible or part time job I could juggle while going back to San Antonio College.

We were extraordinarily blessed to return home from our honeymoon to a house full of gifts from our friends and family. Since we hadn't lived together prior to getting married, it made for a great start, and I immediately slid into my "wife" role. As a teacher, Tomas would leave very early in the morning and return home late in the afternoon. When he walked in the door, I would have all his clothes cleaned, folded, and put away. Dinner was always ready, and our home was perfectly clean. I kept this routine up for months before things changed—not so much with him, but with me.

I honestly couldn't tell you when it happened or how it happened. It just happened. I began to take longer to get out of bed in the morning. Some days I'd miss class. Instead of getting things done right away, I would lie on the couch and watch television or sleep. I just didn't really feel like doing anything. This wasn't the occasional "lazy day" lounging. This was outside of my personality and slowly became a daily occurrence. It got to the point where it felt shameful, and I felt compelled to hide it from everyone like a dirty secret. After all, I should be happy. I was married to the man of my dreams, living a wonderful life with him. What could possibly be wrong?

No matter what I did, I felt like I was unraveling emotionally, but I didn't want Tomas to figure it out. It was similar to how I ended each day, going to bed with makeup still on, fearing without it he would see what I looked like without the "mask" of concealer. More than that, I worried he would realize he married a girl who was broken and leave me to find one who didn't have the sharp edges of more problems than he could count. When the clock chimed like a lookout to let me know it was just a couple hours before Tomas would walk in the door, I'd peel myself off the couch to shower, get the house ready, and prepare dinner. For all Tomas knew, I was productive and thriving.

The cracks showed when I missed too many classes in school and had to drop them. I'm pretty sure I made a flippant excuse to Tomas as to why I dropped the classes. I wasn't liking the professor; the coursework was boring. He had no reason to be suspicious, so he was understanding, and that, perhaps, made the deception hurt even more. Eventually, I also lost my part-time job for the same reason: I'd gone "Missing In Action." I just couldn't get out of bed in the morning. It was like a force keeping me from placing my feet on the ground and taking the proceeding steps needed to start the day.

Growing up with a mother like mine, working hard was a way of life and there was a pride that came from it. Truthfully, all these feelings were so outside of my "normal" personality, I can't even begin to explain it. I felt pieces of my world falling apart, again, like a sandcastle being touched by the ocean. I was too close to the edge of the water. Eventually the waves were going to catch up with me.

They'd taken my education first, then my career. The only thing left was being a wife to Tomas, and I couldn't imagine losing that, too.

Although my mind was constantly punishing me, reminding me I had nothing to be unhappy about, each night I would cry myself to sleep—like a routine of unexplained sadness in the deafening quiet of the night. It became overwhelming since I'd never felt this way before. Even though so much of my life had been an accepted roller coaster, I'd never felt truly depressed. Now, though, I could ask the question: Was this depression? I would have struggled to admit it to anyone, but I could not deny the truth. Sure, before and after my accident, I would have challenging days, but I felt they were no different from anyone else's. It had never dragged me down like this. Then again, I wasn't left alone long enough to let my thoughts take over, either.

After my accident, we were all busy just taking care of the immediate needs, distracted by the everyday challenges of recovery. If I was being honest with myself, I had barreled through life in "go mode" all the way through the wedding. Who has time to process emotions when there are cake tastings and dress fittings to attend to? Our first few months of marriage were the first time my life had taken on some sense of normalcy. Only then could it come to light that I was being held together by scotch tape and gum. My mind and my body were trying to tell me, "Hey, we're not doing well. We need to fall apart for a bit."

Then came the evening when my secret was discovered. Exhausted from a full day of teaching, Tomas typically would fall asleep right away, and I would just lie there next to him, eventually finding myself silently crying. One night, I thought he had fallen asleep, and I was holding my breath—hoping not to be heard while tears were streaming down my face, dampening the pillow under my head. From the darkness, Tomas whispered, "Are you all right?"

Startled, I didn't really know what to say. Pausing for just a moment to gather my breath, when suddenly, the floodgates opened. I was terrified he would see all my vulnerabilities and hightail it for the hills, but the more I talked, the more I didn't care. I needed to let this out, and I was just praying he would understand. We spent the rest of the evening having an open conversation and, by the end, Tomas encouraged me to seek therapy. It was not obvious to me until that moment that I needed it, but for him, it was apparent that I had a lot of unspoken feelings to work through.

Even before my accident and whirlwind of an engagement, the truth was my childhood had been full of crises and "go mode" moments. I thought this rough patch was just another time I could put on a brave face, but Tomas helped me realize that true strength was being able to admit I wasn't alright. With his support, I found the courage to ask for help.

* * *

After many months of therapy, I started to feel like myself again and was ready to get back to work. My therapist agreed.

"Do you feel nervous at all?" she asked during one of our sessions.

"Truthfully, a little," I confessed. "Part of me is itching to feel whole and productive again. I'm just not sure if I always know what 'whole' looks like, but I feel good about trying, and I think getting back to work may help."

"Being your 'whole self' means trying your best to accept every part of who you are, even if some of those parts are still under construction."

"It's hard, though. Sometimes it's easier when I can just hide my scars or hide the way I feel, but I know I just need to remind myself I don't have to put on a brave face for everyone."

"Exactly!" she agreed. "Reconnect with the part of your life that feels the most authentic—the part of your life that keeps moving you forward, for example, your life today."

"I know. Sometimes I get stuck in the past, but I realize I have to accept yesterday in order to have today. Maybe I lost something but gained something else?"

"That can be true. Tomas is a good example of something you've gained in your life."

"He is, and I feel very grateful. I can be exactly who I am with Tomas. He's been so supportive, and he refuses to let me hide." I felt a smile form. "He'll sit with me and talk, even when he doesn't know what to say. Sometimes *I* don't even know what to say." I continued smiling as I felt laughter coming. "But somehow, he manages to make me laugh and eventually lightens the mood. His talking always snaps me out of my fear."

"Remember our earlier conversations," she gently nudged. "It's okay to be messy, imperfect, even a little broken and still be happy, full, or excited about what tomorrow brings. The circumstances of your past don't make up the totality of who you are or even the person you want to become. I think you've made a lot of progress. What do you think?"

"I agree. I definitely feel stronger, clearer even." Seeing my opportunity to lighten the mood, I didn't miss my chance. "I'm ready to jump back in; put me in, Coach!" Laughing, we both stood, and I thanked her as we concluded the session.

She was right. I had made progress. With that, I was ready to take on more of a daily routine in my life, and Tomas was completely supportive. He was proud of what I had accomplished, but it was okay to admit that we were both nervous—that, maybe, adding too much to my day would cause me to revert into a depressive cycle—so, we took it one day at a time.

Before rushing into a course of action, we sat down to talk about what "Operation Reintroduce Christina to Society" would look like for us. I have a strong belief that therapy of any kind is such a unique journey for each person. The type, the process, the recovery —all of it. For me, this was a journey that only I could do on my own, but having support would help me get from one day to the next.

I told Tomas I had two choices: Option 1) I could stay home, and I'd always have dinner ready for him. His dress shirts would always be clean and pressed. The downside would be I'd risk having too much idle time for my mind and possibly slip back into a depression. Or Option 2) we could find a housekeeper who could do the laundry once a week while I went back to work, keeping my mind busy. In hindsight, it seems like a simple choice, but back then we were on a single income and a teacher's salary, at that. However, Tomas and I could both see that continuing down the path we were currently on would only lead to disaster. We both chose "Option 2" so, within a couple weeks, I had found a job and a housekeeper. In the process, I found myself again as well.

We always laughed when someone would poke fun at us for having someone to come help with cleaning the house, or when family members implied we were wasting money. It wasn't their business, but they didn't know what the alternative was. Even when it wasn't a necessary expense for my mental health, it was still what we agreed would keep life moving on a positive path for us.

Throughout those early years of marriage, I would sporadically slip back into that dark place, but I learned to recognize the signs earlier and seek help when needed. That kept a short-lived "moment" of darkness from snowballing into full-blown depression, and it helped immensely that Tomas never lacked positivity and was willing to do whatever it took to keep my mind strong.

What I have learned over the years is how to cope. I'm a fighter. No one needs to tell me; it's what I believe with all my heart. But sometimes I cry and I'm okay with that too. There are no instructions and certainly no rules to living. Sometimes people aren't going to understand my journey, and that's okay. I've learned what things I need to avoid so I can remain in a positive headspace, like too much time in the mirror or letting life get way too busy. I've learned there are days when I'm perfectly content with no makeup to cover my scars, and other days I don't wash my face before I go to bed so I can leave my makeup on. There are also things I know I always must prioritize in my life—time spent with friends and family and enough alone time to remind myself of why I choose life—to remember why every day is so special and why I never want to let depression win.

Chapter Fourteen

Gum.

 Don't miss out on something that could be amazing just because it could also be difficult.

— **Unknown**

When the depression finally loosened its grip on me, I was hungry to work again. If a car accident couldn't keep me down, nothing could. I was feeling a little invincible. Enough of Sad Christina. Confident Christina was in charge now.

A friend had suggested getting a job at an apartment community, thinking it would be a nice, slower pace for me to ease into. Though I had no real estate or sales experience, I applied to two properties, and one called me back, offering me a sales position in the leasing department because it was a relatively new property. This apartment community attracted residents looking for more amenities as it fell into the "luxury" apartment category. Even more impressive, the company had recently updated its uniforms for the leasing staff and management, so each employee was given a credit to purchase matching suit sets and coordinated sweater outfits.

This turned out to be a lifesaver because my professional wardrobe was non-existent. What was probably a standard gesture for my employer turned out to be transformational for me, and I jumped right into the new role.

I'm not sure if it was because the apartments were upscale or it was the nature of the industry, but I never did experience the "slower pace" promised by my friend. Nevertheless, I really fell in love with the job and the staff, especially. I was finding for the first time, in a long time, I was excited to "seize the day." I quickly realized the more active I was, the more I started putting the pieces together and feeling whole again.

One day, the property manager introduced me to one of the new residents who worked near her home. My boss gushed that the resident, Vi, worked for a successful local custom home builder and went on and on about the beautiful model home she called her office. *Custom homes?* Being young and with no experience in construction, except the little I had on that missionary trip, I wondered how that worked exactly? I didn't say anything at the time, but I was intrigued.

Shortly after my introduction to Vi, I leased a short-term apartment to a sweet, young couple who were about my age and were building a house themselves. They completed their application and handed it back to me to input into the lease database. While punching in the routine information, I noticed the two of them also worked for homebuilders as "sales consultants." *Huh. Small world.*

It wasn't until it came to the section for me to enter their income that I stared at the application page in disbelief. My hourly wage, even if I worked a full forty hours a week, equaled just 13 percent of ONE of their incomes. No sooner had the door closed behind them than I opened a new tab on the computer and typed in the name of the homebuilder they worked for. As soon as I clicked on the "Careers" page, I scrolled until I found the job requirements for a sales consultant.

First thing on the list? A college degree. I didn't have it, but I wasn't intimidated. I'd faced plenty of closed doors in the past and always made it through. There had to be another way, and in that moment, I was my mother's daughter, filled with determination and gumption.

I'd already learned the process of taking potential prospects on tours, explaining the benefits and doing all I could to try to "close the deal." I figured homebuilding was probably similar, but on a bigger scale. And whatever I didn't know, I could research, study, and make up for it with grit and hard work. At that very moment, I decided I was on a mission to get a job like this young couple. I just needed a few minutes with Vi, and I knew all the pieces would fall into place.

A week or so passed, and it was time for the apartment community's monthly social evening. As if fate was calling all the shots, there she was. I walked up to Vi and reintroduced myself. We chatted for a bit and then I went right in for the kill. "You know, I'd love to be in the home building industry like you are. Do you have any recommendations on how I can start?"

Vi was so kind and gracious with her time. She told me about home builders she thought I should stay away from, those who had a good reputation and, of course, some details about the industry. After the evening was over, I went home and explained to Tomas how the conversation had gone beautifully, and that I was hooked. I wasn't going to rest until I could land a job in this brand-new world.

Beyond the intrigue of the home building industry, what I was really striving for was financial independence. I have never believed money equals happiness, but I believe it can make life easier. Or at least that's what my childhood told me. Having a job that could offer financial security made me feel there was a possibility of never having to deal with situations that I experienced in my childhood: no electricity, no water, no phone, no vehicle. No stability. Beyond that, I wanted to make Tomas proud.

Vi ended up being a saving grace for me. She introduced me to people in the industry and got me more than one interview. On one occasion, she called me for a position with the builder she was working for, letting me know she had already arranged an interview. I just needed to "land" it.

Vi's advice was to be honest. She recommended that I be upfront with John, the owner of McNair Custom Homes, and tell him that although I was green, I was hardworking and ready to soak up everything I could about homebuilding. She thought he might see it as an advantage that I wasn't coming in with preconceived notions or lazy habits that would need to be unlearned.

On the day of the interview, that's exactly what I did. Feeling confident and super professional, I walked in wearing a black suit (thank you luxury apartment uniform) and introduced myself to John McNair. I gave him my best handshake, like my mama taught me, and he even commented on it. The John I have come to know is the epitome of a Texas gentleman, forever clad in cowboy boots. A graduate of Texas A&M, he's intelligent and never one to mince words in his life. He would tell you exactly what was on his mind within two minutes of introductions.

When he finally asked me about my experience, I was armed and ready with what Vi had prepped me to say. When he was finished with the interrogation, he paused and said, "Well, do you have any questions for me?"

It was now or never. At the young age of twenty-three, I was trying to muster all the confidence of someone with twice my experience. There was one more card I was prepared to play that another resident of my apartment complex told me worked for her every time. I looked John square in the eye without a hint of fear and said, "Yes. When do I start?"

John looked at me with one corner of his mouth upturned and said, "Well, uh, you seem like a pretty good candidate, and I'm tired of interviewing, so sure. When can you start?"

Huh. He didn't seem to care about my scars. *Maybe I shouldn't either?*

Regardless, I almost died inside. It turned out my job at the apartments was a dress rehearsal for what turned out to be a lucrative career over the next ten years in the homebuilding industry, six of which I would spend with John McNair. After we shook hands that day to make it official, it wasn't ever easy. John would visit me for the next few weeks at the model home and, based on his questions, I knew he wondered if he had made a mistake hiring me, such a young girl.

I couldn't blame him. I had no experience, and my counterparts were twice my age. The money was amazing, but the sacrifice was time. Tomas and I didn't take many vacations during the years I worked in home building, and in that world, salespeople work every single weekend. Period. For me, there were no weddings, baby showers, or fun day trips floating down the Guadalupe River. Often, I would work on my days off, which were during the week when Tomas was teaching, so we were always on opposite schedules. Tomas continued his education with a master's degree in Education Administration from Texas A&M University in 2005. He was off for holidays, extended breaks, and the entire summer. I, on the other hand, was in my busiest season during the summer, sweating in the Texas heat while sporting a full suit and heels.

I'd walk homesites full of dirt and often mud, touring prospective buyers with a million questions and needing months to decide. For the next several years, I worked very hard learning all I could to be an expert in my position. I wanted to gain the confidence of my buyers in hopes they would overlook my age and see my industry knowledge, not my youth.

John McNair's words often rang in my head, *If you don't feel like you're the best in your field, then get out.* I knew John had taken a chance on me, so I did all I could to be the best representative for McNair, using each day to earn my position and always prove to him he made the right decision in hiring me. The company John created included some of his family working with him—his sister, Karol, and brothers, Michael and George. Good days and difficult ones, but it always felt like we were all one big family. There were so many lessons I learned during my time at McNair Custom Homes and from John, specifically, that I carry with me to this day and help me in the businesses I now own and operate. The time I spent with John McNair was the first in my life I had pursued a goal, achieved it, and then thrived. It felt good; and it was a huge boost for my confidence.

* * *

Several years had passed since my car accident, and I decided I was finally ready to have an elective reconstructive surgery. While I had undergone emergency surgeries or procedures to help reduce or relieve pain, I was excited for this one since I thought it could improve my appearance. I would go in for a scar revision and brow lift to move my eyebrows into a more normal position. They were over corrected when the surgeon attempted to close the gap between my eyes, and I also wanted a deep dermabrasion to resurface the skin from all the scarring.

I was lucky to find an incredible plastic surgeon who was truly gifted in reconstruction, Dr. Gregg Anigian. For me, I feel like it's one thing for a plastic surgeon to be talented at making something already lovely, a bit nicer. It's another thing entirely to take something that has trauma written all over and make it beautiful. Dr. Anigian has that level of talent and, from the moment I met him, I felt so confident he would be the surgeon for me.

A few weeks after my surgery, a friend called to check in on me. I had gone into hiding, not wanting to see anyone—or rather, not wanting anyone to see me.

"Christina, I miss you! When am I going to see you? I'm excited to see the 'new you'!"

Shakira, who had previously spent many years in the medical field as a Physician's Assistant specializing in emergency medicine, and had now gone into aesthetics, was eager to see me. We had known each other since before the accident and were accustomed to spending most of our free time together since we lived near one another.

221

I hesitated to answer, knowing she would see right through me. "Um. Truthfully, I'm not ready to see anyone right now."

"What? What do you mean? First, I'm not just 'anyone,' but what's wrong? Did something happen?" *Busted.* I could tell her medical brain was already brewing.

"No, nothing happened. I just don't look great. I don't want to be seen like this." Looking at my newly angered scars in the mirror, it felt like déjà vu, reliving the past all over again.

"Well, I don't care. I'm picking you up. You're getting out of the house. If it makes you feel better, grab some sunglasses and a hat. I'm pulling up in five minutes." I could feel her Puerto Rican fire burning through the phone.

"No Shak, you don't get it. I would rather wait until I heal before being out in public." Feeling a flashback of emotion, I listened to my explanation sound eerily like excuses I had made all those years ago after the accident.

"You're right, I don't get it. But let's get some lunch and you can help me understand. I'm here for you. I promise Chuy's creamy jalapeño dip will solve everything. Okay?"

"Fine. I am hungry." I hung up the phone as I went to my bedroom and grabbed a floppy beach hat to pair with the biggest sunglasses I could find before heading out the door.

As promised, she pulled up exactly five minutes later and as I got in her car, she greeted me with her usual loving smile. Shakira tenderly rubbed my arm as she said, "I'm so proud of you. I mean, you look ridiculous in that hat, but I'm glad you decided to come." *Me too.*

Over chips and salsa, I explained to Shakira all the emotions that I had been feeling since the surgery.

"Since my accident, I've been learning to deal with the newness of my face. I know the surgery went well, but I wasn't prepared for the recovery. Honestly, I hadn't even thought of it."

"Christina, I love you, but you gotta give it time. What were you expecting?"

I looked down at my restless hands, sitting on my lap and took a deep breath before continuing, "I don't know, Shak, but the face looking back at me in the mirror is too close to the face I remember after all those surgeries. And I hate it. I hate feeling like this, not even for another minute. I don't think I can do this again."

I was potentially looking at further procedures to help soften the scarring throughout my face, reshaping my nose and straightening it, among other things. Surgery was something I thought I had wanted, but emotionally I was struggling.

"Christina, you're beautiful just the way you are and if it's too much to handle, then don't do it. No one expects it of you. You can only do this for yourself, and if it's not making you happy, then why do it?"

She was right. I didn't think I could handle any more changes. I was learning that any amount of surgery meant I became caught up in worrying about my appearance all over again. And I was done with that version of myself.

So, after that surgery, I decided it would be the last. No more elective "adjustments." I worked on becoming content with what I had. It turned out that self-assuredness could not have come at a better time. After so many surgeries and putting my family through endless hours and efforts of caring for me, I was done with surgeries and "fixing" things for the foreseeable future. Besides, each surgery meant the girl who stared back at me in the mirror was different... again.

* * *

Just before we celebrated nine years of wedded bliss and prior to my thirtieth birthday, I had a vision one morning while getting ready for work. In my vision, I was sitting on a blanket having a picnic in an open park with a little boy running around. It just popped into my head along with the thought "I'm ready." *Where'd that come from?* I kind of shocked myself; I couldn't believe it. It was just about as easy as walking down the aisle. I didn't feel any fear or hesitation. I was ready to have a child. Sort of.

Prior to getting married, I had been diagnosed with endometriosis. While the symptoms I had experienced for years were painful, the most devastating revelation was being told that it would either inhibit my ability to have children right away or make it impossible to conceive at all. Back then, I didn't really process this or discuss it with anyone since, at the time of the diagnosis, I didn't really understand the impact. With already so much I felt I was navigating through, I figured I would cross that bridge when I came to it.

So, when it came time to stop "practicing" and start "trying" to have a baby, the weight of that diagnosis all those years ago finally hit home. I got a little nervous about the idea that it might not happen at all. Quietly, without even mentioning it to Tomas, I started mentally preparing myself for the worst.

Soon after, Tomas and I went on a cruise—a favorite vacation for us. Having one of the best times of our lives, we engaged in as many experiences as we could fit in. This included off-roading with all-terrain vehicles and an impromptu jump off a cliff in Jamaica only to return home and discover I was pregnant… with a boy.

I'll never forget when I shared the news with Tomas. He would have been happy with having children immediately after our wedding vows. Tomas loved kids! He was a teacher after all. However, he respected my decision to wait until we were a bit older. This gave us an extended "honeymoon" to get to know each other better before adding kids to the mix.

The evening prior to discovering I was pregnant, I had a feeling I might be. I didn't want to get Tomas' hopes up, so I didn't mention anything to him. Besides, considering what the doctor had said, the chances were slim that I was right. The next morning was a Monday, which meant I had early morning meetings. I was dying to know if I was right about the feeling of being pregnant, but I would have to wait hours until all the meetings concluded.

The morning seemed to drag on until, gratefully, lunch time arrived. I got in my car and drove down the street to Target. After rushing down the aisles and through the checkout counter, right there in the Target restroom, I found out I was going to be a mom. I couldn't believe it. Knowing I could never keep a secret from Tomas, I came up with a plan to surprise him with the news. After work that day, I headed to the shoe store in search of the smallest pair of Michael Jordan sneakers I could find. Once I made it back home, I gave Tomas a box of black and red "baby Jordans" with my positive pregnancy test tucked on top. Tomas was elated and so was I! We were on our way to becoming parents.

As first-time parents, we did all our research over the next nine months and wanted nothing but the best for our baby. I was obsessed with giving him the best start possible. My childhood had been unpredictable, and I never wanted my baby to experience that. He would never worry where his next meal would come from, and Tomas and I would do everything in our power to make sure we had careers where we would be home for dinnertime and enjoy time together as a family.

We decided a home birth would be peaceful, natural, and away from the hospitals I had learned to dread. Like my own birth story, however, our son's entrance into the world was also a little bit dramatic and exciting.

On August 4, my water broke after waking up in the morning, six days earlier than my son's due date. We called our midwife, and she began her journey from Austin to where we were in San Antonio. Tomas and I enjoyed a beautiful day as we waited for our baby's arrival. We walked and talked, excited to meet this little love bug that had been growing in my belly for so many months. We ordered food and put our prenatal training to use, trying to make these last few moments as a family of two as peaceful as possible. After all, Tomas and I had such unique experiences connecting the two of us, we wanted this one to be drama-free.

I had what I would consider a near-perfect pregnancy until about a month before the baby's due date. At that point, my liver and kidneys were over working, and my skin was sensitive to anything, including the softest touches like that of a makeup brush. My symptoms were consistent with that of Intrahepatic Cholestasis of Pregnancy (ICP). It felt like my skin was always on fire. There were only two shirts and one pair of pants where the clothing seams didn't irritate my skin. I couldn't keep anything down and ate pounds of rice trying to give my baby at least some nutrients.

As the final weeks approached, my tailbone and lower back would ache constantly, so I started using an inflated plastic donut to sit on. Without many options, I started visiting my chiropractor to get some relief, and it seemed to be working. My adjustment from the chiropractor visit the day before may have been what helped my water break early. Either way, as our day together continued, my labor wasn't progressing. It seemed like maybe the baby wasn't ready after all, and our midwife became concerned.

The following morning and after more than thirty hours of labor, I wasn't dilating nor making any headway with the baby's positioning. While most home births go as planned, ours was getting a little scary, as our midwife was having difficulty finding the very faint heartbeat of our baby. Once I began to fall asleep from exhaustion, the decision was made. It was time to transport to the hospital. *Uh oh.*

"Would you like to go to the hospital here?" the midwife asked, referring to the one just three miles from our home. Knowing I had gone through a situation with that very hospital when I was experiencing false contractions just a month prior, she paused and offered a second option: "Or would you like me to take you to this hospital in Austin? There's a doctor I work with there for any transports. He's very supportive."

Tomas looked at me, eyes sick with worry, and said, "You want to go to the one here, right?"

Haha, nope, and there's no arguing with a woman in labor once she's made up her mind.

The moment I entered the tiny backseat of the midwife's hatchback, the pain of labor intensified. Unlike at home, where labor came without discomfort, I moaned in pain the entire hour all the way to Austin. After getting checked into the hospital I ended up being wheeled into surgery for a Cesarean section.

Oh, no. Immediately, my thoughts went back to the story of my mother and me.

When the doctor finally pulled him out, he loosened the umbilical cord which was wrapped around the baby's neck. And unlike my mom, I was gifted with the sounds of my newborn's first cry.

There he was. This little squishy, tiny, and oh-so-cute baby boy. Made from scratch, with the help of God. Not exactly the birth journey I had expected or planned for, but our little Enzo was healthy, and we were certainly in love. We couldn't imagine something so little could bring us so much joy.

Leaving the hospital for the drive back home to San Antonio, Tomas and I both looked at each other and thought we couldn't believe they were going to let us take this baby home. We felt undeserving and underqualified to be given such an enormous responsibility and, honestly, it was a little unreal. We weren't prepared for his first ride home since we had planned for a home birth, so it took us a full forty-five minutes to figure out how to strap the car seat in, for goodness' sake.

With the bassinet next to our bed, Tomas and I slept with the lights on for the first few weeks. We were so scared something was going to happen to him and terrified we would screw this whole parenting thing up. As it turned out, we were pretty darn good at it. The fact that Tomas and I were married for nearly ten years before we had our son meant we were in sync. More than that, I couldn't have asked for a better partner. Tomas was always hands on. In fact, I didn't change a single diaper for the first month. As soon as the baby was fed, Tomas took over burping, changing diapers and was even a wizard at putting our precious little boy to sleep.

There were two main things that came to mind once I got into the groove of raising our son. The first was my desire for him to grow up with confidence, like Tomas. I wanted Enzo to have a sense of worth, always knowing that he didn't have to be anything other than himself because he was enough. It was vital for me to impress upon him that no flaw, blemish, or personal "defect" would make him any less.

The second was a bit more personal: I found myself concerned with whether or not he would notice my scars and be embarrassed I was his mom. As the years made my scars fade from my thoughts, I wondered if they would resurface when he eventually would recognize them. *Would I be the ugly mom?* I could remember a time when my niece was about two years old, and I was holding her. She kept staring at the scar on my nose and cuddling next to me. Finally, as we all sat for dinner, she snuggled up to my shoulder and looked at me ever so sweetly. Raising her little index finger up to my nose, she tapped it two times. *Boop. Boop.* Making a little sound with each tap.

Although it was perfectly innocent and made me laugh, it shocked me a little that she even noticed at all. Of course, I wasn't naive to think no one noticed my scars, but it was the first time I realized that even a child could notice them. Some adults would graciously feign surprise and say they didn't really notice the scars on my face. But I always knew from that point on that if a child could notice, then most adults did as well. Looking back, I honestly appreciated the day my niece opened my eyes because it gave me years to prepare my heart.

Chapter Fifteen

Invincible.

 Challenges are gifts that force us to search for a new center of gravity. Don't fight them. Just find a new way to stand.

— **Oprah Winfrey**

In 2012, after hearing a live mariachi performance, I was reinvigorated with the dream to sing a mariachi song from the evening I met Tomas. I knew it needed to happen soon or it would be another seventeen years before I got up the courage to try again. Now I just needed to pick a date. I thought about it over the next few weeks and then somehow it popped into my mind, clear as day: June 9, the day of my accident.

Normally, every year when that dreaded anniversary would come around, I would stay inside all day. I didn't drive; I didn't get in anyone's car; I didn't make any plans. I just silently moped about, staying at home secretly feeling sorry for myself. As if tragedy could repeat itself on the same exact day, year after year. Somewhere along the way, I decided it would be the one time of the year I would privately allow myself to feel all the self-pity and not apologize for it. Tomas didn't argue with my flawed logic; he was supportive to an extreme degree.

This year, however, I decided I didn't want to remember June 9 with such awful sadness anymore. I wanted to change how I felt about the day. I wondered if I could release the power it had over me by making new memories instead. So, that's what I did. I booked the Arneson River Theater, a historic outdoor amphitheater on the banks of the San Antonio Riverwalk. After hiring a full mariachi band, Los Galleros, I began practicing a few songs in my car.

About a month before the concert, I called a good friend who played the classical guitar to ask if he would accompany me. He was one of the most incredible musicians I had ever met. When Carlos Sanchez played, it sounded like an entire orchestra was backing him, not just a single musician. I always had so much admiration for his ability to hear just a few notes of a new song before he could play it. I, on the other hand, was an untrained vocalist and couldn't even read music, yet he always treated me like a professional. Without hesitation, he said he would be honored to join me for my anniversary concert and even called a few other musicians to help.

With Carlos secured, the only other people I told about my decision to sing were Tomas and my mom. I was still hesitant to tell anyone else about the event, truthfully, because I wasn't sure if I would go through with the concert or not. However, the details were set, and I had a couple of months to decide what I wanted to do. Just a few days before the Sunday concert was scheduled, I emailed my friends and family, announcing the event. *No backing out now.* I explained the reason behind the concert, my accident, and how I wanted to change the meaning of my anniversary from a day of travesty to a day of triumph.

The email was shocking to some. I had many close friends who didn't know I enjoyed singing or hadn't heard the full story of my accident in my own words. Over the years, the pace of life had sped up so that my love for music had been filed away under "Things I Used to Have Time For."

I'm not special, I'd think whenever I considered singing again. But now it was out in the open for all to know. I remember receiving a text message from a friend I had known for several years saying she thought my email was hacked because she received something about a concert. I laughed and replied, telling her it really was from me, to which she responded incredulously, "You sing?!"

Yes, and she playfully teased, "Do I even know you?"

Another very close friend I had known for nearly a decade, Darleen, was equally shocked after receiving my invitation. She insisted I explain everything, then sing for her. Darleen is elegant, poised, and someone who never said "no" to an adventure. Darleen was also responsible for introducing me to a whole new world: the world of luxury. We went to fashion shows, five-star dinners, and sophisticated events around town. When it came time to attend my first gala, she took me shopping and helped me pick out the perfect cocktail dress. Darleen showed me a lifestyle completely opposite to how I grew up. It was, and remains, inspiring to see how she knew exactly what she wanted out of life and never apologized for it.

Darleen shook her head and asked, "How did I not know you could sing?" Not having a good answer, I just shrugged and said, "I don't really talk about it. But you can see me perform at the concert." She was in disbelief that this hadn't come up in all the years we had known each other.

It was entirely intentional on my part. I guess I just hadn't realized after all those years it was another attempt to shy away from the spotlight and hide my flaws, or at least the biggest ones. By this time in my life, if you didn't know me on the day of my accident, I wasn't going to share that piece of my past with you. I thought if you didn't know about it, maybe you wouldn't look at my scars or notice I was different. Noticing them made me remember them and, if I could forget, it was like they weren't there. Ignorance could be bliss for everyone I encountered, and then I didn't have to deal with the pain.

One of my friends, Cynthia Lee, who happened to be a news anchor for a local station, also heard about the concert. With her journalist brain churning, she immediately called me asking if I would be willing to make an appearance on their morning show. While some may relish their chance for fifteen minutes of fame on television, to me it sounded like my worst nightmare. At the time, I disliked being on camera or photographed. The only person I would ever allow to photograph me was Elizabeth.

There was just one thing making me take a moment to consider the opportunity for media attention: the concert would benefit a charity, raising money for children who needed reconstructive surgery. Cynthia made the compelling argument that more aware-ness would mean more donations for them. With that, I agreed. *How could I not?*

We jumped on a quick phone call to discuss the details of my story before going on air, and just before we hung up, she asked me if I knew if any news outlets had covered the accident when it occurred in 1998. I told her I hadn't seen anything, although I could faintly remember someone mentioning they saw something on the news. She told me not to worry; she could look it up in the archives before she saw me for the live show.

The next morning, I was caught up in the flurry of getting ready, knowing I would appear on camera but not allowing myself to truly grasp what I was walking into. When I arrived, I was told they had found footage of my accident that had aired all those years ago on that hot June afternoon. I honestly thought to myself that it was kind of cool; I had never seen it before, and it would be interesting to watch.

With just a few minutes before we went live, I met the sweet host, Cassandra Lazenby, who was so down to earth and put me right at ease. We chatted for a couple of seconds and then went right into our interview. With cameras pointed at my face and the bright lights of the studio shining down, she showed a clip of the video which caught my attention, but what would be revealed next would make me speechless.

In the video, it showed the woman who had pulled out in front of me standing in front of her car. I'd never seen her before. Then my car and people standing around it, including the good samaritan shown without his shirt. I watched as first responders pushed a gurney with my body strapped to it towards a waiting helicopter. None of this I had ever seen before, and I could hardly take it all in. It was like looking the monster under your bed right in the eye. Shellshocked, I just stared at the TV monitor with no words. Sensing my internal turmoil, like an *Oprah Show* moment, Cassandra asked me, "Christina, what's going through your head when you see that?"

What felt like minutes passed while I tried to form a response. *Say something. Anything!* The problem was I had just learned about that video minutes before the show began, but much as I had waited so many years to see all these visuals, I couldn't take it all in fast enough. I forced my gaze from the video back at her, and somehow we continued our interview.

The hardest part about the whole ordeal was this beautiful young lady sitting across from me, trying to keep her own emotions at bay. Her bottom lip was trembling *just* enough for me to notice since I was sitting right next to her. I was trying to keep it together, but seeing someone else emotional is the worst for me. *Do not cry!* I mentally begged my interviewer. If she cried, we were both going down.

When the interview was over, we said our goodbyes and Tomas dropped me off at home. The minute I walked inside, I was met with the silence of an empty house and instantly felt the deepest shame. *Why did I do this interview?* Everyone, people in my life and even those I'd never met before, were going to know about my secret pain I had spent years hiding. They were going to ask me about it. They were going to look at my scars. I wanted to hide. *What had I done?*

Only a few hours had passed, when Tomas called to let me know he was sending a link to the interview via email. I couldn't believe the recording of the show was already posted online. Curiosity mingling with dread in the pit of my stomach, I found his message in my inbox and clicked on the link. Of course, I began criticizing myself only ten seconds into watching the video, grinding my teeth with every "um" and cringing at my momentary silence upon seeing the accident footage.

But despite my bumbling, when the video ended, I sat staring at the computer monitor just taking it all in. I felt proud. Watching us talk openly about the one thing I had tried to hide from the world felt liberating. It wasn't mortifying like I thought it would be. I felt relieved. I felt like I had breathed life into my scars. Talking about them hadn't given them more power over me. In fact, it felt like I had been released from their hold on me.

It's hard to describe and truly make sense of what that one single interview did for me. I'll be forever grateful to Cynthia for pushing me to share my story and finding the original footage of my accident. By sharing with all of San Antonio, I felt proud of my scars. I felt stronger. I felt like my story had meaning and I felt like a warrior by living to tell it. But could I be a warrior with the courage to sing?

Before I could even warm up my vocal cords, I received a call that weekend letting me know a news crew was going to cover the concert. Looking back on the two interview videos, it isn't difficult for someone to see for themselves the impact they had on me. In the first interview with Cassandra Lazenby, I was quiet and soft-spoken. Even my body language was closed off.

The second, with news reporter Christina Coleman, revealed a new person—a metamorphosis. I spoke confidently. I was strong. I was bright and shining. I was new, and I hadn't even performed yet. The two videos show very different women. One showed how her scars were hidden from the light, embarrassed for anyone to see her secrets. The second woman wore her scars like a badge of honor, like battle wounds she took pride in, for they told the tale of her survival. In the interview, Christina said, "With every note her inner strength showed." I believed her.

The concert was on a Sunday afternoon, and my lovely friend, Liz, arrived to do my hair and makeup that day, helping me feel so beautiful. No sooner did we step outside of our car, however, when we felt the sun blasting on us along the downtown Riverwalk. It was something I hadn't taken into consideration, and when I drank from the bottle of water which was placed on the stage for me, it was as hot as fresh coffee. I didn't consider the crowds of tourists who would walk by or my friends and family who selflessly bore the heat of San Antonio to come and support me. I went into my own place that afternoon.

I kept recalling the words of encouragement from Tomas' sister, Keisha: "This is your moment; just be in the moment." And that's exactly what I did. Despite feeling weak from the heat, I sang my heart out, sometimes off-key, often mispronouncing Spanish words and once or twice even completely forgetting the words all together. But I didn't really care; I still loved every moment. Feeling very special, I even did a costume change, one for the band where we sang a few English songs and one for the mariachi.

After the concert, I received a message from a friend who had come to support me. She was one of the friends who had been completely oblivious to my struggle until my fortuitous email. She let me know she was proud of me and how she had her own "scars," and after hearing my story, she felt inspired. My spirit felt renewed, and I felt a sense of purpose surging from within.

From talking with her and more who had been impacted by my story, I have come to realize the relationship I have with my scars is like an arranged marriage: rather than a passion-filled romance from the start; I have grown to love them and, in turn, love myself. I might not have picked them from the start, but I was growing comfortable living with them. Let's be honest. My scars aren't going anywhere; they are a witness to the challenges I have overcome.

And as it turned out, the moment Enzo first asked me about my scars wasn't hurtful or depressing like I'd imagined it would be. It was the night of the concert, after we'd finally made it home and snuggled up under the covers. I felt the warmth of his chubby hand stroking my hair as I read aloud from *Winnie the Pooh*. It's one of our favorites, since I do all the voices *extremely* well. At least, that's what my son says. Having just finished my rendition of Tigger, Enzo looked up and said, "You were in a car accident. You were hurt." I imagine Tomas and him had a conversation about this earlier that day.

"Yeah, right here." I pointed to my nose. It wasn't a question or a query, he was just telling me he knew. He had the innocent curiosity of a child, ironically around the same age as my niece had been when she first noticed my scars, but he was satisfied with the response that Mama had been in a car accident. Far more frequent were the times he would tell me I looked pretty. Like when I picked up a cosmetic bag to do my makeup and Enzo would say, "You don't need makeup, Mommy. You're beautiful *for me*."

Those were the moments I realized the love a child has for his parents can be incredibly special. They forgive any scars you might bare, be them internal or external. I knew a bit about that from my relationship with my mother. And I couldn't deny that it had been largely due to her strength and encouragement that I had found the courage to step on stage and sing earlier that day. Though I don't believe time fully heals all wounds, I know that it gave me the opportunity to learn from them, and more importantly, learn to manage them.

As I stepped onto the soft rug from Enzo's toddler bed to leave him dreaming soundly, I felt the peace of knowing that I was loved by that little human, and so many others. The concert was worth it. It had all been worth it. If there was one person I could help come out of the darkness about their scars, whether inside or out, and feel strengthened by them rather than victimized, I knew I would go through the journey all over again. It was worth speaking up. It was worth being vulnerable. My shattered pieces were no longer everywhere. They were forming a brand-new story that could help others pick up the broken aftermath of their own lives. With Tomas and Enzo, I was happy. But with a reflection in the mirror that I accepted fully, I was whole.

Epilogue

 Every day is not easy, but every day is worth living and you, you are worth everything.

— **Christina Maria Martinez**

In April 2017, the season of Fiesta was upon us. Each year, San Antonio comes alive with the bright colors of confetti and the smell of freshly made churros in the air during this celebration. With a bejeweled, sparkling crown on my head, a sash across my chest, and white gloves made by the same glove maker as Queen Elizabeth II herself, I stepped out of the police-escorted vehicle. I couldn't help but feel like I was dreaming. In true royal fashion, along with the other queens, kings, and royal court, I was ushered to the entrance of the Arneson River Theater representing our respective charity organizations. That year, I stood with my royal "court," better known as my tribe: my sister Nicole and friends, Claudia, Diana, Jennifer, Susie, Veronica and Sandy Saks, entrepreneur and philanthropist whom I lovingly refer to as the Fairy Godmother of Fiesta. Together, we had raised more than

$50,000 for student education scholarships and I had the honor of being crowned La Reina Linda IV or "The Pretty Queen."

Yes, you read that correctly. Me, the girl with the scars on her face, was now royalty. Or at least I was for the year I held the crown. Who would have thought that could happen? What a contrast from the little girl at Hillcrest; my life had changed so dramatically since then. I imagine that is the true beauty (and irony) of life. When things seem a little tougher than usual, I remember, like the diamonds fitted in the crown I wore on my head, we are made under great pressure.

There was a time when I thought my scars were going to define my future. I thought they were something to hide. And I'm not just talking about the ones from my accident. My childhood, which I had to process more than I ever expected in the writing of this book, left me with as many pieces of baggage to unpack as the number of times we moved. I'm living proof that it is possible to have a family who loves you intensely but still leaves you with emotional trauma to work through. But I know that by sharing my story, I'm choosing to shine a light on ALL my life, not just the happily ever after.

While I imagined my trauma to be a solitary battle, Tomas and my mom, along with our family and community of friends, made it their mission to prevent me from wallowing in pity or blaming God for my pain. Instead, I was surrounded by love, which allowed me to find strength, push past my pain, and at long last, love myself despite my scars. This love would, ultimately, carry me through to the beautiful life I live today with Tomas.

Today, I don't spend too much time looking in the mirror, because it doesn't tell me who I am. In fact, the woman I look at in the mirror now is not the same as the girl I was before the accident —not physically, emotionally, or spiritually. Today, I draw courage from my scars, wearing them like a warrior would. I feel like the woman described in Proverbs 31:25 (NLT): "She is clothed with strength and dignity, and she laughs without fear of the future."

I know now that I have been immeasurably blessed to be surrounded by amazing people that, in so many moments throughout my life, saw me on a cliff but didn't let me jump. They sat with me in the dark places, whether it was trying to take a few steps in a hospital or the Majestic Theatre and never left my side. Life has sent me a series of lessons that were learned in the hurting and the pain.

Even when there are gloomy days, I couldn't imagine not being part of this family God has blessed me with. So, today I focus on not what was taken from me, but what was given. I can only hope to encourage others that life does not end with our scars, whether those are physical or emotional. Had I not lived past the moment in the mirror where I wished my life away, I wouldn't have found love for myself and others, and I wouldn't be able to share my story today.

As for my fairy-tale ending? I chose to fight for it, for my green-eyed Prince Charming who didn't rescue me as much as he stood in the fray with me, fighting side by side. I fought through the darkness, and I pray you will as well. If you choose to fight, I promise it will get better. Maybe not tomorrow, but it will. And eventually, you'll find yourself looking back at the dark times and realizing you're no longer defined by them. You're defined by today—the here and now. So let your scars tell your story.

All about me.
My name is Christina and I was born in Lakewood New Jersey on January 9, 1979. I almost died because I was not breathing

Grandpa Vincent
+
Grandma Evelyn

Tomas & Dee

Elsie♡

fireschool

The name of them are states
St. Claude Heights, Dove Park,
John F. Kennedy, Mercury,
Alice Birney. I've been in
four apartment, two houses
and I can't count how
many hotels. My teacher...

Laura - my
1st night
home :"

20th
Anniversary!

Royal
"duties"!

Still my
green eyed
prince

and would be a law
to live this would
my family life be to

Enzo. just born.

Acknowledgments
A Story within a Story

The journey of writing this book began while Tomas and I attended a business conference in California in 2018. During the trip, we had the great honor of attending a dinner hosted by friends, Cathy & Brad Taylor. In a rare opportunity, I rode back to the hotel with Rudy Ruettiger, known for the movie *Rudy*. As we chatted, he shared his story with me, and I felt inclined to share some of mine with him. It was during that ride; it was Rudy, who encouraged me to write my story. Although it was something I had considered before, I couldn't seem to bite the bullet.

Months later, in a conversation with Brad, I shared with him an experience Tomas and I were lucky enough to have: Breakfast with the incomparable Larry King and friends. Every morning, Larry would meet with a group of his closest friends to break bread and share stories. One morning, that group included the two of us. Larry King will always be a legend, who holds the stories of legends, and now holds ours. Tomas & Christina's.

As I tried to distract Brad from what I knew was the reason behind his call, he cut me off and asked, "When are you going to write your book?" Like a teenager caught putting off a school project, I said, "I don't know."

Instead of pressuring me to move forward, he suggested I start off with a "mock podcast" recording with Tomas, one of the best interviewers in the business. I *might* be biased. Brad's reasoning behind the podcast was for me to practice telling my story, thus making it easier to write later on pen and paper. My conversation with Tomas was like any other we've ever had. Easy, flowing, and maybe just a little too honest. By the end of the recording, I became so comfortable, I revealed details of my life, like Hillcrest, that I had never shared before. I didn't think twice about it, though, since the recording would never see the light of day - at least that's what I thought before I boarded my flight.

When the plane touched down in Los Angeles, and I turned my phone back on, you would have thought there had been an emergency with the amount of notifications I had waiting for me. In a way, there was. My "mock podcast" wasn't "mock" at all. The entire thing had been uploaded and published for the world to hear. I panicked. How was I going to explain to my mom I had publicly revealed details of our lives, *her* life, we had fought years to leave behind and forget? *Maybe I should stay in L.A.?*

Thankfully, I didn't have to suffer long. Shortly after my initial freak out, my mom called. To my surprise, there were no tears or feelings of betrayal, but instead, she told me how proud she was of me.

Later that year, my friend Adriana Cova gifted me the book and accompanying journal, *Becoming*, by Michelle Obama. Feeling inspired, I began writing. Sort of.

After one-too-many mental roadblocks, I reached out to my friend and all around beautiful person, Juli Henderson. Juli is gifted in more ways than I can count, but her greatest gift is her generosity. She is generous with her time, resources, and, thankfully, her relationships. Juli facilitated the introduction between me and Andrea Lucado. Besides taking on reviewing my manuscript, Andrea pulled out of me pieces of my story that had been long forgotten. She gave me the confidence to tell my story and to do it my way. Even if that meant a little extra homework. If a publishing/ literary guru like Andrea believed I had something to say - I could believe it too.

My next call was to Aquila Mendez-Valdez, a publicist and visionary in her field whom I have had the pleasure of working with for many years. Working with her, you catch on pretty quick, she is the consummate professional. For whatever reason, she agreed to join me on this crazy adventure, and helped shape my abstract idea of a book with her beautiful words. Apart from the words she gifted me, Aquila, being incredibly organized, kept me on a strict schedule. If not for her timeline, the book you're holding now, or listening to like I would, could still be sitting in my Google Doc drafts.

Karen & Peter Veloz, who opened their home and spent their weekend with me. They may not know it, but they were responsible for perhaps the most eye-opening moment throughout the entire writing process. In one dinner, they helped me understand that my story, and everyone else's, is not just one big moment. It's the accumulation of the hundreds of little moments that come together to mold us into who we are. They helped me understand the gravity of what this book could mean and encouraged me to dig deeper within myself. Again, more homework.

To everyone mentioned in *Shattered Pieces Everywhere*: Thank you. I'm lucky in that I have had too many people to name help me along the way. I'm grateful for each person in this book and for how they played a part in my story. Some of them don't even remember the beautiful thing(s) they did for me, but I do. I will always remember their moments of kindness and generosity.

To all the people who might not have been a part of my past but are such constants in my today. They surround me with love, and because of that support I continue to choose today. I continue to choose tomorrow.

Laura Aguilar, who showed me at an early age what pure, genuine friendship looks like. No matter the distance between us, our bond will always remain.

To the kind Samaritans I didn't formally meet on that hot June afternoon: I may never know who they are, but I will always remember what they did for me, a total stranger. May all of their years be blessed. They've earned it.

To each of the physicians, nurses, technicians and supporting staff at The University Hospital in San Antonio, Texas, in 1998: they gave me, a scared young woman, the ultimate care and comfort, even if it did hurt sometimes. To those who continue the work and legacy today, they're still five-stars.

Jennifer Vega, who was brave enough to read our "Franken-baby Manuscript" before anyone else and before it went to editing. Thank you, and I'm sorry.

Melanie Walker: Copy Editor Extraordinaire. Melanie helped turn a beat-up manuscript into an actual book.

By my side, every step of the way was the care and support from the entire team at Elan Publishing and Division Street Books. We did it!

The most awarded and talented couple I know, Elizabeth & Trey Homan. More than our photographer, we are blessed to call them friends. They have the gift to imagine beauty where no one else might, and the talent to translate it for the world to see.

Matt Carlsen, responsible for the beautifully designed book cover you see before you.

The TPC San Antonio Book Club, our fantastic beta readers: more than just a fun afternoon discussing the book, those lovely ladies gave us an incredible first insight into what a reader might think. Thank you to everyone in the group, including Carrie, Phyllis, Meagan, and Kim for the interest in this project and of course, the honesty shared.

To Dr. Ed Newton, "Your pain is never wasted." He may never truly know the impact of these words of his, but they will stay with me always. Reminding me that God takes broken pieces, and makes masterpieces.

To my siblings, Santina and Eddie: During the most crucial times in our childhoods, we had each other. We may not have always been physically near one another, but our bond was greater than the distance. Through the moments we shared in this book, to the many others that are only ours to know, we had each other.

Mama, her bravery and resilience is beyond that of most. She allowed me to tell parts of her story she never imagined sharing, let alone publishing. I'm so grateful that our relationship has allowed me the freedom to speak freely and without judgment. Thank you; I love you.

My talented sister, and best friend, Nicole Pietramale: She is with me in everything I do. I appreciate her creative direction for *Shattered Pieces Everywhere*. More than anything, I appreciate all the times she lifted me back up when I felt like this journey was more than I could handle.

Krystal Navarro: Without fail, she helped shepherd this book from its inception. Whether it was on the golf course during Enzo's practices or late nights at the kitchen table, she was with me. She is intertwined in the fabric of my life and a part of our family. She helped me draw out some of the deepest and most buried parts of my story, allowed me the time to breathe, and in the absence of words, knew what I was thinking. Together, we celebrate our unique sarcasm and unconventional sense of humor... who cares if no one else thinks we're funny. We do, and that's all that matters :o) Her gifts are too numerous to name; Krystal is a shining light in any room she enters. I look forward to the many years of amazing experiences we will share.

The Martinez / Brugh family, who never stop cheering me on and brought into this world the best thing to enter my life: my green-eyed-dreamboat-of-a-husband, Tomas. Tomas is and has been everything I ever wanted out of this life. There aren't enough words to describe what he means to me, or the love I have for him. Hopefully, the ones written in this book are a good start. To our son Enzo, who makes this life so worth living. I hope, more than anything, he always feels like he's enough. Because to me, he's so much more.

Please consider contributing to the work of Hillcrest Children's Home, a facility who is still transforming the lives of children today. Even the smallest donation can make a massive impact. Like a teddy bear, for example.

Finally, I don't know who you are, but this is for you, the Reader. Thank you for taking the time to read this book. You even made it through the acknowledgements! Please know this is not "The End" as my story is still being written. I ain't done yet... (Sorry for the grammar, Melanie.)

*If you felt inspired by my story, I hope you will share it with someone you would like to inspire. Or, If you'd like to share your own story with me, please email it to **ShareMyStory.SPE@ gmail.com***

Endnotes

Chapter 12

1. Elizabeth Edwards, *Resilience: The New Afterword*